PROTRACTED CONFLICT

HARPER COLOPHON BOOKS

HARPER & ROW, PUBLISHERS

NEW YORK AND EVANSTON

PROTRACTED CONFLICT

A FOREIGN POLICY RESEARCH INSTITUTE BOOK

by ROBERT STRAUSZ-HUPÉ, WILLIAM R. KINTNER,

JAMES E. DOUGHERTY, ALVIN J. COTTRELL

Chapter 1, *The Revolutionary Setting*, appeared in somewhat different form in *Orbis*, Vol. II, Spring 1958, No. 1, Copyright 1958 by the Trustees of the University of Pennsylvania. The Appendix, *The Menace of Communist Psychological Warfare*, appeared in *Orbis*, Vol. I, Spring 1957, No. 1, Copyright 1957 by the Trustees of the University of Pennsylvania.

FIRST HARPER COLOPHON EDITION published 1963, by Harper & Row, Publishers, Incorporated, New York and Evanston

CONTENTS

PREFACE AND ACKNOWLEDGMENTS

A study of protracted conflict was one of the earliest projects undertaken by the Foreign Policy Research Institute, following its establishment early in 1955. Members of the Institute were convinced that existing studies of the Communists' international strategy and tactics, while placing almost exclusive stress upon Communism as a social or economic ideology, almost completely ignored the significance of Communism as a doctrine and a technique of conflict. This study began with an effort to analyze the intermediate range of challenges posed to the Western alliance by the Communists, particularly those operations which enabled the Communists to carry on "nibbling expansion" at the expense of the Free World without ever provoking the United States to unleash the full force of its nuclear power. At the onset of the Cold War American nuclear-air capabilities had deterred the Soviets from launching large-scale military aggression against Europe. Yet, despite American technical superiority and the gradual strengthening of NATO defenses, the general strategic situation of the Western nations, assessed in global terms, seemed to be deteriorating steadily while that of the Communist bloc slowly improved. The first phase of the Institute's protracted conflict study was designed to probe into the manner by which the Communists managed to circumvent the West's primary defenses while conducting their campaign of global power accumulation.

In the fall of 1955, each Associate of the Institute was invited to submit a preliminary statement of the problem as he saw it. Several papers were drafted and later discussed and criticized by all of the Associates: William Y. Elliott, William R. Kintner, Henry A. Kissinger, Hans Kohn, Paul M. A. Linebarger, Norman D. Palmer, Stefan T. Possony, Froelich Rainey, Robert Strausz-Hupé and Arthur P. Whitaker. Drs. Strausz-Hupé, Possony and Kintner undertook to direct further studies into the problem, with the assistance of two members of the Institute's research staff, Alvin J. Cottrell and James E. Dougherty. The title of the study project was suggested by the title of Mao Tse-tung's book, *On the Protracted War,* which probably contains the fullest statement of the protracted conflict strategy to be found in Communist literature.

During the early stages of the project, considerable attention was focused upon the problem of "limited war" in the nuclear age. It became apparent, however, that "limited war" was only one aspect of the larger strategic challenge confronting the West. As further study papers were prepared on the Western idea of war, as compared with the Russian and Chinese Communist approaches to conflict, it was seen that the Western attitude toward conflict differed profoundly from that of the Communists. This fact in itself led to a rethinking of the concept of limited war as it was being articulated in the West, since it was obvious that "limited war" meant something very different to the Communists. The concept of limited war was finally found unsuitable as a framework of analysis. Further inquiries into such subjects as Communist strategic theories, historic instances of Communist conflict operations, the character of guerrilla warfare in the twentieth century, psychological warfare, and the policy-making process in totalitarian as contrasted with democratic societies made it clear that a much broader framework of analysis was needed. This broader framework had to be one which could encompass the strategy and tactics of the Communists on a global scale, and fit into a coherent scheme the various phases and modes of the Communists' conflict operations: political, technological, economic, psychological, sociological and military.

While the quest for this larger theoretical framework was in process, additional study papers dealing with specific facets of protracted conflict were written, circulated among the Associates, evaluated at bimonthly Institute meetings, and rewritten.

The next important phase of the study consisted in relating the strategy of protracted conflict to the systemic revolution which is in progress throughout the newly emergent nations of the world, particularly in Asia and Africa. Starting in the fall of 1956, the Institute inaugurated a series of field trips to American missions around the world, under a grant from the Richardson Foundation. Drs. Kintner, Strausz-Hupé and Rainey separately or jointly visited the following countries and territories: Japan, Korea, Formosa, Okinawa, Hong Kong, Cambodia, Thailand, Vietnam, the Philippines, Burma, India, Pakistan, Iraq, Israel, Cyprus, Egypt, the Lebanon, Libya, Tunisia, Algeria, Morocco, France, Greece, Germany, Austria, Finland and Sweden. The Department of State made advance arrangements for the Institute team to meet with top American political and military personnel in the areas visited and to discuss critical problems confronting American foreign policy. (Copies of a précis of the Institute's study of protracted conflict had been made available to the American missions abroad prior to the arrival of the FPRI team.) The FPRI members recorded summaries of their conversations. The extensive record of the field trips was sifted and analyzed upon the return of the FPRI team and subsequently was published in separate reports for selective distribution. This part of the study was completed by July, 1957.

The FPRI staff then set about developing a code of operational principles of protracted conflict as practiced by the Communists. Selected sections of the manuscript appeared in the spring, 1958, issue of *Orbis*, the quarterly journal published by the Institute. In April, 1958, the five members of the Institute most closely associated with the project conducted a two-day seminar on protracted conflict with the staff and faculty of the Army War College at Carlisle, Pennsylvania. On that occasion, the general thesis of the study was presented to approximately forty staff officers at the War College, whose valuable criticisms contributed much to the final drafting of the manuscript during the late summer and fall of 1958.

This, the first volume of the Institute's study of protracted conflict, does not contain a detailed prescription for future American foreign policy. Nevertheless, our long study led to—almost forced upon us—certain broad, intuitive judgments. These are set down in the concluding chapters of this book and provide guidelines for the further study of U.S. strategy being undertaken by the Institute.

It is to be hoped that this book will help to establish a conceptual consensus among American policy-making groups and opinion elites on the protean nature of the Communist challenge. The second phase of the study will deal, in the light of the present analysis, with the range of U.S. responses. The second phase of the study, the most important and urgent undertaking of this Institute, will seek: (1) to develop a conceptual framework for American and Western foreign policy; (2) to clarify the definition of the national objective of the United States; (3) to determine methods for the effective integration of the various instruments of U.S. policy; and (4) to identify more effective organizational means for formulating and executing an American conflict strategy that accords with world political necessities and the ethos of American society.

In the preparation of this study, the authors have received advice and assistance from many persons.

Walter F. Hahn, Executive Editor of *Orbis*, the quarterly journal published by the Institute, has contributed invaluable editorial assistance to the making of this book. Countless conversations with him have helped us to refine many of the ideas appearing within these covers. In the fall of 1958, Mr. Hahn gave unstintingly of his time and energy in the reorganization of the manuscript. His intellectual imprint appears on many of the pages which follow.

The skillful editorial criticism of Cass Canfield, Jr., has done much to shorten and sharpen the text.

The authors are deeply indebted to George E. Pettee of the Operations Research Office, Johns Hopkins University, for suggesting one of the key concepts of this book. Early in 1957, Dr. Pettee prepared for the Foreign Policy Research Institute a background paper which greatly stimulated our thinking on the relationship of Communist strategy to the "systemic revolution" sweeping the world. Dr. Pettee's deep insights into the revolutionary character of the present era were fully borne out during the extensive field trips made in conjunction with this study.

Over the course of nearly three years, incalculable benefits have been derived from the regular semimonthly discussions of the Institute in which the following participated: Professors William Y. Elliott of Harvard University; H. Field Haviland, Jr., of the Brookings Institution; Henry A. Kissinger of Harvard University; Hans Kohn of the City College of New York; Paul M. A. Linebarger of the School of Advanced International Studies of Johns Hopkins University; Norman D. Palmer of the University of Pennsylvania; Arthur Smithies of Harvard University; and Arthur P. Whitaker of the University of Pennsylvania.

Special thanks are in order for two Associates of the Institute. Dr. Stefan T. Possony of Georgetown University was helpful in supervising the research on specific phases of the project, in making available hard-to-find materials from his own Sovietological collection, and in urging us to "rethink" our analysis, especially with respect to military-technological problems. Dr. Froelich G. Rainey, Director of the University of Pennsylvania Museum, proved to be a most thought-provoking companion on one of the treks through the peripheral areas of the world. His incisive observations were all the more valuable precisely because he was not always in full agreement with the authors' analysis.

The authors wish to express their appreciation to the Departments of State and Defense for facilitating their discussions of the concept of protracted conflict with officials of American missions and commands stationed adjacent to the periphery of the Sino-Soviet bloc. Particularly valuable was the co-operation of Mr. Richard B. Finn, Special Assistant to the Deputy Undersecretary of State, and of Karl Harr, Jr., then Deputy Assistant Secretary of Defense for International Security Affairs, in making arrangements for the field trips. While these discussions abroad furnished the authors with an excellent opportunity to put to the test their ideas of Communist strategy, the views contained in this book are entirely their responsibility. It should not be inferred, moreover, that this study reflects the views of either of the two departments of government.

The authors are profoundly grateful to the staff and faculty of the War College, especially to Major General Max S. Johnson, Commandant, and Brigadier General E. C. Doleman, Deputy Commandant, who offered helpful critiques at the conclusion of the seminar. For the administrative planning of the seminar at Carlisle, the authors extend their cordial thanks to Colonel Chester L. Johnson.

Lieutenant General James M. Gavin, former Chief of Research and Development, Department of the Army, and Dr. Ellis A. Johnson, Director of the Operations Research Office, Johns Hopkins University, made arrangements which considerably expedited the completion of the study. The Foreign Policy Research Institute also wishes to acknowledge the financial assistance of the Richardson Foundation, whose grant established the Institute and largely sustained its operations from 1955 through 1958. The Donner Foundation has also supplied generous support for the general operations of the Institute since 1957. The University of Pennsylvania made a specific grant for the study of protracted conflict.

Useful and illuminating background papers on specialized topics falling within the scope of the study were submitted by

Donald Kellett, L. Cabot Briggs, Paul Sapieha, Vladimir Petrov and Virgil Ney.

This project gave rise to an endless round of deciphering and typing reports, background papers and completed manuscripts. Mrs. Joy M. Cottrell, for three years, has acted as secretary of the project and has supervised these tedious logistic operations with consummate patience and skill while simultaneously bearing much of the brunt of the Institute's regular administrative activity. In this task, she has been ably assisted by Miss Joanne Walter. To them, the authors extend their abiding personal gratitude.

Philadelphia   Robert Strausz-Hupé
March 15, 1959   William R. Kintner
                                                            James E. Dougherty
                                                            Alvin J. Cottrell

PREFACE TO THE COLOPHON BOOK EDITION

Protracted Conflict was intended to provide an analysis of the operational code whereby the international Communist movement carries on conflict in an environment of unrelenting systemic change—or, put differently, a study of how the Communist "scavengers of revolution" endeavor to make history work for themselves and against the West. Although material was drawn not only from Communist literature but also from numerous historical episodes over a forty-year period to illustrate the principles of strategic behavior which seem to guide the Communist leadership, the work was never meant as a history of the Cold War. Hence it is not necessary to update every aspect of the Communist-Western strategic confrontation since 1959.

We, the authors, do not believe that, after four years, our earlier examination of Communist strategy requires significant modification. We do not pretend that if we were rewriting the book today we would make no changes in the interpretation of certain events. Neither the scholar nor the publicist can afford to indulge in such intellectual obstinacy. It was necessary, for example, to revise the section in Chapter Five dealing with the Sputniks. There was reason to be skeptical of Soviet weight claims in 1958, in view of the Russian refusal to make detailed scientific data available to the outside world, but it has since become evident that the U.S.S.R. does possess the rocket thrust which it boasted. Other changes might have been made here and there throughout the book, but instead of a thorough revision it was decided to allow the work to stand as originally published.

We have, however, added an epilogue reviewing some of the major international developments and significant strategic trends of the last four years. These, we believe, will serve to show that the essential thesis embodied in *Protracted Conflict* was based upon the consistent internal logic of Communist strategy, not upon mere ephemeral impressions of world events.

The authors are well aware that recent years have brought important changes within the Western alliance, the Sino-Soviet bloc, and the underdeveloped countries—indeed, within the international strategic environment as a whole. Nevertheless, we regard the original analysis as still fundamentally sound. We submit that the strategic diagnosis spelled out four years ago still furnishes a realistic and useful interpretation of the strategic methodology by which the Communist leadership hopes to achieve its international goals.

August, 1962

ROBERT STRAUSZ-HUPÉ
WILLIAM R. KINTNER
JAMES E. DOUGHERTY

PROTRACTED CONFLICT

CHAPTER 1 THE REVOLUTIONARY SETTING

Protracted conflict is a historical phenomenon. It attends upon every systemic breakdown and the ensuing quest for a new equilibrium. Every revolutionary movement issues from a position of physical inferiority vis-à-vis the defender of the *status quo*. The revolutionary movement, to assure its final victory, must perforce rely more upon the breadth of its vision than the strength of its arms. Its strategy derives from a superior understanding of the total historic situation; the spectrum of revolutionary conflict techniques is as wide as the entire scale of social change. Within that spectrum, a central intelligence organizes and phases the instruments of conflict—political, economic, psychological, technological and military. That central intelligence discerns potential weapons where the defender of the *status quo* sees only the tools of peace; in short, it turns plowshares into swords.

The concept of "protracted conflict" was given classic formulation by Mao Tse-tung. Mao must be ranked not only among the greatest strategists but also the greatest theoretician on war of all times. His book *On the Protracted War* sums up very well the principles of revolutionary conflict. Its central thesis, which deals with the ambiguity of "war" and "peace," shows clearly that, in this age, those terms do not suffice to describe the complex realities with which the statesman and the soldier must grapple.

The strategy of protracted conflict postpones the decisive battle and calibrates its challenges to a calculus of risks—until the balance of power has shifted overwhelmingly to the side of the revolutionary forces. Indeed, this is—and always has been—the strategy of the Russian and Chinese Communists, who have been able not only to accept but even to thrive upon conflict as the normal condition of the twentieth century.

The salient characteristics of the doctrine of protracted conflict are: the total objective, the carefully controlled methods and the constant shifting of the battleground, weapons systems and operational tactics for the purpose of confusing the opponent, keeping him off balance and wearing down his resistance. The doctrine of protracted conflict prescribes a strategy for annihilating the opponent over a period of time by limited operations, by feints and maneuvers, psychological manipulations and diverse forms of violence. But this strategy should not be mistaken for one of limited war in the style of European warfare in the eighteenth century. It does not rule out the final and total knockout punch. In Communist theory, various techniques of political warfare and graduated violence are so co-ordinated as to form a spectrum that reaches all the way from the clandestine distribution of subversive literature to the annihilating blow delivered with every weapon available.

For the Communists, protracted conflict brackets all possible relationships between states and groups—political, economic and cultural—and some that, from our point of view, signify the exact opposite of conflict.

War, in our epoch, is not an isolated, capricious phenomenon which flouts the "normal" peaceful process of history. Wars occur in series: World War I and World War II were serially connected, as were the smaller contests which preceded and followed them, from the Russo-Japanese War (1904–1905) to the Korean War almost fifty years later. While the major wars form a single current, a number of lesser military conflicts parallel or join the major stream. Thus, for example, the wars in the Middle East and the guerrilla campaigns in colonial areas during and after both world wars were, in many respects, distinct and independent from the operations in the principal theaters of war. Yet the fortunes of the larger struggle affected—and were, in turn, affected by—the outcome of local and peripheral conflicts. And a series of uprisings and revolutions, although it did not issue into international conflicts, was both distinct from and connected with the multiple series of wars.

Ever since 1914, the countenance of peace has been as blurred as that of war. Throughout the lifetime of this generation, peace has been little else than a paraphrase of Clausewitz' celebrated dictum, namely the continuation of war with other means. Peace has not been a state of international repose and contentment. Peace has been a phase of—or, so to speak, a variation on—the power struggle. At peace, this struggle has been waged with nonviolent means. Within this over-all category of "peace," there has been a series of propaganda campaigns, political warfare operations and economic wars which impinged and fed upon each other, and which themselves were meshed with the chain of military and violent conflicts.

Thus, conflict undertakings are invariably linked with one another. A propaganda campaign may be waged to support political warfare or a guerrilla attack. Propaganda operations as, for example, a peace offensive or appeals for the cessation of weapons-testing may aim at neutralizing the technological superiority of the opponent. Once the technological gap has been closed, propaganda maximizes the psychological impact of the achievement (Sputnik). In a broad sense, all the violent and all the nonviolent techniques are interconnected. Acts of violence are always supported by nonviolent activities.

Second, any one conflict undertaking in one geographical-cultural area is correlated with any other conflict undertaking in the same environment. Thus, for example, a propaganda campaign in the Middle East is geared to the economic, political and military penetration of the region—regardless of whether these operations are launched simultaneously or successively.

Third, conflict undertakings in one area exacerbate strife in other areas. Thus, for example, conflicts in the dependent territories not only tax the military resources of the European colonial powers but also precipitate psychological and political disturbances within and among the countries of the Western alliance, including those nations who boast of an impeccable anticolonial record.

The term "protracted conflict" is as convenient as it is precise. The current struggle for the mastery of the globe has been waged for five decades, albeit by diverse contenders. It will continue to plague mankind for many more years. Even if the present parties to the conflict would seek, by mutual consent, to compose it now, the liquidation of most contested issues would not be completed within the life span of this generation. Hence we must reckon with the extension—the protraction—of the world conflict into the next century.

In order to survive or win this conflict, strategies must be planned to the scale of decades, not years. An individual conflict should not be viewed as an isolated phenomenon but as a phase of the total struggle, an integral part of a multiple series of interrelated conflicts. One conflict triggers the other; there are no decisive defeats or victories except the last.

How does the notion of "limited war" fit into the context of the "protracted conflict"? Not all military struggles are of the same intensity. Some will be more "total" than others. The intensity of war will be dictated by circumstances of geography, sociology, technology and political structure, and by the importance, within the framework of the over-all conflict, of the specific objective at stake. It is conceivable that a war may start on a limited scale and gradually become "total." It is just as conceivable that a war may erupt with the utmost ferocity and gradually subside into a sharply circumscribed tournament, in which only the chosen few need suffer injury. It is possible, moreover, that some wars remain limited throughout and others remain total. But protracted conflict should not be equated with limited war, and not all of its phases will remain "limited."

The term "limited war" has been used indiscriminately. What

is meant by the term? Does it describe the type of war which was waged in Korea, or Indochina, or Greece, or Egypt, or Algeria? The image of a war between major contenders, each of whom adheres strictly to certain "ground rules" and keeps large-yield weapons in storage, might be more pleasing than the gruesome specter of total war. Unfortunately, the immense strides in weapons technology alone rule out the possibility that the major powers will forego, in an armed clash with one another, the use of nuclear weapons and wage strictly "conventional" war. Soviet military theoreticians have explicitly rejected the notion of limited war, and the United States can ill afford to espouse such a doctrine unilaterally. Conceivably, the major powers, if and when war breaks out between them, will accept some practical limitations on the use of superweapons. But the war, nevertheless, because it may utilize the full spectrum of available weapons, will be total in character.

The successful strategists of modern warfare are those bold commanders who do not share the preconceptions and scruples of their more timid opponents and defeat their enemy with strategies and weapons which the latter deem too "unorthodox" and too fraught with unacceptable risk.

The problem of contemporary conflict defies solution by a neat maxim on the limitation of war. The manifold and unruly realities of protracted conflict cannot be contained by one simple formula. To fasten attention upon one species of war to the exclusion of the great variety of likely conflict situations is to confuse the part with the whole.

We do not assert that the term "protracted conflict" applies to all aspects of international relations in this century; nor do we believe that protracted conflict need be the eternal lot of mankind. We assert that every effort must be made to rid international society of its oldest scourge—on terms, however, which safeguard freedom. We do not hold that conflict is necessary to human progress; we certainly do not favor war. Yet, the festering sores on the international body politic cannot be healed by pious homilies on the blessings of peace. Medical scientists who sought to control infantile paralysis did not pretend that this disease did not exist; nor did they refuse to study it in all its manifestations. Precisely because they studied it, they found a cure. Political thinking will make little progress if it discards scientific method and fails to assess properly the facts of global crisis, however repugnant these may be. The facts which matter today yield their meaning to the theory of "protracted conflict." Without such an informing theory, the crisis of our times is meaningless.

CHAPTER **2** A NEW LOOK AT COMMUNIST STRATEGY

In the conflict between the U.S. and U.S.S.R., two alien systems confront one another. This confrontation takes place in space and in time; the contest is over the domination of the earth and, now, its outer space and over the future of human society. It is the climactic phase of the systemic revolution through which the world has been passing ever since 1914. It is thus a power-political as well as a social contest, a war as well as a revolution.

So absorbing has been the search for the ideological consistencies or inconsistencies of Communism that, by comparison, not enough attention has been given to Communism as a method.[1] Communism is a method of conflict in space over a sustained period of time, i.e., of protracted conflict. This neglect of the method as against what Communism really is (or says it is) is due to many causes. Some of these are inherent in the Communist method itself—to deceive the opponent as regards the nature of the method is part of the method; others are inherent in our own society, which is neither revolutionary nor aggressive nor monolithic. Our society does not subordinate all its aspira-

[1] The principal exceptions are Stefan T. Possony's *A Century of Conflict*, Chicago: Henry Regnery, 1953, William R. Kintner's *The Front Is Everywhere*, Norman: University of Oklahoma Press, 1950, and Philip Selznick, *The Organizational Weapon*, New York: McGraw-Hill, 1952.

tions to considerations of power; Communist-dominated societies do. And the struggle being what it is, namely a revolutionary one, Communism presses all men and all things into the service of one cause: the overthrow of the existing social order and the establishment of a Communist society. It is only within this context that we can read meaning into Communist strategy and develop counterstrategies that will bracket the range of the Communist threat and not merely seek to fill the breach opened by the latest Communist thrust.

In the language of politics, the term "revolution" stands for a certain kind of historical change: an old order dissolves and a new one emerges; old rulers are replaced by new ones; men feel that the tempo of events is quickening and that, willingly or unwillingly, they are breaking with the past; and the transition is enlivened by more or less spectacular bursts of violence. Indeed, these were the characteristics of the French Revolution and the Russian Revolution, the most familiar examples of "revolution" in modern history. Both these cataclysms lasted for known spans of time; both were national insofar as they occurred within historical states. It is plausible—and by now platitudinous—to say that the two world wars were revolutionary wars. This they were. It is easy to identify the milestones of the "Revolution of Our Times." It is more difficult to relate these discrete events— national revolutions and international revolutionary wars—to a general development which, in different ways, occurs in all countries, affects all men and lasts over an indefinite period of time.

Cycles of history, completed long ago, afford us a better insight in the nature of the unfolding world revolution than do the more recent happenings which we call revolutions and which are, in fact, mere tremors, albeit sometimes momentous ones, of a vast and lasting disturbance. Such a vast and lasting disturbance seems to have shaken the ancient world. It started with the Peloponnesian War and reached its climax in the Roman Civil Wars which pitted first Pompey against Caesar and then Caesar's heirs against one another. The revolution, although its most celebrated stages were Athens and Rome, was not confined to any one city or country. It rolled over the entire Mediterranean region—the universe of the ancients. We may call it a *systemic* revolution. When it had run its course of four centuries, the state system had changed from one of many city-states into one of a single universal empire. A new order had been established, not only for Rome or Athens, for Italy or Greece, but for all peoples of the Mediterranean region, and even for those peoples who had never known the rule of the city-state. Similarly, the slow-motion "fall" of Rome was a revolution that spilled over the bounds of any one clearly identifiable state or, for that matter, any one clearly identifiable civilization. The state system that issued from this lengthy process, which its eyewitnesses must have found interminable as well as senseless, bore hardly any resemblance to the Roman state. A new order of political and moral values submerged the institutions and mores of the Romans. Then again, at the time of the Renaissance and Reformation, Europe was recast. The emergent system of nation-states marked a break with feudalism as radical as that which sundered the universal Roman state from the polis of antiquity.

In each of these systemic revolutions, states fought great wars among each other. These wars between states were also civil wars, for the disturbance of the system spread into all its parts, erasing the distinction between civil and external, national and international. Each of these great upheavals traced a definite pattern of events that baffled the participants although it became meaningful to posterity. The process of the systemic revolution, like that of the business cycle, is woven from the actions of masses of men who neither understand nor desire what they are about to fashion. Design there is, but it is a design that is neither conscious nor rational. Most certainly, it has not been planned by anyone. It holds for those who are caught in its meshes, the contemporaries, an unfathomable riddle.

This generation faces a bewildering and unprecedented paradox: new and virtually unlimited resources are within our reach, and we stand at the threshold of a new rich and universal civilization; yet the survival of civilization itself has been put in doubt. So terrible is our dilemma and so pressing are the demands of the hour, that we incline to mistake each bend of the road for a historic turning point. Unique as is our situation, it is but the latest episode of a long story. No one knows how this story will end and whether the leading characters of the current installment will figure in the next. We can but surmise that destiny has placed us in the midst of a revolutionary epoch, comparable, on a global scale, to those which embraced the passing of the city-state, the "fall" of Rome and the breakdown of European feudalism. For many decades, historic institutions and their sustaining faiths all over this earth have swayed and broken under the impact of revolutionary forces. The nature of the process is still largely veiled to our eyes, for the complete returns are still not in and our judgment is clouded by passion. We may trace, with some semblance of accuracy, this or that root cause: the truths unlocked and the powers unleashed by the natural sciences; the global spread of industrialization; the rapid growth of populations; and the ever accelerating mobility of men, ideas and things. Yet the political and social crisis of this century remains as ineffable as the human condition to which it has given rise.

The conflict between the United States and the Soviet Union now holds the center of the historical stage. Yet, this confrontation is the mere contemporary expression, the vast powers arrayed in each camp notwithstanding, of pervasive conflict that encompasses all lands, all peoples and all levels of society. The United States and the Soviet Union are now the leading protagonists; the struggle which is civil as well as international cleaves all societies. Hence any effective strategy for waging the ubiquitous protracted conflict must be, by necessity, a revolutionary strategy: to wit, a strategy that puts the revolutionary forces-on-the-loose in politics, economics, culture, science and technology to its own use and denies their exploitation to the enemy. Insofar as Communist strategy has been able to do just that, it has been effective. The Communists have benefited from the errors of their opponents who let themselves be bemused by the Marxist myth of revolution and remained blind to the realities of revolutionary strategy.

The Russian Communists, saturated with a dynamic philosophy of history and astride a formidable territorial base of operations, saw what the West did not: that "the august, unchallenged and tranquil glories of the Victorian age," tarnished by World War I, were to depart forever amidst the rising commotion of Asia and Africa.

The West's rapid expansion to all continents challenged gravely the authority of all the world's surviving civilizations. Western society pressed its forms upon all societies; it planted everywhere the seeds of its creativeness—and of its own dissensions. Thus revolutionary change within the historic West is inextricably linked with the transformation of the non-Western societies. The concurrence of the crisis of the West itself and the impact of Westernization upon the rest of mankind impart irresistible force to the secular and universal, the *systemic* world revolution.

For instance, the Russian Communists did not create the "revolutionary situation" in Asia and Africa; that "situation" had been taking shape for a long time. The Communists, however, were quick to exploit it and "to push what was falling." First hampered by ideological preconceptions, they soon adjusted their sights to political realities: the colonial peoples would forge the political ideas which they had received from the West into instruments for dislodging the Western powers from their imperial holdings. Although the incipient breakdown of the colonial system would be paced by economic and social transformation, the prospect of proletarian revolution held, for the Kremlin, less attraction than the strategic prize: to inflict upon the Western powers, who were, in point of time, the principal opponents of the Soviet Union, heavy losses in political prestige, markets and raw material resources and to weaken them through the debilitating effects, military, economic and moral, of colonial wars of attrition.

Although the Communists thought of themselves as the vessels, so to speak, of the "inevitability of history," they were determined to be also its agents. Hence they were not content to contemplate the unfolding of events. Throughout the European colonies, nationalist movements were still amorphous, weak and unsure. Forty years ago, it was by no means certain that they would harden into implacable hostility against the West. Lenin tailored Marxist doctrine to the realities of the systemic revolution and launched the Soviet strategy for the subversion of the colonial world. This masterpiece of dialectical legerdemain and political improvisation is Lenin's greatest legacy to the Russian Communists.

The Congress of the Peoples of the East, convened at Baku in 1920, affords a preview of a Communist strategy designed to outflank, so to speak, the capitalist order by carrying the revolution to the colonial empires.[2] At Baku, the Bolshevik leaders met with the nationalist revolutionaries of Asia. The Congress resolved dutifully upon a program for the subversion of the European colonies. The fact that many of the participants played, up until the present, leading roles in Asia's revolutionary movements bespeaks the importance of the Baku Congress. Indeed, ever since Baku, the Communists have been in the van of those rising forces that, within less than forty years, triumphed in the expulsion of the West from the Asian Continent. But the immediate results of Baku disappointed the Bolsheviks. During the 1920's, one revolutionary attempt after the other ended in failure, partially because the Communists had not allowed sufficient time to prepare the professional core of trained revolutionaries so essential to their method. In China and the Dutch East Indies, the Communists suffered heavy losses. In North Africa, the nationalist movements organized by the French Communist party not only failed to dislodge French colonial rule but ran into the resistance of powerful tribal groups and local chieftains. The Bolsheviks could no longer blink the fact that the resources of Russia were grossly disproportionate to the task of spreading the global revolution and even to the task of keeping Communism

[2] Captain Malcolm Kennedy, *A History of Communism in East Asia,* New York: Praeger, 1957, pp. 120–124.

alive in its first historic abode, namely in Russia. The eclipse of
the ideologues had become a necessity. Stalin assumed the management of Russia and bent the energies of his reluctant country-
men to the establishment of socialism in one country, namely in
their own. In this first phase of ideological ebb tide, the emphasis of Soviet foreign policy rested necessarily upon Europe.
For Europe was the source of whatever power-political threats
faced the Bolsheviks. The first mission of international Communism was to safeguard the Soviet base.

Stalin was no ideological purist. Outside of Russia, the Communist party was expendable. In Europe, Stalin sanctioned cheer-
fully such ambiguous devices as the popular front and outright
alliances with Fascism. Outside of Europe, Communist initiative
was limited to the oblique and far from generous support of Communist movements that had managed to survive the defeats of
the 1920's and the recurrent purges of their respective commands by Stalin. Only in one respect did Stalin prepare the
grounds for the resumption of the offensive in Asia and Africa:
he launched a long-range program for the training of native
Communist cadres, to be deployed under more favorable circumstances.

After World War II, Stalin set out to repair the damages
caused by German invasion and to modernize the Soviet armed
forces. Soviet strategy in the immediate post-World War II period
was essentially defensive. Stalin appears to have anticipated
further crises in the Western state system.[3] Although the Communist parties throughout the West were alerted to exploit such
an eventuality, it is highly doubtful that Stalin, well aware of
America's nuclear power, contemplated large-scale military ac-

---

[3] Joseph Stalin, *The Economic Problems of Socialism in the U.S.S.R.*,
Moscow, 1952. In this, his last important work, written prior to the Nineteenth Party Congress, Stalin warned his comrades not to assume that the
world conflict had yet reached the stage of direct confrontation between the
socialist and capitalist state systems. He contended that new internal crises
within the capitalist system would inevitably arise as the result of imperialistic rivalry, and he implied that Communists should seek to exploit these
contradictions more fully.

tion against the West even had a world economic collapse borne
out his prognosis. Stalin's principal objective was to deter the
West from contesting the Soviet gains in Eastern Europe and
from thwarting, by means of a preventive war, the Soviet Union's
gigantic effort to close the military-technological gap. Until Stalin's death, Soviet policy remained relatively inactive throughout the rimlands of Asia, including the Middle East and the Arab
world. Although it can be argued that Stalin pursued a positive
policy in China, there is strong evidence that Mao Tse-tung often
took his own counsel and even proceeded sometimes in opposition to Stalin's wishes.[4]

American foreign policy, from the late 1940's onward, was
presumably designed to counter the Stalinist policy in Europe.
American policy sought to contain what it conceived to be the
main thrust of Soviet expansionism directed at Central and
Western Europe. Its principal tools were the Marshall Plan
and the Atlantic Alliance. Although the bland doctrine of containment was cast in a global mold, its principal objective was to
stop the Russians in Europe. If Stalin sought to consolidate his
gains and repair the war-damaged fabric of his empire, the
United States sought to repair the war-damaged fabric of Western and Central Europe. As an aftermath of the Korean onslaught it also worked to create, for the first time, a military
counterpoise to Russia west of the Elbe River. The analogy,
which does not lack an element of high comedy, does not stop
here: just as Stalin expected the West to run into heavy weather
economically, so the proponents of containment counted on the
contradictions besetting the Communist world as their strongest
ally. In truth, Stalin and those who proposed to contain Stalinist
expansionism were at one insofar as each side expected that the
other would defeat itself. As a matter of fact, the West had its
spate of economic troubles—only to overcome them with another
burst of capitalist productivity. The Communist bloc was riven
by internal contradictions—only to overcome them by a reorgan-

[4] Benjamin Schwartz, *Chinese Communism and the Rise of Mao*, Cambridge: Harvard University Press, 1951, p. 5.

ization of the system of controls, the demonstration of military-technological power and the application of force abetted by the still inexplicable passivity of the West.

In January, 1954, American policy, by reinforcing the doctrine of containment with the doctrine of "massive retaliation," [5] sought to redress the strategic balance in Europe and signified implicitly the United States' determination to fight for the preservation of the *status quo* in Europe as well as in Korea. Secretary of State Dulles' new deterrent doctrine replaced his predecessor's hypothetical "positions of strength" with the declaratory policy of "massive retaliation."

The policy of deterrence forced the Communists to desist from such direct challenges as they had presented in Korea and to devise more subtle modes for the penetration of the "gray areas." Neither Mr. Dulles' "massive retaliation" nor, for that matter, the doctrines of "limited war" advanced by his critics coped adequately with Communist strategy which now had shifted into new political and paramilitary dimensions. Moreover, the growing nuclear power of the Soviet Union put in doubt the United States' readiness to invoke "massive retaliation" unless confronted by a clear threat to national survival.

The 1955 Geneva Summit Meeting was made possible, if not unavoidable, by prevailing Western public sentiment—weariness with the exactions of the Cold War and a characteristic craving for final and formal settlements—and by mounting disagreements among the Western allies.

The Soviet leaders, although they were fully aware of Western motives and integrated them in their own calculations, were led to the encounter at Geneva by motives which differed from those inducing their Western opposites to meet with them at the summit. With the demise of Stalin disappeared a formidable obstacle to liquidating a number of demonstrably unproductive ideological positions. The thesis of capitalist economic crisis could now be put conveniently into storage. The petty feud with Tito

[5] John Foster Dulles, "Policy for Security and Peace," *Foreign Affairs,* Vol. XXXII, April, 1954, p. 358.

had been composed, and the Yugoslav leader's alleged heresy could be turned from an ideological liability into a diplomatic asset. More important still, the long overdue reorganization of the Communist system, blocked by Stalin's personal idiosyncrasies, could now be launched under comparatively favorable conditions. By conceding that "many roads led to socialism," the Soviets hoped to attract the Afro-Asian neutrals whom Stalin had neglected and whose aversion to totalitarianism sprang not so much from rooted democratic convictions as from distaste for Stalin's unsophisticated methods. By shifting the international cadres of Communism from close-order to open-order drill— by purporting to loosen the reins of Moscow's control over the Communist parties outside of Russia—the Khrushchev "collective" sought to check the West's military build-up and occasional psychopolitical stabs at the Soviet Empire in Eastern Europe. In effect, the new combine proffered to the West the prospect of a quasi-neutral zone of Titoist states from the Black Sea to the Baltic Sea.

To be sure, de-Stalinization was intended also to relieve mounting internal pressures and to mask the struggle for power within the Soviet hierarchy. But its companion piece, the apparent devolution of Soviet Russian controls over the satellite states or, rather, the local Communist parties, was made to serve Soviet diplomacy playing for the "relaxation of tensions," to wit the relaxation of Western defense efforts and unity of political purpose. The West, since it was beginning to see—in the light of Soviet nuclear advances—no alternative between total peace and total war, between the "balance of terror" and nuclear apocalypse, snatched eagerly at the salve to its uneasy conscience: "national Communism," although the Communists themselves emphatically rejected the term, seemed to the Western statesmen the next best thing to "liberation," if not the best last hope of the satellite peoples.

It is doubtful that the summit meeting at Geneva marked a turning point of history. In the protracted conflict between two vast systems, no single event, be it conference or battle, can be decisive. The real significance of the Geneva meeting seems to lie not so much in the importance of the issues under negotiation as in the insight it afforded in mental states: The Western statesmen, whatever might have been their private reservations, were carried to Geneva on the crest of their peoples' perennial hopes for a settlement with finality and surcease from strife; the Soviets came to establish another position of maneuver in the protracted conflict. The Soviets adroitly avoided, as they always had done before, a showdown with Western strength and shifted their weight, as they always had done before, to bring it to bear against Western weakness. The West's key position—NATO— was too strong to be taken by frontal assault; the Communists moved to outflank it. The chosen field of maneuver was the area not explicitly covered by the system of Western alliance treaties. The first probing thrust, which was launched shortly after the fatuous Geneva communiqué, was the Czech arms shipment to Egypt. Had the West responded vigorously, the Soviets might have disavowed their satellite or met a sharp Western riposte— such as the capture of ships carrying Czech arms—with a verbal protest. Nothing illustrates more graphically the West's disregard of the canons of protracted conflict than its supine acceptance of Soviet penetration, first by proxy and then directly, into the Middle East. By the time the numbness induced by Geneva had worn off, the West saw itself confronted with a phenomenon unprecedented in modern history: the emergence of Russia as a Middle Eastern power.

In the West, the summit meeting at Geneva was vested with a meaning that transcended the reticent phrasing of the declarations issued by the assembled statesmen: the United States and the Soviet Union, having recognized the catastrophic horrors of thermonuclear war, had reached a *de facto* agreement to renounce force. If this had been indeed true, a new epoch of international relations would have opened at Geneva.[6] The idea that

[6] The post-Geneva comments indeed reflected the optimistic belief that a new era had opened. Secretary of State Dulles said that "for the predictable future we can subject our differences to the patient processes of diplomacy

the Soviets now eschewed *all* violent conflict in favor of "peaceful" competition was pleasing to the Western mind. To the Western mind, conflict as a conscious, managed struggle, the goals of which are mutually incompatible, is an unpalatable idea, for it does not fit the Western image of modern, civilized society. By contrast, regulated competition, because it is impersonal and unconscious in its operation among individual groups bidding for a share of economic goods, is conducive to economic welfare and, if conducted with propriety, to good feeling. It is therefore not surprising that the West has thus far failed to grasp the central role of conflict in Soviet operational doctrine and the variety of forms which it may take. After Geneva, the West construed the term "peaceful, competitive coexistence" in the light of its own concept of competition, just as in the past it was willing to accept other samples of Communist semantics such as "popular democracy," "free elections," "imperialism" and "colonialism" as though they meant the same thing to the Soviets as they did in Western parlance.

There is much to be said for a return to traditional diplomacy and against "open covenants, openly arrived at." The Soviets themselves are careful students and skillful practitioners of the time-honored art of diplomacy. They have shown themselves keenly aware of the virtue of self-enforcing agreements and piecemeal settlements of sticky issues; we can do worse than to

---

with less fear that war will come to them." *New York Times,* July 27, 1955. Lester B. Pearson, then Canada's Secretary of State for External Affairs, remarked: "The results achieved there have been rightly hailed throughout the world as marking the beginning of an effort by the leading nations of the two power blocs to adjust by discussion and negotiation their conflicts of national interest and ideological difference which have divided and distressed the world during the last decade." "After Geneva: A Greater Task for NATO," *Foreign Affairs,* Vol. XXXII, October, 1955, p. 14. "Once full scale war becomes a suicide pact, it can no longer be regarded, even by the most cold-blooded aggressor, as the continuation of policy by other means. Even before the July conference in Geneva, it was evident that both the Western and the Soviet governments had grasped this fact; at that conference they had a chance to convince each other that both has grasped it. They seem to have succeeded." "Graduated Deterrence," *The Economist,* November 5, 1955, p. 457.

dust off the manuals of cabinet diplomacy and bargain with the Soviets to mutual advantage. But the limits of negotiation with the Communists are sharply drawn by their own conflict doctrine. To negotiate for a cessation of protracted conflict *before* the Communists have rejected their operational doctrine and Messianic aspirations would be tantamount to negotiating for surrender. At Brest-Litovsk, forty years ago, the Communists, although they yielded, did not capitulate. Then, their writ extended no farther than the suburbs of Leningrad and Moscow. Today, they hold one-third of the globe. It is unlikely that Nikita Khrushchev or his successor will do what Leon Trotsky refused to do. Conflict to the bitter end is the stuff from which Communism draws its very sustenance. Negotiation is merely one technique, albeit a highly effective one, prescribed by the doctrine of protracted conflict.

We can now see how the Communists have applied this doctrine to the strategic situation confronting them from 1945 to 1957. The problem was to annul the Western democracies' technological and strategic superiority while presenting them with no challenge sufficiently decisive to trigger that type of straightforward military response which Hitlerian strategy forced upon them. At first, the American atomic monopoly deterred Russia from presenting the United States with a forthright military challenge. Later, even after they had developed their own nuclear power, the Western air base system which formed a ring around the Communist heartland kept them at a strategic disadvantage. Through this period, they confined their military challenges to the indirect and irregular type, employing proxies to do their work.

The Kremlin leaders depended primarily upon psychological warfare to counter the effect of the American-sponsored economic and military programs which were designed to strengthen Western Europe. Communist propaganda succeeded in conditioning European popular opinion to be increasingly sensitive to American objectives. A considerable segment of European opinion—liberal, pacifist, socialist and neutralist—was alienated by the continuation of the U.S. nuclear experiments, the decision to rearm Germany, the cost of NATO defenses and the construction of U.S. air bases on Europe's soil. Meanwhile, the Soviet Union, attempting to effect a tactical juncture between its objective of shoving the West out of Asia and Africa and its objective of bringing about the disintegration of the Western alliance, tried to maneuver the United States into an uncomfortable middle position between the national aspirations of the colonial peoples and the commercial-strategic interests of the European colonial powers.

In June, 1950, the troops of the Communist puppet regime of North Korea, striking across the Thirty-eighth Parallel, put to test the firmness of American intentions in the Far East. Moscow parried the affirmative American response to that aggression by persuading the Chinese Communist regime to enter the war. Even though the U.S.S.R. supplied arms to the North Korean-Chinese forces, the Russians did not allow themselves to become drawn directly into the war. When, after a year of combat, the Communist forces in Korea were unable to win new ground and the American-North Korean build-up permitted potentially decisive offensive operations, the Russians, far from threatening the West with a general war, suggested, in 1951, that negotiations for a truce be opened.

After the Communists had worn down the West's will to fight in Korea by two years of devious armistice discussions and had blanketed the Free World with their peace propaganda, mounted elaborately and financed largely by the contributions of *Western* Communists, fellow travelers and pacifists, the Korean truce signaled a stepping up of the operational pace in Indochina. Here France fought an "old" war, heavily encumbered by ambiguous political and moral issues which militated against any vigorous Western response. The Soviet Union thus embroiled the West in Asian wars waged by its Korean and Chinese as well as its Malayan and Indochinese protégés. Their barefaced connivance notwithstanding, the Soviets dodged the responsibility for the actions of their proxies. In this farce, they were assisted by the legal-mindedness of the Western nations and the political naïveté of many of the "uncommitted" Asians.

Following the Soviet forced march into the realm of thermonuclear power, the Kremlin leadership felt capable of introducing important innovations into its postwar tactics. Initially, the Soviets sought to penetrate contiguous areas. In this endeavor, they depended upon the Sino-Soviet superiority in conventional armies and guerrilla warfare methods. Now for the first time in their history, the Soviets were able to "leap over" the Western treaty barriers into the more remote areas to which they had always been denied strategic access. By cannily devising proxy arms deals, the Soviet Union was able to extend its influence to Guatemala, Egypt, Syria and, through Egypt, to Algeria.

Since 1945, the Communists have succeeded in their efforts to confine, on the whole, the Cold War to the "war zone" of the non-Communist world, while keeping the "peace zone," namely the Communist bloc, virtually closed to Western intervention and, incidentally, the ministrations of the United Nations.[7] The West was willing to give a round and take a round. If the West won a round as, for example, in Korea and Jordan, it was in the defense of the *status quo.* When the Communists won a round as, for example, in Czechoslovakia, China, Indochina and the Middle East, they gained access to ground previously closed to them. At best, the West stood its ground; but the Communists in winning their rounds made a net gain. At Geneva, the West accepted, together with the "balance of terror" thesis, the Com-

---

[7] ". . . The Communists, like the early adherents of Islam, divided the world into an abode of peace and an abode of war; the 'peace territory' is to be constantly extended outward as a result of conflict in the 'war territory.' It is significant to note that, since 1945, the Communists have made the non-Communist world the 'war territory,' and they have attempted, with a good deal of success, to confine the Cold War to that part of the world outside their own borders." Alvin J. Cottrell and James E. Dougherty, "Hungary and the Soviet Idea of War," *The Russian Review,* Vol. XVI, October, 1957, p. 19.

munist-devised rules of the game, namely to play it anywhere but in the Communist "peace zone," and to content itself with winning and losing the alternate rounds elsewhere.

Communist psychological warfare has conjured up an extraordinary image that resembles an old master's representation of heaven and hell: the non-Communist world is shown as the nether world of international conflict, while the Communist orbit is aglow with peace and stability. To this day, the Western peoples have not been able to break this hypnotic spell woven by the wand of Communist propaganda. The simple fact is that the Soviet conflict managers have either instigated or aggravated almost every international dispute which has gripped the postwar world. For their own part, the Soviets have been immune from outside intervention because American policy-makers have stuck to the mystique of the containment doctrine which established—semiofficially, so to speak—the boundaries of the Communists' untouchable "zone of peace." Even in the Hungarian crisis, the United States took pains to reassure the Soviet Union that it had no intention of exploiting the only real international conflict which had yet occurred within the Communist zone of "peace and stability."

The Soviet Union has foisted upon the world the notion that only those international disputes which originate in the relations of the West to the colonial or formerly colonial areas are of world political concern. Thus, the Communists have managed to manipulate the United Nations as a lever against the *status quo* in the non-Communist world. The majority of the Asian and African members of the United Nations, being newcomers to the community of sovereign states, are keen to vindicate their own legal rights and to rescind whatever rights the Western nations still claim within their remaining overseas possessions or ex-colonies. The Soviets exploit this situation by carefully assessing and then stirring up the latent conflict potentialities within a given region. As the crisis develops, it may drain the resources of a Western nation or undermine its political prestige; it may, by its repercussions, set off a political crisis within that nation itself, or produce tensions among the Atlantic allies; and it is bound to be raised as a propaganda issue within the United Nations. Yet, in the most flagrant instance, since World War II, of the suppression of the right of national self-determination—Hungary—the Soviet Union managed to bully the U.N., for all practical purposes, into accepting the dispute as an "internal matter." Legalists may cavil at this interpretation; the Soviets have learned to count on—and to discount—their opponents' legalistic scruples.

The integration, in the early 1950's, of nuclear striking power into the Communist military establishment marked the first significant closing of the gap between the Communist and Western military-technological power. The acquisition of atomic capabilities and delivery systems signaled several important and, for the West, ominous changes in the Communist strategy of protracted conflict. These changes have been not so much in the kinds of techniques used as in the degrees of pressures brought to bear upon the West.

Ever since the Communists had to abandon their hopes for a simultaneous world revolution, they relied primarily on the psychopolitical modes of protracted conflict. Their strategy, in the broadest terms, has been to eschew the massive use of hardware and to produce psychological disturbances within the West, while at the same time keeping the uncommitted nations uncommitted or drawing them into the Communist orbit. In the development of their psychopolitical methods they are deeply indebted, although they have omitted any acknowledgments, to Pavlov and Freud. The Communists have applied Freudian techniques in order to induce a guilt complex in the West about such things as armament, colonial possessions and foreign bases, and thus to paralyze the West's will to take a resolute stand anywhere. Then again, we might compare the alternations between Khrushchev's avowals of peaceful intentions and threats of nuclear destruction with the alternate ringing of high- and low-frequency bells which, in the Pavlovian experiment with dogs and rabbits, were gradually brought closer together until the animal became paralyzed by terror or went berserk.[8] Since Geneva, the intervals between the bells have become shorter and shorter (Note 1).*

The acceleration of pace and increase of pressure of Soviet strategies do not signify a change in Soviet objectives. These remain the same. They are, in the short run, first, to force the withdrawal of the West from its strategic footholds, especially from the SAC network of bases; secondly, to compel the West to divert vital economic and military resources from Europe; thirdly, to take Western pressure and attention off Eastern Europe; and fourthly, to exacerbate the divergencies within the Atlantic Alliance. The long-run Soviet objectives, too, are the same: namely to isolate the West, deprive it of its sources of strategic raw materials and markets, and to encircle it via Asia, the Middle East and Africa, until the West, its economic roots having withered, will fall under its own weight.

Soviet objectives, long-run and short-run, have been plain enough to impress the West with the need for a policy, if not for appropriate counteractions. There is now fairly general agreement that we have not been doing enough and that we must do more. But on the question as to what it is that more should be done about, opinions still divide radically. There is one line of reasoning—it still seems to be the predominant one in Western councils—which runs as follows: first, the nuclear stalemate and the "equilibrium of terror" preclude war; second, the Soviet Union will not risk the "inevitability of history" on the nuclear battlefield; third, the boundaries of the Cold War in Europe are frozen and the only area of maneuver left to us and to the Communists is the uncommitted world; fourth, we can compete with

---

[8] I. P. Pavlov, *Conditioned Reflexes*, translated by G. V. Anrep, Cambridge: Oxford University Press, 1927. Cf. especially Lecture XXIII, "The Experimental Results Obtained with Animals in Their Application to Man," pp. 395–411. The implications of Pavlovian psychology for Soviet international policy are discussed by "Ferreus," "The Menace of Communist Psychological Warfare," *Orbis*, Vol. I, April, 1957, and by Robert C. Tucker, "Stalin and the Uses of Psychology," *World Politics*, Vol. VIII, July, 1956.

* See Notes, p. 153 ff.

the Communists effectively because our material, social and spiritual wares are superior; and fifth, we can win over the underdeveloped areas by helping them toward economic growth, which, in turn, will engender political and emotional stability.

In essence, this plan of action abjures force as an instrument of Western policy, except perhaps in the case of "brush-fire" wars of indeterminate origin, i.e., small wars which the Communists, acting discreetly through one or several middlemen, suddenly start or keep going in out-of-the-way places. In any case, force, if it has to be used at all, must serve to maintain the *status quo*. Force, as either military power-in-being or military power-in-action, must not be applied as the instrument of a diplomacy which seeks to reverse the *status quo*, carry the Western offensive into the Communist "peace zone," and win new ground. The task of diplomacy thus must be to keep the peoples-on-our-side on our side and, since there really is no other alternative, to seek an accommodation—or even "disengagement" [9]—with the Soviet Empire. Once this premise is granted the Western sphere of action narrows down to the so-called uncommitted world, for in this world the West stands to incur grievous losses in addition to those which it has suffered, since the Cold War began, there and elsewhere. Since the West's retreat from colonial empire proceeds at an ever accelerating pace and the United States, in particular, does not propose to coerce the new Asian and African states into "commitment," there remains friendly persuasion and massive economic assistance as the only means of keeping the uncommitted peoples out of the clutches of the Communists. We can hope to enlist their good will by respecting their "legitimate" national aspirations and by conceding that their posture is tantamount to true neutrality as long as they do not

[9] The most popular and the most general proposal for disengagement in Europe can be found in George F. Kennan, *Russia, the Atom and the West,* the Reith Lectures delivered over the B.B.C., New York: Harper & Brothers, 1958, Chapters III and IV. A more limited form of disengagement, calling for a partial withdrawal and redeployment of American forces on the European Continent, is suggested in Alvin J. Cottrell and Walter F. Hahn, "A New Strategy for Europe," *The Yale Review,* Vol. XLVII, Autumn, 1957.

accede to external or internal Communist control. Furthermore, we can derive comfort from the fact that their cultural and religious heritage endows many noncommitted countries, particularly the Islamic ones, with a high degree of immunity against Communist ideology. In brief, the struggle for the mind of the uncommitted peoples is not yet lost. Western humanism, reinforced by economic assistance, can carry the day, particularly since we are rich enough to outbid the hard-pressed Soviet economy in the competition for the custom and good will of the Afro-Asians.

This line of reasoning, highly popular throughout the West, derives from the classic doctrine of containment—which is probably the principal reason why it is still so widely accepted. Indeed, it has everything to recommend it—except the fact that it does not meet the challenge of protracted conflict. Its arguments are fallacious because, first, the "equilibrium of terror" is not a *stable* equilibrium as long as the technological race continues, and the "equilibrium of terror" does not preclude war and is itself an instrument of Communist protracted conflict management; second, the attrition of protracted conflict has put the superiority of our material, social and spiritual wares in doubt—and in grave doubt at that; and third, the new nationalisms are directed against the West. The non-Western peoples are passing through various stages of Westernization. Yet, Westernization has been far from engendering pro-Western sympathies. To the contrary, it has given rise to a psychological transference to the Western peoples of the feeling of guilt for the abandonment of traditions and mores. A whipping boy must be found who will atone for the dislocations caused by Westernization. The most convenient one is the West itself.

The West is bent upon the crucial problem of its survival in the face of the Communist threat. The West thus offers a ready and profitable target for blackmail. The "backward" peoples' common, albeit naïve, admiration for Communist performance, especially for the Soviets' short cut in industrialization, has been deepened by the Soviets' recent technological triumphs and the

West's patent discomfiture. The neutrality of Asian countries such as India, Indonesia and Egypt tends toward diverse shadings of benevolence toward the Soviets. This brand of neutralism is quick to take offense at any Western initiative—except the West's proffer of gifts "without political strings."[10]

In most of Asia and, to some measure, in most underdeveloped lands, the "forces of history" are not on the side of the West: they favor the Communists. In the short run, at least, Western chances of effecting a decisive improvement in Eastern standards of living are slim. Conceding even the dubious thesis that economic improvement stands in any palpable relationship to the growth of democratic institutions, or, for that matter, of any political institutions, it is unlikely that whatever the West manages to accomplish within, let us say, the next twenty or thirty years in assuaging the aspirations of the underdeveloped peoples will alter significantly the power relationship between itself and the Communist bloc. At best, the Communists will not grow stronger; the West will not grow weaker.

In the face of these hostile tides, the West can only hope to defeat the Communists by learning to counter the strategy of protracted conflict—to manage conflict in space and in time.

The development of proper Western attitudes toward protracted conflict will be immensely difficult. The Communists possess a mentality that is much better suited to protracted and controlled conflict than that of the Western peoples. According to Marxist-Leninist theory, history has been always on the side of Communism. The Russian Communists are, by now, convinced that, indeed, it is. They are patient and tenacious in their efforts to win the inevitable victory.[11] They must make certain that they do nothing foolish, nothing that might jeopardize their chances of ultimate success. They are capable not only of accepting but

10 Robert Strausz-Hupé, Alvin J. Cottrell and James E. Dougherty, *American-Asian Tensions*, New York: Praeger, 1956, especially Chapter I and the General Conclusions.

11 George F. Kennan, "The Sources of Soviet Conduct," Appendix I in *American Diplomacy, 1900–1950*, Chicago: University of Chicago Press, 1951.

also of exploiting a tactical defeat, if such a defeat leads their opponent to relax his guard and thus to neglect his defenses. Furthermore, a monolithic structure enables the Communist rulers to execute their foreign policies with a unity of purpose and a ruthless efficiency that are unparalleled among modern governments.

The West has neither a doctrine of protracted conflict nor an international conspiratorial apparatus for executing it. What is more, we do not want such a doctrine or such a political apparatus, for it would be a tragic piece of irony if the men of the Free World, in trying to combat the Communists, should become like them.

What we need now more than anything else is an understanding of the comprehensive, complex, subtle and consistent strategy of our opponent. Later chapters, therefore, will set forth some of the principles of protracted conflict as applied by Moscow and Peking, and define some of the implications of Sino-Soviet strategies.

CHAPTER 3 THE COMMUNISTS' VIEW OF CONFLICT: THE LARGER STRATEGIC VISION

Within four decades, Communist power grew from a gleam in Lenin's eye to the absolute domination of nearly a billion people. One of the principal reasons for the Communists' enormous gains has been their ability to conceive of the struggle for power—its terms, its theater, its methods and its goals—in larger dimensions than their opponents.

The dialectic theory of history, first formulated by Marx and Engels, is a theory of universal and protracted conflict: the whole world is transformed into a battlefield upon which socio-economic forces are locked in a titanic contest of indefinite duration. Marx and Engels bequeathed to the revolutionary Communists a conceptual framework which enabled them to relate the meaning of events here and now to a wider historical process governed by immutable laws and moving toward a predictable end. Lenin acknowledged the debt of Bolshevik political and military strategy to Marxist historical analysis:

Marxism asks that the various types of struggle be analyzed within their historical framework. To discuss conflict outside of its historical and concrete setting is to misunderstand elementary dialectic material-ism. At various junctures of the economic evolution, and depending upon changing political, national, cultural, social and other conditions, differing types of struggle may become important and even predominant. As a result of those sociological transformations, secondary and subordinate forms of action may change their significance. To try and answer positively or negatively the question of whether a certain tactic is usable, without at the same time studying the concrete conditions confronting [the movement at] a given moment [and] at a precise point of its development, would mean a complete negation of Marxism.[1]

This strategy, as developed and refined by revolutionary Communism, transforms the entire globe into a theater of war, and nations are mere salients to be reduced and continents mere flanks to be turned.[2] While the military commander confines his analysis of the logistical situation to the immediate theater of war, the Communist conflict manager extends his evaluation to the performance of entire rival economic and technological systems. The morale of one's own forces is a question of education, training, indoctrination and other modes of social control; the morale of the enemy is marked as the target of psychopolitical attacks, especially through the enemy's own media of mass communications. In this broader dimension, it is not sufficient to study a single leader, his character, his training and his strategic preconceptions. The strategist of global, protracted conflict must seek to gain insights into the society which he is bent on conquering: its cultural matrix, its institutional structure, its popular emotions and neuroses and its decision-making machinery. Moreover, he must vary the modes of his approach—military, paramilitary, political, psychological, technological and economic—and suit them to the place and the time. He must phase his tactical operations over large geographical areas and long periods of time, and he must subordinate all operations to the larger strategic goal; a

---

[1] V. I. Lenin, "Partisan Warfare," *Orbis*, Vol. II, p. 196. The above is a translation of the article "Partisanskaya Voina," which has been reprinted in all four Russian editions of Lenin's *Sochineniya* (*Collected Works*).

[2] The party must make all appraisals "on a sufficiently broad scale, that is, precisely on a world scale." Nathan Leites, *The Operational Code of the Politburo*, New York: McGraw-Hill, 1951, p. 15.

local military victory, for example, may have to be forfeited for the sake of more enduring political gains.

As the geographic setting of conflict analysis widens, the time needed to consummate the strategic operation must be lengthened and broadened commensurately. In turn, the extension of scale calls for suitable organizational techniques and instruments. In protracted conflict strategy, five-year logistical plans are meshed with decades of the tactical movement of forces and the careful phasing of political, economic, psychological and military or paramilitary operations. Hence, the side which knows how to conceive of the conflict in the appropriate dimensions of time enjoys the advantage—and can even afford the luxury of policy mistakes for the opponent is ill equipped to recognize and comprehend their significance in time to exploit them.

From the outset, Communist conflict doctrine revealed a remarkable affinity to military thought. The idea that military and political instruments are interchangeable in the execution of one vast strategic plan, central to Clausewitz' thought, is the pith of Communist doctrine. In his personal copy of the great German theoretician's famous book, *On War*, Lenin underscored the following passage:

If War belongs to policy, it will naturally take its character from thence. If policy is great and powerful so also will be the War, and this may be carried to the point at which War attains to its absolute form.

It is only through this kind of view that War recovers unity; only by it can we see all Wars as things of one kind and only thus can we attain the true and perfect basis and point of view from which great plans may be traced out and determined upon.

There is upon the whole nothing more important in life than to find out the right point of view from which things should be looked at and judged of and then to keep to that point, for we can only apprehend the mass of events in the unity from one standpoint, and it is only the keeping to one point of view that guards us from inconsistency.[3]

[3] Cf. Byron Dexter, "Clausewitz and Soviet Strategy," *Foreign Affairs*, Vol. XXIX, October, 1950, pp. 49–50.

In sum, war, be it fought with military hardware or with non-violent, political and psychological instruments, is a unity. "Hot" and "cold" are phases of intensity in one and the same war.

Advances in technology and psychology have permitted the Communists to widen the range of conflict instruments far beyond the dreams of Clausewitz, who wrote in an age of hand tools and slow communications. But the principal insights of Soviet strategy into the politics-war continuum can be derived from *On War,* written over a hundred years ago.

Friedrich Engels, Karl Marx' faithful collaborator, was a close student of the German military theoretician Karl von Clausewitz, a half-century before Lenin annotated his copy of *On War.* Lenin's familiarity with the writings of Clausewitz is a matter of record. He wrote of Clausewitz' celebrated dictum on war as the continuation of policy: "The Marxists have considered this axiom as the theoretical foundation for the meaning of every war."

If Clausewitz was the unwitting prophet of the Communist doctrine of protracted conflict, its most incisive modern spokesman is Mao Tse-tung. The wide strategic vision of the Chinese Communist leader derives at least in part from the Oriental tradition of warfare.

As conceived by Mao, the strategy of protracted conflict is the lever for effecting a gradual change in the relative strength of the two sides—the revolutionary and the *status quo.* As the war is prolonged, various forces—political, economic, psychological and military—which are unfavorable to the enemy and favorable to the revolutionaries can be set in motion, shaped and nourished. The Communists will grow in military experience, technology, organizational ability and gain increasingly the international mass support. Conversely, the Communists' foes will suffer changes for the worse: exhaustion of resources, disintegration of morale, the alienation of world opinion and confusion over the proper policy to be pursued.[4] At every turn in the protracted war,

[4] *Selected Works of Mao Tse-tung,* London: Lawrence & Wishart, Ltd., 1954, 5 vols., Vol. II, p. 189.

the Communists can, by adopting all kinds of deceptive measures, effectively drive the enemy into the pitfall of making erroneous judgments.[5] Mao, in one famous passage, distilled the essence of his extended strategy to sixteen words: "Enemy advances, we retreat; enemy halts, we harass; enemy tires, we attack; enemy retreats, we pursue." [6] The import of Mao's writings is that both time and wisdom are on the side of the Communists and that, inescapably, the forces of the *status quo,* lacking a conceptual framework of the conflict, will succumb in the enveloping tide of revolutionary Communism.

In keeping with the broad strategic vision advocated by Clausewitz and Mao, the Communists have acquired a spectrum of weapons much more variegated than that which composes the arsenal of the West. They discern weapons where the West sees only the implements of peaceful international relations (Note 2). According to the Communists doctrine of protracted conflict, war, politics, diplomacy, law, psychology, science and economics—all form a continuum and all are closely integrated in the conduct of foreign policy.[7] Moreover, the Communists have developed political, psychological and organizational

[5] *Ibid.,* p. 216.

[6] *Ibid.,* p. 164. "Throughout 1946 and 1947, communist policy was one of avoiding decisive battles and of building up fighting strength with troops and equipment captured from small segments of the Nationalist armies. During this stage guerrilla warfare was pushed on all fronts. Gradually, the Reds were enabled to merge into a war of maneuver involving larger bodies of troops." F. F. Liu, *A Military History of Modern China 1924–1949,* Princeton: Princeton University Press, 1956, pp. 251–252.

[7] Although writing primarily for Soviet military strategists, M. V. Frunze exhibited a keen appreciation of the "Spectrum of Weapons" concept in the following passage: "The Red commander must learn to the fullest extent to master those methods of thinking and the art of the analysis of phenomena which is provided by Marxist teaching. The substance of this method comes to this, that for us there cannot be anything absolute or ossified; everything flows and is changing, and every means, every method must find its application in certain circumstances. The proficiency of the commander manifests itself in the ability to select, from the variety of means at his disposal, those which give the best results in a given set of circumstances." M. V. Frunze, *Izbrannye proizvedeniya,* Moscow: Voennoye izdatel'stvo Voennogo ministerstva Soyuza SSR, 1951, p. 190.

strategies far more sophisticated than the mere physical seizure
of territory. They have mastered the technique of staging aggression against social institutions and human minds, without
physically violating political borders and thus posing a *casus
belli.*

What particular method or mixture of conflict methods is to be
used depends upon given capabilities and opportunities. Psychologically prepared for an indefinitely prolonged struggle, the
Communists are steeled against temporary setbacks. They remain
undaunted in the face of adversity, for they are convinced that
their reverses are only partial, or local, or short-lived. If the Communists suffer an acute loss in one area, they can take comfort from the victories wrought in another. All reversals are thus
seen as relative; new strength can be drawn from the lessons
which they contain. Every retreat becomes a "strategic retreat,"
calculated to produce greater gains subsequently. If plans are
blocked and rendered invalid by unanticipated events on the
terrain of conflict, these events can sooner or later be reconciled
to the global blueprint, or else the blueprint can be modified to
accommodate them. This concept, i.e., the "ebb and flow" of the
world revolutionary tide, is fundamental in Communist strategic
thought.[8]

Brest-Litovsk constitutes one of the earliest and most interesting applications of the "ebb and flow" concept. Lenin, upon
coming to power in 1917, confronted one overarching problem,
namely, how to end Russia's participation in the world war as
quickly as possible, so that the Bolsheviks could concentrate their
resources on consolidating their first territorial foothold, the
launching platform of future conflict operations. Lenin realized

---

[8] "The communist movement never should swim against the trend of the
historic cycle. During revolutionary ebbs and non-communist tides, it should
avoid risk and protect its position while simultaneously accumulating
strength." Stefan T. Possony, *A Century of Conflict*, p. 394. "The law of
'ebb and flow' implies that unless the whole of capitalism collapses under
the present revolutionary wave, the surviving remnant will temporarily
stabilize itself a few years after the end of the war and an ebb in the tide
of revolution will set in. . . ." "Historicus," "Stalin on Revolution," *Foreign
Affairs*, Vol. XXVII, January, 1949, pp. 212–213.

that unless peace were made soon, the fledgling Soviet state might be crushed in the vise of foreign war and internal armed resistance. So far as Lenin was concerned, the internal enemy—i.e., the White Russian forces—was more to be feared than the external foe. In order to guarantee the continuation of his Communist regime, he came to terms with Germany at a heavy cost to Russia. Under the Treaty of Brest-Litovsk, Lenin ceded 32 per cent of Russia's arable land, 34 per cent of her population, 89 per cent of her coal resources, and 54 per cent of her total industrial capacity.[9] Lenin, however, perceived his strategic problem in larger dimensions than did the "triumphant" leaders of Imperial Germany. The severe conditions of the Treaty of Brest-Litovsk did not disconcert Lenin in the least. In fact, the Soviet leader, by yielding to the demands of the victorious, albeit exhausted Germans, showed a consummate mastery of a strategic technique which was by no means new in Russian history—trading space for time. This technique, as applied by Lenin, reflects what may be aptly termed a "four-dimensional" approach to conflict. No retreat or loss need be considered fatal for Communism, if Communism thereby strengthens itself or enhances its capabilities of carrying on future conflict. In due time, everything that has been conceded will be taken back.

An excellent illustration of the Communists' larger strategic vision—their ability to widen the global dimensions of the battlefield on which the protracted conflict is being waged—can be found in their policy toward the colonial areas. At the end of the First World War, the Communist leadership realized that the Asian and African continents were entering a period of revolutionary transformation. They proposed to harness the power of the social forces which were about to inundate the colonial regions. The Communists perceived that developments impending in these regions would have a direct and important bearing upon the success of their strategy against the West. As early as 1921, Stalin called attention to this relationship:

[9] John W. Wheeler-Bennett, "The Meaning of Brest-Litovsk Today," *Foreign Affairs*, Vol. XVII, October, 1938, p. 139.

If Europe and America may be called the front, the scene of the main engagements between socialism and imperialism, the nonsovereign nations and the colonies, with their raw materials, fuel, food and vast store of human material should be regarded as the rear, the reserve of imperialism. In order to win a war, one must not only triumph at the front but also revolutionize the enemy's rear, his reserves.[10]

Perhaps Lenin never actually uttered the famous aphorism which is so often attributed to him: "The road to Paris lies through Peking." Whether he did or not, it is clear that Lenin and his successors saw the important part which the anticolonial struggle would play in softening up the West for the final, decisive phase of the protracted conflict (Note 3). Today, few would deny the significant role played by the colonial areas in the struggle between Communism and the West. Yet, Lenin foresaw this role as early as 1916, when he quoted the following passage by Rudolf Hilferding:

The thousand-year-old agrarian isolation of countries situated outside the main current of history is broken, and they are dragged into the capitalist whirlpool. Capitalism itself gradually procures for the vanquished the means and resources for emancipating themselves. And they set out to obtain the objective which once seemed to the European nations to be the highest objective: national unity as a means to obtain economic and cultural freedom. This movement for national independence threatens European capital in its valuable field of exploitation, where the radiant prospects are opening up before it, and in those places European capital can only maintain its domination by continually increasing its military forces.[11]

The conduct of the Soviets immediately prior to and during World War II furnished instructive examples of the manner in which the Communists apply their conflict strategy to concrete historical situations.

[10] Joseph Stalin, *Marxism and the National and Colonial Question*, New York: Marxist Library, International Publishers, n.d., p. 115.
[11] Cited in V. I. Lenin, *Imperialism: The State and Revolution*, New York: The Vanguard Press, 1929, p. 101.

The Communists, when waging actual military operations, are not guided by the same set of canons that inform Western wartime policy (Note 4). Americans in particular, once they have thrown themselves into the effort to defeat the enemy with sheer physical power, are inclined to postpone consideration of political objectives until after the cessation of hostilities. Thus American leaders in World War II planned and conducted an exclusively military strategy which was designed to produce a crushing victory as rapidly as possible. It is indeed a paradox of our time that democracies, once fully mobilized for military conflict, are apt to outdo the dictatorships in waging total military war—the war for unconditional surrender. This paradox derives from the democracies' instability of mood—the oscillation between the aversion against all things military and a war psychosis that can be appeased only by total victory and the severe punishment of the enemy.

When the war against Germany entered its final phase and the Soviets took the offensive, Stalin became increasingly concerned with Russia's postwar position in Central and Eastern Europe. Earlier, at Teheran, he had exerted his influence to bring about a Western "second front" in France rather than in the Balkans, where an attack would have thwarted Russia's postwar objectives. His primary objective of winning the war already assured, Stalin now concentrated his efforts upon the problem of how to exploit the war in its closing stages in order to maximize Russian political gains. Instead of maintaining unrelenting pressure upon the retreating German forces, the Soviets paced their military operations to the attainment of political objectives beyond military victory: They sought to ensure Moscow's postwar domination of the Eastern European governments. An eyewitness of the Soviet conquest of Hungary wrote:

These operations were directed solely by political expediency and as a result of that, they were momentarily illogical from a military point of view. . . . The aim of all these operations was to eliminate the existence of strong pro-Ally and anti-German resistance forces in Poland, Bulgaria and Hungary, which, after the liberation of their countries,

*could have been significant obstacles on the avenue to Bolshevization,
due to their non-communist character. The military procedure applied
was that of indirect extermination, indirect cooperation with the German Army.*[12]

The U.S.S.R. disdained the opportunity to negotiate armistices
with the indigenous governments of the former Nazi satellites
which were anxious to end their participation in the war as
speedily as possible. Instead, the Soviets sought, even at the risk
of delaying their westward military advance, to create a political
vacuum in each of the East European countries which could later
be filled by a Communist provisional government. The best-
documented incident of this truly Machiavellian strategy occurred in Poland. As the Red Army approached Warsaw in
July, 1944, the Soviet Radio repeatedly urged the underground
army of Polish patriots in the capital, led by General Bor, to
rise up and fight the Nazis. But when the Poles launched their
insurrection, the Soviet forces immediately brought their offensive to a standstill outside Warsaw and waited patiently while
the Nazis liquidated General Bor's forty thousand men. The Russians refused to make the slightest effort to extend aid and declared that they would not allow British and American aircraft
to use Soviet airfields if they attempted to fly supplies to Warsaw. As a result of Stalin's policy, the Polish uprising proved a
complete failure. After the Home Guards had been totally destroyed, the Red Army resumed its advance, "liberated" Warsaw
and established the hand-picked Lublin Communist government
in power (Note 5).

The manner in which the Soviet Union dealt with Japanese
peace overtures in early 1945 furnishes another instructive example of controlled warfare. Although the first Japanese attempt to
obtain Soviet mediation was made in Tokyo during February,
1945, the Soviet government concealed this information from the

[12] John A. Lukacs, "Political Expediency and Soviet Russian Military
Operations," *Journal of Central European Affairs*, Vol. VIII, January, 1949,
p. 402.

United States until the Potsdam Conference, five months later. Obviously, Stalin did not wish to see the Pacific war end "prematurely." He intended to exploit it in two ways: first, by extracting maximum concessions from the United States for his promise to enter the war against Japan, and second, by using his actual participation in the war to establish his claim to a major voice in the Far Eastern postwar settlement. There is now little question that the Soviet Union held it within its power to take a step which could have led to the termination of hostilities even before the dropping of the atomic bombs (Note 6). Japan had sought Soviet help in obtaining from the West a less severe armistice formula than "unconditional surrender." But the Soviet Union could not accede to such a request without forfeiting the chance to profit politically from having taken a belligerent's part in the defeat of Japan. Nor could the U.S.S.R. flatly reject Japan's overtures without prompting Tokyo to make a more direct appeal to the West. Thus Stalin shrewdly led the Japanese to believe that there was some chance of softening the harsh terms of unconditional surrender. At the same time, Stalin assured the Western leaders of his loyal adherence to the policy of "unconditional surrender." That he fully intended to enter the Pacific war at the most advantageous juncture is borne out by the hasty Soviet military assault on Japan just forty-eight hours after the first American atomic bomb dropped on Hiroshima.[13]

Thus, unlike most Western strategists, who have traditionally equated war with the clash of arms, Communist leaders are trained to think of conflict in much larger dimensions. Military action for them is but one of many forms of warfare. Other forms of conflict—political, sociological, ideological, psychological, technological and economic—are just as important or, under certain circumstances, even more important. Quick, decisive military victory, which for centuries has been the prime objective of Western strategic planning, does not hold an equally exalted place in Communist conflict science. The Western strategist is

[13] Paul Kecskemeti, *Strategic Surrender* (a Rand Corporation Research Study), Stanford: Stanford University Press, 1958, pp. 155–211.

inclined to consider his job done once crushing victory has been won on the battlefield; the responsibility for advancing the nation's political objectives is then shunted conveniently from the military commanders to the diplomatists. This delineation of functions reflects Western democracy's traditional image of war: an aberration from international normalcy, resulting from a breakdown in orthodox diplomacy. For the Communists, by contrast, policy and war are but two sides of one coin. The coin is strategy.

In any healthy and dynamic system of thought, theoretical principles serve to facilitate positive, rational action, not hamper it; hence the simpler they are, the better. Not a single operational principle of Communist strategy, looked at separately from the others, would deserve to be ranked as anything more than a common-sense proposition. One need not ascribe diabolical cunning to men who, in a contest for power, adapt their policies to the simple dictates of common sense. Indeed, both the pattern of the contest for power and the strategic rules by which it is governed are timeless. These strategic rules have been understood for many centuries, most often implicitly rather than explicitly, by men who have commanded troops and led them into battle. But whereas the West, for complex cultural reasons, has come to identify strategic principles almost exclusively with the staging and the fighting of the immediate military engagement, the Communists have fallen heir to a less circumscribed and more ambiguous Oriental concept of conflict, in which political and psychological modes are not sharply differentiated from the purely military ones. The Communists, in brief, have learned to project strategic principles onto a wider screen. It was of more than philological significance that Stalin, when speaking didactically on the subject of international politics, used language which abounded in military metaphors.

The guide lines of Communist strategy, described in the following four chapters, are not set forth as an explicit "unified war" code worked out by the Communist high command. Soviet leadership has never published its operational codes to the world; certainly, the thought processes of conspiratorial leaders cannot be easily discerned through their formal pronouncements. The Communists may indulge in endless theoretical digressions, but they never render candid accounts of the rationale of their actions. Nevertheless, their strategy is not completely impervious to analysis by deduction. We can know something of the inwardness of Communist strategy by tracing its pattern through an abundant record of operations since 1917. A careful analysis of this pattern permits us to fit together, piece by piece, at least a few basic operational principles. The authors of this study are of the opinion that these few closely related principles—the indirect approach; deception and distraction; monopoly of the initiative; and attrition—indicate a set of preferences which influence the Communists in their strategic and tactical choices. We are not prepared to argue that the Communist leaders always adhere consciously to these principles or scrupulously strive to observe them in every instance. The classical "principles of war," it should be noted, were intuitively followed by military commanders for centuries before they were ever written down in systematic form.

To some, this effort to formulate the principles of protracted conflict as practiced by the Communists may appear as laboring the obvious. But to reduce the obvious to order is the first prerequisite for establishing a common conceptual framework for analyzing the problem before us. If we have suffered defeat upon defeat at the hands of Communist strategy, our plight is due less to the lack of available information than to the absence of a wide and pondered agreement as to what the obvious characteristics of Communist strategy really are. At the present time, the concept of protracted conflict could furnish Western policy-makers the most useful tool of analysis available for an understanding of the challenge posed by the Communists.

CHAPTER 4 THE INDIRECT APPROACH

The Communist strategy of protracted conflict seeks to avoid a general, direct, decisive encounter with the enemy unless and until overwhelming physical superiority, sufficient to ensure the enemy's complete destruction—and his alone—has been acquired. To avoid this encounter, fullest possible reliance must be placed upon indirect, irregular, unconventional strategies.[1]

Any army or revolutionary organization pitted against an opponent commanding superior forces will avail itself of the stratagem of evasion. The conflict must be kept indecisive at any one time or place until the achievement of ultimate victory has become feasible.

Tsarist policy-makers were not unaware of the potentially disruptive effects of war upon Russia's social structure (Note 7). These trepidations were shared by their Soviet successors, particularly during the first two decades of Communist rule. The qua-

---

[1] "To tie one's hand beforehand, openly to tell the enemy who is at present better armed than we, whether and when we shall fight him, is stupidity and not revolutionariness. To accept battle at a time when it is obviously advantageous to the enemy and not to us is a crime." *Selected Works,* New York: International Publishers, 1943, X, 119. "The Communist Party must develop into a militant organization capable of avoiding a fight in the open against overwhelming forces of the enemy." *Thesis and Resolutions Adopted at the Third World Congress of the Communist International, June 22–July 12, 1921,* New York: Contemporary Publishing Association, 1921, pp. 110–111.

si-isolationism of Soviet Russia during the interwar period was prompted by compelling reasons. Communism took the reins of power when Russia lay prostrate. The next two decades were devoted to curbing the Russian people and to establishing a powerful base for future conflict operations. In this period of internal consolidation and "capitalist encirclement," Soviet leadership regarded the avoidance of frontal military action as a cardinal rule of survival.[2] Karl Radek, one-time secretary of the Executive Committee of the Comintern, wrote in 1934: "The object of the Soviet Government is to save the soil of the first proletarian state from the criminal folly of a new war. . . . The defense of peace and of the neutrality of the Soviet Union against all attempts to drag it into the whirlwind of a world war is the central problem of Soviet foreign policy."[3]

Avoiding a premature military showdown was the key to Soviet diplomacy during the gathering storm of the 1930's. Stalin, as he watched the gathering war clouds in Europe, was bent on postponing as long as possible Russia's participation in the inevitable conflict. At the same time, he skillfully exploited the

[2] Marshal M. N. Tukhachevsky, one of the greatest Soviet military strategists, emphatically opposed the *blitzkrieg* doctrine, holding that no major war could be decided by a single strike. *Voina i voyennoye iskusstvo, v svete istoricheskoye materializma*, ed. M. N. Gorev, Sbornik statei, Moscow-Leningrad, 1927, p. 125. The former Soviet Commissar of War, Mikhail V. Frunze, contended that a political-economic-military strategy of attrition was more feasible for a Communist state, whereas capitalist forces are superior in pursuing a strategy of quick victory by annihilation. A. Golubev, *M. V. Frunze o kharaktere buduschei voiny*, Moscow: Voyennaya Akademiya RKKA imeni M. V. Frunze, 1931, p. 50. Frunze also wrote: "Strategy is the highest military art which must consider not only the purely military elements such as the numbers of armies, etc., but also the elements of the political situation." *Ibid.*, p. 33. Communist military writings make it clear that Communist commanders are supposed to fight in such a way that their major forces are always protected and deployed in a manner that allows easy disengagement. While all available forces should be thrown into the conflict, the main strength should never be exposed to extreme risks. A corollary of this doctrine is that the security of the Communist heartland should not be seriously jeopardized for the sake of a marginal gain along or beyond the periphery of the heartland.

[3] Karl Radek, "The Bases of Soviet Foreign Policy," *Foreign Affairs*, Vol. XII, January, 1934, p. 206.

crisis within the non-Communist world. His purpose was to divide the Western powers into two warring groups and to drive them against each other in a war of attrition. The Soviet Union, *tertius gaudens,* was to play the part of the "holder of the balance." By concluding the Nazi-Soviet Non-Aggression Pact of August, 1939, Stalin made certain that Russia would be a bystander in the early stages of the war. Thus Russia would be able to build up her relative strength while the Western nations were expending *their* strength in an internecine conflict. Then, the Soviets could later enter the war and compel one side or the other to accept them as allies whose help was indispensable to winning the war (Note 8). Furthermore, by entering into a neutrality pact with the Japanese in 1941, the Soviet Union staved off involvement in the Far East while girding itself for the war on the Western front. These two nonaggression pacts—with Germany in 1939 and Japan in 1941—effectively warded off the nightmare of Soviet strategists: an attack on two fronts by the combined might of Russia's enemies.

Future historians will record as the most significant consequence of World War II not the defeat of Germany nor the "victory" of the West, but the emergence of Russia as the world's second most powerful nation. The defeats of Germany and Japan conferred upon the Soviet Union hegemony in Europe and Asia. Moreover, France and Britain, gravely weakened by the war, were unable to halt the disintegration of their empires. At the same time, the war and its aftermath quickened the pace of the systemic revolution in the dependent areas once controlled by the West. Thus, in the turn of a half-decade, the "capitalist encirclement" of Russia was breached by stretches of "no man's land," the ideal terrain for the operations of Communist strategy. With the rapid demobilization of Allied forces in Western Europe, few major obstacles stood in the way of the Soviets.

Yet one development, unforeseen by Stalin, threatened to rob the Communists of their gains, real or anticipated. One Western military writer described the Soviets' discomfiture as follows: "Overhanging the Soviets' prospects was the grim shadow of the

mushroom cloud. The United States had both atomic weapons
and the means of delivering them to targets inside Russia. The
Soviet Union lacked such capabilities. The Soviet air defense was
a shambles, most of the Soviet air effort having been absorbed by
tactical close-support aviation as the Luftwaffe's bombing threat
withered." [4]

The United States—and the United States alone—held the
"absolute weapon," and thus the Soviets remained inferior to the
West. Stalin, until he could redress the military balance, was
determined not to provoke the West into war. Hence the principle of avoiding direct military conflict with a superior opponent
retained its force.

This principle was applied for the first time after World War II
in Iran. In 1946, the United States showed signs of stiffening
when the Soviets failed to meet the deadline for the withdrawal
of allied troops from Iran. Stalin ordered the Russian troops to
leave rather than risk an open conflict with American forces.[5]
The Soviet leader doubtless recognized the fact that the West
regarded the Middle East as an area of vital strategic and economic interests; and that hence he could not risk an overt military
challenge.

In Europe, too, the Communists confined themselves, during
the days of the Marshall Plan, to psychopolitical warfare.
While pushing the development of their own atomic bomb, the
Kremlin leaders nimbly sidestepped the danger of a military
showdown with the United States. In early 1948, they subverted
Czechoslovakia by a nonmilitary *coup*. In the face of the Western
response—the North Atlantic Alliance and German rearmament
—the Soviets stepped up their psychological warfare against the
United States, but made no move for a smash-grab of Europe be-

[4] George Fielding Eliot, "The X-Factor in Disarmament," *Orbis*, Vol. II,
Fall, 1958, pp. 305–306.
[5] On August 25, 1957, Harry S. Truman, writing in the *New York Times*,
said of the Iranian crisis: "The Soviet Union persisted in its occupation until
I personally saw to it that Stalin was informed that I had given orders to
our military chiefs to prepare for the movement of our ground, sea and air
forces. Stalin then did what I knew he would do. He moved his troops out."

fore NATO could build its strength. Meanwhile, they shifted
their attention to the Far East. Civil war was already raging in
Indochina and China; the Communists started guerrilla warfare
in Malaya in 1948; and, in 1950, they committed overt aggression
in Korea. During the first five years after the end of the Second
World War, the Soviets felt that they could safely foment
troubles in Asia without touching off general war. Communism
was emboldened to advance because the United States apparently did not consider the peripheral countries of Asia as lying
within the zone of its vital interests.

In Europe, the Soviets faced greater obstacles. Despite the
overwhelming superiority of the Russian ground forces in Central and Eastern Europe, Western fears of a sudden Russian
march to the Channel appear, in retrospect, to have been ill
founded. The idea of such an overt, aggressive thrust, at the time
when the weapons balance favored the West, ran counter to one
of the basic tenets of Soviet strategy, namely, to abstain from
military action in an area where war could not be localized. The
Soviets were bent upon extending their writ as far as possible—
short of war.

The Berlin blockade furnished an illuminating example of
how the Soviets conduct psychological warfare and yet keep the
psychological gambit from provoking an unwanted military showdown. The Soviet decision to impose a blockade around West
Berlin was a daring move. The blockade temporarily cut off the
military forces of the Western Allies, stationed in the Berlin en-
clave, from overland sources of supply reinforcement. Thus the
Berlin blockade, though a nonviolent move, imperiled the isolated American, British and French security missions. The Soviet
leaders doubted that the United States would consider the move
a *casus belli*; many psychological factors, especially in American
domestic politics, militated against a forceful response. The Russians may well have thought that, under the circumstances, the
Western Allies had no alternative but to withdraw their Berlin
contingents west of the Stettin-Trieste line, thereby relinquish-

ing their foothold in the German capital and thus losing an important round in the political struggle for Germany.

The United States realized that it could not yield West Berlin without shaking the faith of its European allies. American policymakers were confronted with a delicate problem: to maintain the U.S. garrison in West Berlin and not to commit the cardinal error of diplomacy, namely, leaving no other alternatives but war or retreat with loss of face. The President, acting on the advice of his National Security Council, decided to supply the Berlin garrisons and population with a "nonmilitary airlift" of unarmed transport planes. Fortunately, the Potsdam Agreement had granted the Western powers free access by land and air. The United States adroitly shifted back to the Soviet Union the choice of war or peace. Although American planes had been shot down over or near Communist territory for alleged border violations, not a single plane in the airlift operation was downed. Apart from several buzzing incidents and threats of Soviet intentions to hold maneuvers in the vicinity of the air corridor, the Soviets carefully refrained from obstructing the flights of American aircraft which were assigned to missions where U.S. honor and prestige were at stake.[6]

It was probably fear of an incident in the corridor which finally prompted the Soviets to take the initiative in suggesting a settlement of the Berlin crisis. If there is a lesson to be learned from the experience of the Berlin blockade, it is that the West can counter Soviet psychopolitical challenges without triggering war.

It might be argued that Communist "forbearance"—i.e., the

---

[6] As W. Phillips Davison points out in a definitive Rand Corporation Study on the Berlin blockade: "Though the Soviets continued their threats to limit flying in the corridors or to close them entirely, these threats clearly failed in their purpose." According to Mr. Davison, "a 'responsible officer' said that the United States fliers would ignore any Soviet declaration barring flights in the corridors and added: 'The only way they could stop us is to shoot us down.'" *The Berlin Blockade: A Study in Cold War*, Princeton: Princeton University Press, 1958, pp. 154–155.

principle of avoiding direct military conflict—was abandoned when North Korean forces struck across the Thirty-eighth Parallel on June 24, 1950. For the first time, Communist and Western forces met on the field of battle. It seems likely that the Communist attack on South Korea was based on a miscalculation, for it occurred in an area where the West's "vital interests" had not been clearly defined. Secretary of State Acheson, in a speech to the National Press Club in January, 1950, had excluded specifically South Korea from the perimeter which, in case of attack, the United States would defend unilaterally.* The withdrawal of United States forces from South Korea must have gone far to convince the Communists that they could take our announced policy at face value.

Some analysts have gone so far as to suggest that the North Koreans, while they had been armed, trained and supplied by the Sino-Soviet bloc for a take-over of South Korea *once the global strategic balance had shifted in favor of the Communists*, staged their attack prematurely.[7] Be that as it may, the Soviet Union never became an overt participant in the conflict. The fighting was done entirely by Sino-Soviet proxies, a circumstance which will be discussed in greater detail further on.

Looked at from the standpoint of Communist operational doctrine, however, the genesis of the Korean War is less significant than the behavior of Moscow and Peking once the fighting was under way. Did the Communists fear a general conflagration over Korea as much as did the United States and its allies?

The longer the conflict dragged on, the more clamorously the critics of the United States' Korean policy raised the specter of general war. Suggestions that the United States take steps to regain the military initiative were invariably rejected on the grounds that they might provoke general conflict. It is, however, almost inconceivable in retrospect that, in 1950–1951, the Soviet Union would have allowed itself to be drawn into a total war

[7] Wilbur W. Hitchcock, "North Korea Jumps the Gun," *Current History*, Vol. XX, March, 1951, pp. 136–144.

* The authors use the word "unilaterally" advisedly in order to be historically accurate. The idea that Mr. Acheson, by describing a unilateral U.S. "defense perimeter" in the Far East, wished also to place Korea outside the area of our mutual security interests has been accepted too readily.

with the West had the United States applied additional pressure
on Moscow's Chinese ally.

During the closing stages of the Korean War and the two
years leading up to the Geneva "summit" conference in mid-1955,
Western commentators frequently referred to the "balance of
terror" which had existed since the Soviet acquisition of atomic
weapons. The West, just as it had previously exaggerated the
threat of an attack by quantitatively superior Soviet ground
forces, now overestimated Soviet atomic capabilities, crediting
the U.S.S.R. with nuclear parity almost from the day the Russians
detonated their first atomic bomb. Strategic nuclear power, however, depends not merely upon the possession of atomic weapons,
but also upon the size of the weapons stockpiles, the effectiveness
of the delivery systems, and defense capabilities. After 1949, the
West, by virtue of its global chain of air-nuclear bases, continued
to hold a decisive strategic superiority over the Soviet Union—a
fact of which Moscow, if not Western public opinion, was fully
aware. Soviet leaders were conducting foreign policy from a position of strategic inferiority. It is inconceivable that the Soviet
rulers would have initiated a general war merely because they
had it in their power to destroy some European and American
cities. In such an event, the Soviet Union could not have escaped
crushing retaliation from a global network of Strategic Air Command bases, against which a simultaneous knockout blow by the
Communists was impossible.

Yet, even while the United States held the atomic monopoly,
the West had played "psychonuclear" warfare against itself: the
revelation of Soviet nuclear capabilities served only to deter, so
to speak, the American power of deterrence. Within the Western
nations, the conviction grew steadily that the Soviet Union, since
it *could* wage nuclear war, *would* wage nuclear war rather than
accept any local defeat, either military or political (Note 9).

There is no question that, in Korea, the West's self-imposed
limits rescued the Communists from the horns of a dilemma:
defeat in a general war or retreat with loss of face. The Com-

---

It should be remembered that the U.S. had assumed commitments in accordance with the United Nations Charter to defend all member nations
against armed attack, as Mr. Acheson pointed out in his speech. The American intervention in Korea, which Mr. Acheson so vigorously championed,
was carried out in support of the principle of collective security and con-
sonant with our obligations to the United Nations Charter.

munists were determined not to place themselves into so awkward a situation again.[8]

After 1954, the Communists shifted to more subtle tactics.
The area in which these tactics bore the richest fruit proved to
be the Middle East where, as elsewhere in the underdeveloped
world, they could exploit the systemic revolution. But here, too,
they shrank from direct embroilment in general war.

A case in point was the Jordanian crisis, precipitated in the
spring of 1957 by pro-Communist elements. After King Hussein
had forced the resignation of pro-Soviet Premier Nabulsi, Jordan
was the target of combined pressure from Syria and Egypt, the
Palestinian refugees and Radio Moscow. The prospects for the
survival of King Hussein's government were bleak. The skies
cleared when the United States despatched the U.S. Sixth Fleet,
carrying fifteen hundred marines, to the Eastern Mediterranean.
After this display of American force, the crisis quickly subsided.

It is important to see the factors involved in this crisis, as
Soviet strategists saw them. The fact that the Jordanian Arab
Legion remained loyal to King Hussein meant that the Jordanian
government could not be overthrown without some kind of military action, presumably from Syria. Since the Jordanian Army,
supported by the American Sixth Fleet, would have been able
to defeat Syrian intervention, Moscow would have been confronted with an embarrassing dilemma: either come to the direct
aid of Syria or stand by and watch Syria, then the most pro-
Soviet among the Arab states, go down to defeat. The U.S.S.R.
could not blink the fact that the United States, with an ostenta-
tious display of naval diplomacy, had placed itself in an irreversible position. The Syrians, seeing that the United States had
committed itself to the Jordanian government, realized that they

[8] True, the Communists stepped up their military offensive in Indochina
after the conclusion of the Korean fighting. Yet this action did not contradict
the Communist operational principle of avoiding a premature military
showdown with the West. For a number of complex reasons, which will be
discussed below, the Communists deemed it safe to press their campaign in
Indochina during the early spring of 1954, pending scheduled negotiations
for the settlement of the conflict.

could press no further without being assured of a similar military commitment by the Soviet Union. The crisis subsided quickly, for the Soviet Union was reluctant to extend such a commitment.

A few months later, the Soviets attempted to reduce Syria to satellite status. The prospects seemed bright, for they could rely on powerful pro-Communist factions in the Syrian Army. Turkey became seriously alarmed at this potential flanking maneuver. Given Turkey's geographical position and growing fear of encirclement, Soviet charges that the Turks were planning a military move against Syria, although they may have lacked substance, were plausible. If the Turks meant to intervene, Soviet policy had no other choice but to avert such a development, lest the Turks easily occupy Damascus and seriously damage Soviet prestige among Arab nationalists. At that time, despite Premier Khrushchev's veiled threats against Turkey, an actual Soviet attack was out of the question, since the Turks were NATO partners of the United States.[9] Faced with the prospect of a situation which the Soviets could not fully control, the Kremlin abandoned, at least temporarily, its attempts to establish a satellite state in the heart of the Arab world. After Khrushchev, while attending a reception at the Turkish Embassy in Moscow, had announced that the crisis was over, the Soviets left Syria free to align herself with Egypt.

Soviet adherence to the principle of avoiding direct military conflict with the West was again demonstrated during the summer of 1958 when fighting in Lebanon and a military *coup* in Iraq again plunged the Middle East into crisis—a crisis brought about partly by Moscow's encouragement of the forces of radical Arab nationalism. For years, Soviet propagandists had decried the feasibility of limited war in the nuclear age. The Soviets

[9] Khrushchev declared that the Turkish government was unwise to deploy so many of its forces along the Syrian border as to leave its own border with the U.S.S.R. relatively unguarded. The U.S. Department of State immediately answered this threat by warning Moscow to be "under no illusions" but that the United States would fully honor its obligations to Turkey in the event that the latter were attacked.

sought to condition the West to the belief that military counter-action would inexorably lead to general war. They now emitted a steady stream of threats to forestall Anglo-American intervention in the Middle East. Ominous warnings that the Soviet Union "could not stand idly by" while Western military forces were deployed so near its borders did not, however, deter the Atlantic Allies from intervening in Lebanon and Jordan. Once it became clear that the Western Allies had no intention of retreating in the face of the Kremlin's fulminations, the Communist leaders were forced to face the facts: a bulwark had now been erected in the Middle East which could not be breached without risking a direct military clash with the United States. This was the first time that the West had called a Soviet military bluff. Soviet prestige suffered a blow, but the Soviet leaders preferred a temporary political setback to the risk of World War III.

Soviet reluctance to cross the critical line that separates political warfare gambits from general war was demonstrated during the deliberations in the United Nations over a settlement of the Lebanese-Jordanian crisis. While the Soviets had hurled their standard invectives against the American landing in Lebanon, the tenor of their condemnation of the British action in Jordan was more restrained. The reason for this was clear. A pro-Nasser coup in Jordan, following close upon the one in Iraq, would almost certainly have provoked Israel into countermeasures which might have set the Middle East aflame. Moscow could not countenance a conflagration which might have ignited the fuse of general war. Thus the Soviet representatives in the United Nations supported a resolution which called for the "early" (not "immediate") withdrawal of Anglo-American forces from Lebanon and Jordan.

The Communist leadership, while shunning the premature, decisive military showdown, does not, of course, turn its back upon military conflict as such. At a given stage, the strategy of protracted conflict may call for a direct military encounter. Should, however, this need arise, the action must be planned carefully, the challenge presented cautiously and the pressure increased gradually—so that the enemy remains uncertain as to the full dimensions of the operation and is not provoked into committing his full capabilities to the struggle. The tactic of *the gradual challenge* thus represents in essence a localized protracted action within the broader setting of the protracted conflict. Gradualness in the expansion of the totalitarian challenge encourages temporizing on the part of the democracies. The latter are slow to assess the threat properly, especially if it is disguised under the cloak of what many Westerners deem, consciously or not, a "legitimate" cause such as "nationalism." There will be a growing cleavage among democratic elites over the issue. Democratic policy-makers will make halfhearted *ad hoc* efforts—"too little and too late"—to deal with the threat.

Since the end of the Second World War, the Communists have shown a marked preference for the gradual challenge. Until such a time as they are ready for total war, they cannot launch a direct attack in Europe—in fact, in Europe even a graduated challenge would run the almost immediate risk of all-out war. Moreover, the geopolitical environment of Western Europe is not conducive to a slow military build-up: no anti-Western nationalist groups can screen Soviet-supported guerrilla operations.

By contrast, the Communists have found, in the "gray areas," a favorable terrain for launching carefully calibrated military challenges. Whenever the Communists cast their lot with a militant national liberation movement in Asia and Africa (regardless of whether they actually control it), they can usually count on profound and time-consuming disputes among Western policy-makers as to whether it is authentic or spurious and whether it should be accommodated or fought. This factor is of incalculable importance in the strategy of protracted conflict. So long as the West is primed for old-fashioned aggression, it is much safer and much more profitable for the Communists to present their conflict challenges gradually and ambiguously. As the new weapons technology has increased the risk of regular warfare, irregular warfare has become the safest method of waging war against

the West. Guerrilla warfare, which lends itself to the careful cali-
bration and gradual build-up of a violent challenge, has smol-
dered in varying degrees throughout the "gray areas" despite
the so-called balance of nuclear terror. In fact, guerrilla war is
rapidly becoming the Communist tactic best designed to skirt
the trip wires of major nuclear conflict.

A recapitulation of the salient features of the Indochinese War
will serve to illustrate the effectiveness of the graduated challenge, especially when employed against the West.

The postwar instability of Indochina furnished the Communists with an excellent opportunity to present to the French a
graduated challenge disguised as a national liberation movement, the Viet Minh. So deceived and confused were the French
as to the nature of the problem which faced them in their overseas territory that they failed to take decisive action until the
situation no longer could be controlled.

Léon Blum, two days before his assumption of the premiership
in 1946, declared that the only way to preserve French interests
in Indochina was to negotiate with the Viet Minh on the basis
of national independence.[10] The first stirrings of Ho Chi Minh's
insurrection in December, 1946, were weak and uncertain, and
the attacks sporadic. Throughout 1947, Paris and Saigon were
rife with rumors of impending settlement and peace. Indeed,
each time the French government stood on the verge of vigorous
action, the prospect of a "political settlement" inhibited decisive military action. By the end of 1947, the French were convinced that Ho Chi Minh's original stocks of arms and ammunition were nearly exhausted and that peace in Indochina was
around the corner.

The Communists put the time gained to good use. By manipulating three currencies—piaster, franc and dollar—on the Saigon
black market and the Paris Bourse, they were able to amass

[10] Ronald Matthews, *The Death of the Fourth Republic*, New York:
Praeger, 1954, p. 277. For a discussion of the divided state of French
opinion during 1947 as to whether the Viet Minh was a Communist movement, cf. Ellen J. Hammer, *The Struggle for Indochina*, Stanford: Stanford
University Press, 1954, pp. 194–197.

funds needed to purchase additional military supplies. Meanwhile, the guerrilla movement proceeded to build up its own economic, social and political "infrastructure."

At the root of France's desultory approach to the Indochina War was a failure to grasp the new postwar guerrilla strategy developed by the Communists, especially Mao Tse-tung (Note 10). This strategy, as applied in colonial areas, seeks to cultivate widespread community support or to compel such support through the prodigal use of terror. Community support, once established by Communist guerrillas, is not easily broken.[11] If the established government tries to wean the indigenous population away from the rebel cause, the guerrillas invariably step up their terrorist campaigns to force the local community back into line. Since the guerrilla fighter's effectiveness depends upon his ability to remain "invisible," he can be ferreted out only through a laborious screening of the local population. Such a policy inevitably involves abridgments of individual liberties which deepen the hostility of the indigenous populace. Brutality committed by the rebel forces often goads the troops of the established government into counter-atrocities, and this, too, further alienates the community—both local and international. The guerrilla movement, as it tightens its grip upon the people, appears to enjoy increasingly spontaneous acceptance. At the same time, the responsible Western power becomes the butt of an international propaganda campaign, invariably instigated and sustained by the Communists, which pictures the *status quo* power as the brutal repressor of "legitimate" aspirations to independence.

The French, misled by the initially unimpressive military strength of the Viet Minh, failed to take the measure of the tightening vise which Ho Chi Minh's forces were fixing upon the Indochinese people. In many parts of the country, the people were governed by what amounted to a Franco–Viet Minh "condominium"—Viet Minh agents governed practically under the

---

[11] The British, who have had considerable experience in dealing with irregular warfare, did find a way to break the guerrillas' community support in Malaya, by relocating a half-million Chinese in new villages.

noses of the ruling French.[12] Not until after the Communists had come into power in China and Ho Chi Minh had established a communications link with Mao Tse-tung did the Viet Minh emerge as an open belligerent, with fully organized armies supported by artillery (but, significantly, not by planes).[13] Thus, five years after the Communists initiated the conflict, the French reluctantly concluded that they were combatants in a full-scale war in Indochina—a war which was to cost them more than the total economic aid they received under the Marshall Plan, not to mention nearly forty thousand casualties. In the fall of 1953, just after the end of the Korean War, the French won several consecutive victories. But the optimism which these advances engendered proved the final undoing of France, now weary of war. When, early in 1954, the Chinese Communists diverted their forces from Korea to Viet Minh, the Indochinese crisis approached its climax and the outcome of the conflict was no longer in doubt.

The use of proxies is one of the proven vehicles of the indirect approach in the strategy of the protracted conflict. The Communists' heavy reliance upon this tactic is partly a matter of sheer convenience. The Soviet Union, as the power center of a revolutionary movement, disposes over a formidable array of forces globally deployed and ready at any given moment to do Moscow's bidding. The international Communist party, with approximately five million members in the Free World, is probably

[12] It was reported that 20,000 regular Viet Minh soldiers operated in the Tonkinese Delta, which was considered French-controlled territory, and that they trained 50,000 other members of the movement virtually under the direct observation of the French. Hammer, *op. cit.*, p. 292.

[13] The use of planes by the Viet Minh would have made it clear that the Chinese Communists had entered the war as overt participants. It should be recalled that Secretary Dulles had said that "massive retaliation" would not be invoked unless Red China gave evidence of open aggression. By refraining from using planes, the Communists played upon American defensive mentality: the Americans, on their part, would hesitate to initiate air warfare lest such action widen the conflict. Thus they insinuated into the battle a set of rules favorable to themselves, since the United States' capacity to intervene depended largely upon its superior air power.

the most effective unofficial instrument of foreign policy at the disposal of any state in modern times.

There is, however, another and more compelling reason why the use of proxies has figured so prominently in the strategies of Moscow and Peking.

Long ago, the Communists discerned how the legalistic preconceptions held by the West could be turned to their advantage. The Western states, throughout their history, have adhered to the concept of direct responsibility of government for their conduct. Indeed, this is one of the central tenets of that international law which is a product of Western culture.[14] The nation-states of the West, when they have gone to war, have usually done so only after fastening, to their own satisfaction, the precise legal blame upon the culprit government directly responsible for violating international legal rights. Therefore, the Communists take pains to present their challenges indirectly or by proxy.

Two general categories of proxies can be distinguished: controlled proxies such as countries, organizations and individuals directly under the writ of the Communists; *ad hoc* proxies, such as "independent" governments, parties and groups which, wittingly or not, further the objectives of Moscow and Peking. The latter may be "neutral" elites and governments, fellow-traveling parties (e.g., the Nenni socialists in Italy), ethnic minorities and indigenous rebel groups within the territory of the Free World —indeed, anybody who is prepared to undercut Western policies.

Through the apparatus of national Communist parties, the Soviet leaders are able to carry out an exasperating daily intervention in the political life of Western or neutral states. The Communists can rally to their banners a sizable segment of the discontented in such states as Italy and India. Communist members of legislative bodies invariably vote as a bloc on all significant issues. Thus Moscow holds, in several free countries, the

---

[14] Cf. Clyde Eagleton, *The Responsibility of States in International Law,* New York: New York University Press, 1928.

parliamentary balance of power on major foreign and domestic
issues. During the first postwar decade, the French and Italian
Communists, on the strength of an average total of ten million
popular votes, usually held about one-quarter of the seats in the
national parliaments and voted in complete accord with Soviet
directives. As a minority party, they failed, more often than not,
to defeat the legislative proposals of the government. Nevertheless, they nearly always managed to obstruct the legislative process, to turn parliaments into propaganda forums and to embitter
interparty relations. The Communist party, wherever it has
mustered sizable parliamentary strength, has worked with all the
resources at its command to paralyze the mechanism of parliamentary government and to foment confusion, strife and unrest.[15]
On occasion, it may be ordered to adopt a course of intransi-
gence, violence, or even treason against the policies of the government in power—to oppose a program of national defense
or economic reform by strikes, sabotage, espionage, riots, demonstrations and the spreading of defeatist propaganda. The Communist party, even where it is illegal, as it has been in most of the
Arab states since they gained independence, nevertheless serves
as an invaluable tool of Moscow, planting Soviet propaganda
among journalists, students, teachers and policy-makers.[16] Should
the local party be suppressed by the national government, the
U.S.S.R., significantly enough, never intervenes on its behalf
through diplomatic channels, for such an action would break

[15] As Aldo Garoschi points out, the Communist party's "most dangerous
characteristic in a country like Italy, which has a tendency to stagnate, is
precisely its contribution to the perpetuation of the country's lethargy, and
its success in blocking any forward movement, especially any step in the
direction of social progress and development, by holding the masses, whose
active and friendly participation in such a development is indispensable,
under lock and key." Mario Einaudi, Jean-Marie Domenach and Aldo
Garoschi, *Communism in Western Europe,* Ithaca, N.Y.: Cornell University
Press, 1951, p. 218.
[16] It is through the university student community that the party, over the
years, has probably exerted its greatest impact in the Arab countries. Cf.
Walter Z. Laqueur, *Communism and Nationalism in the Middle East,* New
York: Praeger, 1956, pp. 13–18.

down the contrived distinction between the party and the Russian government.

The international Communist movement, more than a mere political handmaiden of Sino-Soviet strategy, constitutes a major military and paramilitary cog in the Communist conflict machine. In the postwar decade, Communist parties have been used to instigate and fan attritional civil war in China, Greece, Laos and Malaya. Their primary usefulness to Moscow and Peking derives precisely from an unprecedented flexibility which allows them to change, with relative ease, from respectable parliamentary parties into proscribed guerrilla movements, and back again. No one can seriously question the fact, for example, that the hard core of Western Communist parties would, in the event of a general conflict, transform itself into a fifth column at the disposal of the Communist high command.

The Communist parties furnish the link between Moscow and the satellite states of Eastern Europe. The satellites have served Moscow as proxies in many subtle ways. The Kremlin has charged them with exacerbating conflict in areas where Russia has seen fit to avoid direct involvement. One of the methods used has been the shipment of arms.

The supply of arms to the pro-Communist regime in Guatemala is a case in point. Between 1951 and 1954, the Communist party gained considerable ground in Guatemala under the regime of Lieutenant Colonel Guzman Arbenz.[17] As anti-Communist resentment mounted throughout the country, the U.S. State Department announced, on May 17, 1954, that a shipment of arms from the Communist bloc had arrived at Puerto Barrios, Guatemala. A shipment of nearly two thousand tons of military equipment gave a Communist-dominated Guatemala superiority over her neighbor republics. The Soviet Union had to exercise extreme caution in supplying the arms: an overt effort to establish a Communist territorial foothold in Central America could

[17] Cf. Daniel James, *Red Design for the Americas: Guatemalan Prelude,* New York: John Day, 1954, pp. 281–284. Cf. also R. M. Schneider, *Communism in Guatemala,* New York: Praeger, 1959.

have been easily interpreted by the United States as a violation of its hemispheric security, traditionally couched in terms of the Monroe Doctrine. The shipment originated at the Skoda works in the "sovereign" state of Czechoslovakia. It was loaded at the Polish port of Stettin aboard the *Alfhem*, a vessel of neutral (Swedish) registry, which had cleared first for the French West African port of Dakar.[18] These ambiguities made it difficult, to say the least, for the United States to raise with the Soviet Union any question of legal responsibility for what was really a clear-cut case of intervention in the American zone of security. Similar tactics were employed by the Kremlin when, in 1955, the Czech arms deal with Egypt sparked the successive crises which have rent the Middle East and North Africa.

Arms shipments via satellite proxies are thus a proven method of fanning existing conflict. There are occasions, however, when direct military pressure is called for and when satellite proxies are either unavailable or unprepared to undertake armed missions. To fill the gap between intervention by satellite proxy and direct intervention, the Communists have developed the novel concept of "volunteers."

This concept is closely related to the idea of "legal neutrality." By relying on "volunteers," a Communist state is able to maintain in the midst of a conflict an official posture of neutrality or nonintervention. It is, in short, able to participate in a conflict without being a legal party to it.

The Soviets first employed the "volunteer" tactic during the Spanish Civil War. That war has often been described as a training exercise, especially for the Germans and the Italians, in the use of new weapons. Less attention has been paid to the Spanish War as a proving ground for new organizational techniques. Three European powers—Germany, Italy and the Soviet Union —had a stake in the outcome of the Spanish struggle. The Fascist

---

[18] Philip B. Taylor, Jr., "The Guatemalan Affair: A Critique of United States Foreign Policy," *American Political Science Review*, Vol. I., September, 1956, pp. 793–795. Cf. *Department of State Bulletin*, Vol. XXX, June 7, 1954, pp. 873–874.

and the Communist dictatorships alike intervened in Spain while purporting to be legally uncommitted. Both, too, relied upon the formation of "international brigades" and "volunteers." [19] In the Spanish War the Soviet leaders learned a valuable lesson: it is possible for a country to take an active part in a war without having to decide the troublesome question of openly declaring war, thus exposing itself to charges of "intervention" or "aggression." These terms have unsavory connotations; the term "volunteers," on the other hand, has considerable propaganda potential; "volunteers" are brave men who "spontaneously" traverse great distances and endure hardships to fight for justice, national independence and peace.

The most celebrated case of "volunteers" was the Korean War. When, in late 1950, the North Korean Army was being pushed by the United Nations forces to the Yalu River, the Russians, reluctant to come directly to the aid of their satellite, left it to the Peking regime to support the North Koreans. Mao Tsetung, who had barely gained control of the Chinese mainland, was in no position to confront the world's strongest power with a frontal military challenge which might have plunged him into all-out war. He was too cautious a strategist to commit his army officially against American forces in Korea, thereby risking a war which would, as a matter of course, have been extended to the soil of China. Mao intervened surreptitiously, and left himself an avenue of retreat. He did not dispatch his regulars, he permitted his "volunteers"—500,000 strong—to do or die in Korea.

Had the United States despatched an ultimatum to the Peking government, informing Mao that the United States would not

---

[19] David T. Cattell, *Communism and the Spanish Civil War*, Berkeley: University of California Press, 1952, p. 82. The Soviets were reported to have sent 5,000 Russian personnel to Spain. The same author remarks elsewhere that the Soviet Union, as much as possible, used the Spanish partisans as "mercenaries," but when they proved insufficient, "the communists recruited young liberals in the democracies and unwanted foreign communists to fight for the Loyalist cause." *Soviet Diplomacy and the Spanish Civil War*, Berkeley: University of California Press, 1957, p. 35.

accept the fictitious distinction between "volunteers" and "regulars," Mao could have withdrawn his "volunteers" without loss of face. Since Mao was allowed to dissimulate the Chinese Communist role in Korea under the guise of "volunteers," he was able to condition the United States and its allies to accept the concept of "privileged sanctuary" north of the Yalu River. After the end of the war in Korea, Mao was able to perform, with even greater success, a similar maneuver in Indochina.[20] The United States spelled out obligingly its policy: it would retaliate against Communist China only in the case of "overt military aggression." [21]

Having graphically demonstrated the effectiveness of the "volunteer" technique in Asia, the Communists, at the time of the Suez crisis, employed the mere idea of "volunteers" as an instrument of psychological warfare against the Western powers. On November 6, 1956, Moscow Radio broadcast an appeal from the Egyptian government for aid and volunteers (Note 11). An Egyptian Embassy spokesman said that "a number of Soviet reserve officers" had applied to the Embassy in Moscow and were accepted.[22]

The use of various types of "controlled proxies" has enabled

[20] "Those fighting under the banner of Ho Chi Minh have largely been trained and equipped in Communist China. . . . Military and technical guidance is supplied by an estimated 2,000 Communist Chinese. They function with the forces of Ho Chi Minh in key positions—in staff sections of the High Command, at the division level and in specialized units such as signal engineer, artillery and transportation." Address by Secretary of State Dulles, March 29, 1954. *American Foreign Policy 1950–1955*, Department of State Publication 6446, December, 1957, Vol. II, pp. 2374–2375.

[21] Secretary Dulles repeated this qualified assurance six times in the course of an address on June 11, 1954. *Ibid.*, pp. 2394–2395.

[22] Chronology, *Middle Eastern Affairs*, Vol. VIII, January, 1957, p. 35. Two weeks later, President Nasser declared that Egypt had made no request for Russian volunteers. *Ibid.*, p. 38. This statement came just after Acting U.S. Secretary of State Herbert Hoover, Jr., had told the U.N. General Assembly that the U.N. would be "obliged to take action" if Soviet "volunteers" were sent to the Middle East and that "the United States would fully support such action." *New York Times*, November 17, 1956. Cf. Department of State Publication 6505, August, 1957, pp. 215–216.

Sino-Soviet leadership to cover conflict operations with a cloud of legal ambiguities. As the protracted conflict progresses, however, this cloud is being increasingly dispersed. The hard experience of the Cold War—particularly the bitter memories of Korea and Indochina—has caused the West to shed, or at least to modify, some of the legalistic scruples which Communism has exploited so successfully in the past. Secretary of State Dulles' indictment, during the Lebanese crisis in July, 1958, of "indirect aggression" in the Middle East is symptomatic of a gradual revision in Western concepts of responsibility for aggression.

As the battle lines of the Cold War have become less fluid, the Kremlin has been forced to limit, or forgo temporarily, some of its earlier tactics: the use of "controlled proxies," a relatively "safe" deployment of these proxies and the decreasing effectiveness of the disguise. The Communists, therefore, have cast about for more subtle instruments of conflict and areas more suitable for conflict operations. "*Ad hoc* proxies" have been the answer (Note 12).

The Algerian *fellaghs* served as an "*ad hoc*" proxy for the execution of Soviet strategy in North Africa. More likely than not, the Algerian rebels were led by Arab patriots who were not Communists (Note 13). But a distinction must be drawn between conflict situations which the Communists contrive and those which they shrewdly exploit. While the exact origins of the Algerian rebellion remain clouded, it appears to fit better into the latter category. At the pith of the Algerian conflict was a paradox: The rebels fought in the cause of Arab nationalism and yet advanced, wittingly or unwittingly, the cause of Moscow in a gigantic maneuver directed against the Western Alliance and at the domination of the Middle East and Africa. Until the Communist bloc furnished arms to Egypt, President Nasser's government was in no position to send substantial military aid to the Algerian rebels. The Communists armed Egypt on the main assumption that she would use them to foment trouble for the West throughout the Arab world.[23] In a sense, nationalist guerrilla movements figure as an important element in Soviet strategy. The Communists seek to turn the forces of neutralism against the West. The Soviets give diplomatic, financial and military aid to nationalist movements which, upon attaining independence, are expected to assume a pro-Soviet neutralist posture. The policy of aiding ostensibly nationalist guerrilla movements is a violent prelude to a *nonviolent* strategy of pressing neutralism into the service of Soviet foreign policy.[24]

Egypt acted, for all practical purposes, as an *ad hoc* proxy of the Soviet Union in the conflict which erupted over the nationalization of the Suez Canal Company in the summer and fall of 1956 (Note 14). Whether the final decision to nationalize the company was made spontaneously in Cairo or was made at the suggestion of Moscow is debatable (Note 15). What *is* clear, however, is that Nasser was emboldened to defy the West because he knew that he could count on Soviet backing. In the words of an American diplomatic historian: "Of all the elements that entered into the decision to nationalize the Suez Canal Company and thus to precipitate one of the most serious crises since World War II, the assurance of Soviet support was certainly the most important." [25]

[23] Cf. Osgood Carruthers: "President Nasser has declared he wants to be friendly with both East and West, seeking to get as much help as he can from each to build up his own Arab empire. The price the West asks for such help is that President Nasser curb his penchant for making trouble in the strategic Middle East. The Soviet bloc more shrewdly conceals the price it is asking for its support, but clearly it is that the Arab ruler create as much trouble as possible, especially for the West." *New York Times*, May 4, 1958.

[24] "Once the West has been driven out . . . there will be nothing to stop the movement of the entire area into the communist orbit. Then will be time enough to begin installation of puppet regimes and to become concerned once more with preaching orthodox ideology." Dwight J. Simpson, "Soviet Policy in the Middle East," *World Affairs Quarterly*, Vol. XXIX, April, 1958, p. 23.

[25] Cf. Grove Haines, commentary on Bernard Lewis, "The Middle East in World Affairs," in *Tensions in the Middle East*, ed. Philip W. Thayer, Baltimore: Johns Hopkins Press, 1958, p. 65.

The indirect approach is the standard stratagem for military forces as well as revolutionary movements confronted by a more powerful enemy. As long as the enemy possesses superiority, a premature frontal military encounter must be avoided, even at the cost of temporary setbacks.

The Sino-Soviet Communists have perfected this technique and made it into a formidable instrument of the Cold War. Their success in applying this instrument is derived precisely from their broader strategic vision—their ability to view the conflict in all of its dimensions. It is derived also from an intimate knowledge of the enemy: his disposition of forces, strategic doctrine and, last but not least, his psychological make-up. The latter includes the legalistic preconceptions which have enabled the Communists' conflict machine to proceed almost completely unhindered against the outposts of Western strategic power.

By thus moving imperceptibly and deviously, the Communists have managed to evade that unambiguous and direct legal responsibility which a large and influential segment of Western opinion must be able to pin on the aggressor in order to establish in good conscience a clear-cut *casus belli* (Note 16). Obviously, a cautious respect for the legal sensitivies of the West does not by itself forestall the possibility of Western counteraction. The existence of the so-called "balance of nuclear terror" plays an extremely important role in rendering the Western nations reluctant to become involved in actual military hostilities under almost any circumstances. But the "balance of nuclear terror" is a two-way street. The Communists are, if anything, even less eager than the West to participate in an overt military conflict which might extend into all-out war. At the same time the Communists are determined not to let the "balance of nuclear terror" operate, as one might expect it would, to the advantage of the *status quo* powers.

The problem confronting the Communists is, as we have seen, how to extend their sway without provoking Western riposte. The strategy of the indirect approach relies on proxies for the accomplishment of certain missions. It permits the Communists to execute their strategy of protracted conflict, leaving the Soviet Union and Communist China free to disown the legal responsibility for their aggressive actions. It also enables the Western nations to back away from a firm position without appearing to capitulate to Communist initiatives.

CHAPTER 5 DECEPTION AND DISTRACTION

The importance of military deception is well known to the military scientist. All great commanders have practiced upon their enemies the art of deception (Note 17). Within the Communists' unified concept of conflict, however, deception has more than merely a military application. It has been one of the hallmarks of Sino-Soviet strategy in all phases of the protracted conflict. The Communists have used two primary methods of deception: policy shifts and exaggeration.

Ever since the Bolshevik Revolution, Western observers have disagreed fundamentally over what Communism really is and what Communists really want. One segment of Western opinion has never faltered in its deep hostility toward the Soviet system, and has cited Soviet conduct as abiding proof of the unbending nature of the Soviet system. Another school of Western thought has never abandoned hope that imminent changes would modify or topple the monolith of Communist society. This school has tended to interpret the various shifts in Soviet policy as harbingers of a Soviet *Thermidor,* an "evolution toward freedom" in Communist society.

The Communists have exploited adroitly the legend of their approaching conversion to "liberalism." Each ostensible reversal of their internal and external policies provoked intense debates over the "changing nature" of the Communist system. It would be presumptuous to assert that each detour in Soviet domestic policy represents a Machiavellian attempt to confound the non-Communist world. Indeed, many Soviet policy shifts were prompted largely by the deep-seated ills of Soviet society. Nevertheless, the Soviets, guided by Lenin's axiom of moving "one step backward, two steps forward," overcame each successive internal crisis. In the process, they managed to turn, as a windfall benefit, so to speak, their own embarrassments into stratagems of deception. They deftly played upon the West's hopes for a better world.[1]

The zigzags of Communist domestic policy which have given rise to confusion over the character of the Soviet regime can be illustrated by three historical examples of policy reversals inside the U.S.S.R. In each instance, the Communists altered internal policy under the pressure of necessity and, for the sake of concrete immediate gains, temporarily deviated from doctrine. In each case a substantial segment of Western opinion placed the most optimistic interpretation upon the "change." The system, so the argument ran, was "mellowing." Unfortunately, it was Western well-wishers, not the Communists, who had "mellowed." The benign climate thus created helped the Communists to advance their objectives, both domestic and foreign.

The first example was the New Economic Policy (NEP). Following the failure of the experiment known as "war Communism" (1917–1921), Lenin, in order to lift the national economy out of its postwar chaos, shelved doctrine and restored Russia to

---

[1] Soviet Communism has in this respect fallen heir to the tsarist tradition of impressing the neighbors of Russia with the benevolent nature of the Russian state. Few writers have ever described this phenomenon as trenchantly as Friedrich Engels: "Enlightenment was the slogan of Czarism in Europe during the 18th Century as was the National Liberation in the Nineteenth. There was no land-grab, no outrage, no repression on the part of Czarism which was not carried out under the pretext of enlightenment, of liberalism, of the liberation of nations. Russian diplomacy alone was allowed to be legitimist and revolutionary, conservative and liberal, orthodox and enlightened in the same breath. One can understand the contempt with which a Russian diplomat looks down on the 'educated' West." Friedrich Engels, "The Foreign Policy of Russian Czarism," *Readings in Russian Foreign Policy*, Chicago: American Foundation for Political Education, Vol. I, p. 79.

a quasi-capitalist status.[2] Many in the outside world welcomed the NEP as a sign that the Soviet leadership recognized the fallacy of Communism and now reverted to a system halfway between socialism and the market economy. Undoubtedly, the readiness of Western capitalists and technicians to come to the aid of the decrepit Soviet economy was spurred by high hopes of Russia's reconversion to a mixed system of private and public initiative. The Communists, needless to say, did nothing to dispel this illusion.

In the middle 1930's, a period of "ebb tide" in the Communists' fortunes, Stalin instituted another "new" policy which put a "nationalist"—and hence a more pleasing—countenance on Communism. Once he had liquidated the "Old Bolsheviks," whose adherence to the strict letter of the Communist doctrine rendered them inflexible, Stalin fostered the resurgence of Russian national patriotism and introduce—on paper—a facsimile of democratic institutions. The restoration of Alexander Nevsky, Ivan the Terrible and Peter the Great to the Russian history books, coupled with the promulgation of the new Soviet Constitution in 1936, made many in the West wonder whether Stalin was not, indeed, abandoning the Marxist-Leninist ideology. Western statesmen hoped that the revival of historic Russian culture would serve as a brake upon the revolutionary tendencies of the Bolshevik regime. But the West once again failed to perceive the true import of the policy shift. Stalin, a masterful tactician, sought to suffuse the Communist ideology with the nationalism of "Mother Russia" in order to strengthen the Communist power base for the impending struggle in Europe. The "great retreat," as this maneuver was called,[3] accomplished in the realm of culture what the New Economic Policy (NEP) had done in the realm of economics fifteen years earlier. The move was designed not to weaken, but to strengthen Communism.

[2] Sir Bernard Pares, *A History of Russia*, New York: Alfred A. Knopf, 1930, p. 488.
[3] Cf. N. S. Timasheff, *The Great Retreat*, New York: E. P. Dutton, 1946, Chapter 7.

The third fundamental reversal of policy within the Soviet Union took place after the death of Stalin—the now famous "de-Stalinization program." Under the pressure of popular discontent both in the U.S.S.R. and in the Communist fiefs of Eastern Europe, Stalin's successors sought to modify the more unsavory aspects of the Stalin regime in order to shore up the political foundations of the Soviet Empire and, incidentally, their own personal power. Confronted with the struggle for Stalin's mantle, unrest in the satellites and the crisis of the Soviet economy, Nikita Khrushchev took the most obvious and easiest path: de-Stalinization. His secret speech to the Twentieth Party Congress opened officially a new campaign for domestic and international respectability.

While de-Stalinization was thus primarily the product of formidable pressures within the Soviet Empire, the leaders of the Kremlin were quick to realize its potential as an effective foreign policy gambit. On the international level, de-Stalinization represented an obvious effort to turn Communist internal weaknesses into diplomatic assets. In order to promote his global campaign of "peaceful coexistence," Khrushchev attempted to disassociate Soviet Communism from the hard-fisted policies of his predecessor. Yet Stalin's operational methods were not rendered obsolete by the process of de-Stalinization, for protracted conflict strategy is concerned not so much with ephemeral Marxist theorizing as with permanently valid techniques of conquest and expansion. It is possible to argue that Stalin himself, master opportunist, set the stage for de-Stalinization. Before his death, Stalin realized that his policies—the conversion of Eastern European countries into Soviet satellites, the Korean War, and the activities of the Communist parties in Western Europe—had produced an alarming degree of unity and preparedness in the West, thereby bringing to an end the happy wartime "flow period" of Communism. It was necessary, therefore, for Stalin to warn his followers that the tough policy had been pushed to the point of diminishing returns. The time had come for a *détente* which would allow new seeds of dissension to be sown within the Western coalition.[4] De-Stalinization—the disassociation of the system from its most reprehensible symbol—served admirably this purpose.

The myth of de-Stalinization was exploded by the brutal Soviet repression of the Hungarian uprising. Nevertheless, only a few months later, Mao Tse-tung managed similarly to beguile Western optimists with his policy of "letting a hundred flowers bloom." This policy, which many Western friends of China welcomed as a tender shoot of "liberalization," served ultimately the purpose of ferreting out potential dissidents. Such flowers as had bloomed—and had bloomed, as we now know, in the artificial climate of Mao's ideological garden—soon withered.[5] Within a year after Mao's dulcet call for diversity-in-unity, the Peking regime established the system of militarized communes which shocked not only Western opinion but also Western Communist ideologists and their fellow travelers.

These internal policy shifts were undoubtedly dictated in no small part by sheer necessity. Yet, in the Communist state, internal and external policy goals are more closely meshed than in any other modern state. In advancing the goals of security and development of the socialist base, Communist leaders have learned to depend upon a benevolent attitude on the part of Western elites. The manner in which the various periodic shifts within Soviet society have been propagated in the outside world leaves little doubt that the Soviet leaders have sought, as an important by-product of policy changes which were forced upon them by the pressure of events, to reap the benefits of deceiving Western observers.

Every revolutionary movement develops dynamically and rapidly during its early phases, but sooner or later the pace begins to slacken. Yet, the strategy of protracted conflict seeks dili-

[4] See Stalin's thesis for the Nineteenth Party Congress, *Economic Problems of Socialism in the U.S.S.R.*, Washington: Embassy of the U.S.S.R., 1952.
[5] Cf. Robert C. Herber, "Mao and Polycentric Communism," *Orbis*, Vol. II, Summer 1958.

gently to create the illusion of increasing dynamism. This trick can be turned by showmanship and mass advertising. The Communists are masters in displaying such exhibits as military power and technological achievement. They are also experts in the art of planned misinforma⁺ion.

Deliberate falsification of economic data has been always an important weapon in the Communist panoply of psychological warfare. The appeal of revolutionary Marxism draws its power from a vision of economic beatitude. The Bolsheviks once installed in Russia, had to demonstrate the virtues of Communism not only to their doubting subjects, but to a hostile and contemptuous world. They could do so only with "concrete" accomplishments. When deeds fell short of advertised goals, statistics filled the gaps.

As the First Five-Year Plan was launched in 1928, Stalin decreed that henceforth all statistical data regarding Soviet economic growth had to be cleared through the Secretariat of the Politburo prior to publication. Data on annual economic increases were given in percentages, not volume by commodity. The percentages were based on total national productivity, expressed in rubles. Hence the figures contained a built-in inflationary factor.[6] According to official Soviet statistics, the national income increased by 500 per cent in the period 1928–1938. In fact, real Soviet national income had risen probably by no more than 50 per cent.[7] Figures on agricultural output between 1937 and 1939 were inflated by the simple device of changing the reports from *net* crops, i.e., volume after the deduction of transport and storage losses, to *gross* crops. Postwar agricultural statistics included the yield from 670,000 square kilometers of territories which had been incorporated into the Soviet Union between 1939 and 1945. Since this fact would have detracted from the

[6] Harry Schwartz, *Russia's Soviet Economy,* New York: Prentice-Hall, 1950, pp. 122–123.
[7] Colin Clark, "Russian Income and Production Statistics," *Review of Economic Statistics,* November, 1947, p. 216.

apparent significance of the increase, no reference was made to it when the statistics were published.[8]

The ambiguity of Soviet economic statistics has continued to plague outside observers.[9] The Communists persist in publishing percentage data, the significance of which is vague. Not infrequently, they release statistics in such a confusing manner that they can be taken to indicate overfulfillment of the planned goals when they actually point to deficits and failures. Western analysts, unfortunately, have often been misled to accept the more glowing, though unfounded, interpretation.[10]

[8] Harry Schwartz, *op. cit.*, p. 307.

[9] Calvin B. Hoover called attention to this problem at the time a new Soviet statistical abstract was published. The new abstract, he said, does not prove that the earlier data were correct, and it "does little to correct the strong inflationary bias in the statistics of past performance of the Soviet economy. . . . Past official estimates of the annual increase in national income have probably been from two to three times too high. It is now admitted that agricultural statistics have been defective. . . . It is certain that aggregate figures which purport to show increases in the output of consumer goods have been greatly exaggerated." "Soviet Economic Growth," *Foreign Affairs*, Vol. 35, January, 1957, pp. 257–259.

[10] Soviet deception-by-statistics can be illustrated by the data published for the Fifth Five-Year Plan and the beginning of the Sixth. For the leading consumer goods industries for which data were available (cotton, wool, shoes, meat, fish, vegetable oil and sugar), actual increases for the period 1950–1955 fell below planned increases by percentages ranging from 18 to 58. The planned percentage increase for all consumer goods industries under the Fifth Five-Year Plan was to be 65 per cent. Nevertheless, the draft directives for the Sixth Five-Year Plan in *Pravda* on January 15, 1956, reported the production increase as 76 per cent! *Bulletin, Institute for the Study of the U.S.S.R.*, Vol. III, March, 1956, p. 416. The figure of 76 per cent probably represented the proportion of the planned increase actually achieved. In other words, the Soviets had planned to increase their consumer goods production by 65 per cent and had achieved 76 per cent of that goal. But the figures were juxtaposed in such a way as to make it appear that the *actual* rate of production increase had exceeded the planned rate. The actual rate of production growth in the consumer goods industries was probably about 49 per cent (i.e., 65 per cent multiplied by 76 per cent). It is disquieting to find specialists on the Soviet economy adopt uncritically the figure of 76 per cent as the rate of consumer industries production growth under the Fifth Five-Year Plan. Cf. E. Clovinsky, "The Twentieth Congress and the Soviet Economy," *Bulletin, Institute for the Study of the U.S.S.R.*, Vol. III, April, 1956, p. 42.

The purpose of these observations is not to imply that all the Soviet claims to economic progress are fabrications which should be lightly dismissed. There can be no doubt that, despite recurrent dips, dislocations and crises (caused by "war Communism," collectivization, World War II losses and postwar agricultural failures), the general movement of the Soviet economy has been upward. The U.S.S.R., indeed, has become the second greatest industrial power in the world.

This does not detract, however, from the evidence that the Communists, for several decades past, have conjured forth an image of accomplishments which is out of all proportion to the actual rate of Soviet economic growth. The purpose of their deliberate campaign of misinformation has been to overawe the West with the economic strength underlying Soviet power and to dazzle the emergent peoples of the world with a magic formula for speedy industrialization.

The Communists, using the device of methodical misinformation, have been equally successful in the military realm. It is coming to light only now, for example, that the Soviets deliberately maneuvered the West into concentrating upon the production of long-range bombers at the cost of its embryo missiles program.

At the end of World War II, Soviet Russia possessed practically no strategic air force, most of her aircraft production having been absorbed in the manufacture of tactical airpower to support her huge conventional ground forces. The United States, on the other hand, commanded both atomic weapons and the strategic means to deliver them. The Soviets could not hope to exploit their superiority on the ground without first neutralizing the West's aerial delivery capabilities. It was toward this end that the policy-makers of the Kremlin hit upon an ingenious stratagem (Note 18). General James M. Gavin has suggested the following explanation of Soviet legerdemain:

There is a considerable quantity of intelligence to support the view, a view held by a number of people in the intelligence business, that in the competition to develop Long-Range Striking Forces, the Soviets have led us to believe that they were building a sizable long-range bomber force, whereas, in fact they were investing most of their national product for their long-range forces in long-range ballistic missiles. The Soviets merely built and displayed before Western observers particularly during May Day festivities in Moscow sufficient long-range manned bombers to cause apprehension, and consequent reaction on our part. We in turn embarked on a very expensive long-range manned bomber program. If this actually has been the Soviet strategy, then billions of dollars have been invested in aircraft that will never be used in combat. If we had spent those billions of dollars in missiles and satellites, we would be well in the forefront of the missile-space race today.[11]

Similarly, the Western nations for a decade prior to the Hungarian uprising despaired of their ability to match Soviet conventional military power which was ostensibly deployed for an attack in Europe. Up until 1956, the Russians managed to convince Western strategists that the Western borderlands of the Soviet Empire has been so thoroughly communized that some 70 indigenous army divisions of the satellite states could be added to the regular Soviet strength of approximately 175 divisions. The apparently unbridgeable difference in the size of conventional military forces-in-being produced within the NATO alliance a deficiency of will which stymied all efforts to fulfill the manpower goals originally set by NATO.[12] Against proposals for German rearmament, it was frequently argued that an additional 12 divisions raised by the Bonn government would be "a drop in the bucket" when compared with the 245 Communist divisions poised in Central and Eastern Europe.[13] The Hungarian rising in October, 1956, exploded the myth of Soviet-satellite military unity. The revolt made it clear that a chief purpose of

[11] James M. Gavin, *War and Peace in the Space Age*, New York: Harper & Brothers, 1958, p. 241.

[12] B. H. Liddell Hart, "Military Strategy vs. Common Sense," *Saturday Review*, March 3, 1956, p. 49.

[13] Axel von dem Bussche, "German Rearmament: Hopes and Fears," *Foreign Affairs*, Vol. 32, October, 1953, p. 70.

the presence of the Red Army in Eastern Europe had not only been, as the West believed, to pose an aggressive threat against Western Europe but rather to safeguard the Communist regimes in the satellites. That the Western powers despaired of ever matching the Soviets' ground forces and relied increasingly on nuclear weapons—thus forfeiting the ability to fend against a Russian ground attack with conventional means—was due in no small part to the contrived image of a military "colossus" behind the Elbe River.

In August, 1957, the Soviets, while engaged in disarmament talks in London with Great Britain, France and the United States, announced the successful firing of an intercontinental ballistic missile (ICBM). The implicit claim by the Soviets that they had mastered, in one fell swoop, all the complex phases of rocketry met with deserved skepticism in Western capitals. In the fall of 1957, however, the launching of the "Sputniks" was accepted by most Western observers as the final proof that the Soviets did possess an operational ICBM as they had claimed. Again, the West took Soviet claims at face value: the placing in orbit of two earth satellites supplied no proof that the Soviets had solved the "re-entry" problem; nor did the satellite launchings substantiate Soviet claims for the accuracy of their alleged missiles. The Russian achievement in outer space did not, in any event, modify substantially the West's strategic superiority, based as it is upon an effective global dispersion of air-nuclear power. Yet the Soviets had, through astute showmanship, conveyed the general impression that, by launching the first successful earth satellite, they had somehow instantaneously revolutionized the world military balance.[14]

The Soviet Sputniks constituted as much a psychopolitical as

[14] Hanson W. Baldwin, *New York Times*, February 7, 1958. "The alarm induced by the spectacular evidence of Soviet technological and military progress prompted a popular but exaggerated opinion that the balance of world military power had shifted to the Soviet Union and that the United States, after a brief reign as global 'top dog,' had now become a secondary power." This was also widely reported to be the implication of the conclusions contained in the top-secret "Gaither Report."

a genuine scientific achievement. Indeed, there is much evidence pointing to the fact that Moscow subordinated scientific investigation to political exigencies. In order to steal a march on the United States, the Soviets had played the part of disinterested latecomers to the satellite field.[15] In order to make it as difficult as possible for the West to obtain an accurate estimate of their newly unveiled space capabilities, the Soviets, contrary to the International Geophysical Year agreement, furnished no advance notice of satellite launchings to Western tracking stations and filed no significant scientific information with IGY headquarters at Brussels (Note 19). Despite the fact that American scientists believed that the Russians had used the same type of rocket in all the early launchings, the Communist political news agency, Tass, went to great lengths to make it appear that Sputnik II and Sputnik III each represented great technical advances over Sputnik I.

The U.S.S.R. paraded its space achievements as proof of the intrinsic superiority of "socialist science" over "capitalist science." The Communist world undoubtedly scored substantial psychological gains in the international contest to impress men's minds with the notion that the tide of history was running with the Communist system. The United States sought refuge in the unconvincing argument that it had not been engaged in an outer space race with the Soviets. President Eisenhower, however, conceded that the United States had failed to anticipate the full impact that the first successful satellite launching would have upon international public opinion.[16]

The Soviets' sputnik successes, embellished as they were by a Barnum-like propaganda campaign, cast into some doubt the hitherto unquestioned assumption that the United States enjoyed a commanding superiority in the realm of military technology.

[15] Although the United States announced in mid-1955 its intention to launch a satellite during the IGY, the U.S.S.R. maintained complete silence on the subject for two additional years. Cf. V. N. Petrov, "Soviet Participation in the International Geophysical Year," *Bulletin of the Institute for the Study of the U.S.S.R.*, Vol. IV, September 1957, pp. 3-10.

[16] State of the Union Message, January 9, 1958, in the *Department of State Bulletin*, Vol. XXXVIII, January 27, 1958.

With the confidence of America's allies shaken, at least temporarily, the Communists felt emboldened to undertake a more risky
and dynamic foreign policy during the late 1950's. Although most
careful United States observers did not believe that the U.S.S.R.
had brought about any revolutionary change in the world balance
of strategic military power, Premier Khrushchev in succeeding
years seldom missed the opportunity to drive home the grim
lesson of Soviet scientific accomplishments by drawing a connection between the "stars of peace" and the Communists' intercontinental ballistic missile capabilities. There can be no question but
that the Soviet leader exaggerated the immediate military significance of Soviet space achievements, but that he managed to par-
lay them into considerable gains. This was especially the case in
1959, when Khrushchev adroitly took advantage of three Soviet
"firsts" in outer space [17] to impress his own people with the Communists' new technological power, to dazzle the underdeveloped
nations, to buttress his demands for a change in the status of Berlin, and to punctuate dramatically his visit to the United States
and the United Nations.[18]

From the very first day of the space age, the Soviets have been
at some pains to persuade the world that, in sharp contrast to the
United States, they have experienced no rocket failures. Naturally,
if the claim of perfect rocket reliability is true, it is strategically
significant. Yet, despite the fact that all of the U.S.S.R.'s rocket
programs have been shrouded in official secrecy, the Western press
has transmitted the Communists' claims to the public with a relatively straight face. Compared with the live television coverage
of the orbital flights of John Glenn and Scott Carpenter, the
Soviets withheld all public announcements of the Gagarin flight
until after its completion and released the first visual record of

[17] These were the first "solar satellite"; the first "direct impact upon the
moon"; and the first "lunar orbit."
[18] On January 2, 1959, the first cosmic rocket known as "Lunik" was
launched, apparently intended to go into orbit around the moon. When this
first "interplanetary flight" missed the lunar orbit and continued its flight toward the sun, the Soviets named it "Mechta" and hailed it as the "first artificial
planet."

Titov's trip only at a subsequent date. This was an amateurish film which portrayed Titov's rocket emerging from a cloud of smoke without providing the viewer with any convincing evidence that Titov was actually being borne aloft by the vehicle, inasmuch as the entire sequence of pre-flight preparations was omitted. Certainly the Soviets' technological ability to put a human being into orbit cannot be prudently questioned. But whether they succeeded in their first attempts, or whether Gagarin and Titov were actually the first two cosmonauts—these must remain matters of faith so far as Western observers are concerned until better methods of verifying Soviet claims of sensational technological achievements become available. The open societies of the West are not wise to permit Soviet space feats performed in secrecy to go unchallenged and thus to be accorded the same credibility as those which, of necessity, must be carried out under the full glare of publicity in the free world. The willingness of the United States to admit the whole TV-viewing world to the drama of its space exploits invites a comparison between two social systems which cannot but redound to the West's advantage. Incidentally, the Soviets, in handling the exploits of the "twin cosmonauts" in the summer of 1962, attempted to emulate the live coverage techniques of American public relations.

The revolutionary side in the protracted conflict must distract the enemy from its most vulnerable points and draw him on to a wider battleground where the terms of battle run against him and where he will be compelled to disperse and, ultimately, to dissipate his manpower and resources. Thus distraction is the twin of deception.[19]

The Soviet Union's "Achilles' heel" remains Eastern Europe, where—despite the Soviets' elaborate attempts to forge its peoples into a homogeneous Communist society—the forces of his-

---

[19] "He is skillful in attack whose opponent does not know what to defend; and he is skillful in defense whose opponent does not know what to attack. . . . The spot where we intend to fight must not be made known; for then the enemy will have to prepare against a possible attack at several different points. . . ." Sun Tzu, *The Art of War*, translated by Lionel Giles, Harrisburg: Military Publishing Co., 1944.

tory, in the shape of powerful nationalisms, continue to run counter to the Kremlin. The Communists must invest large resources in Eastern Europe to maintain their fortuitously established position. Communism could not have come to power in Eastern Europe had it not been for the presence of the Red Army; nor could the Communist regimes, such as those, for example, in East Germany or Hungary, retain control without the support of massive Soviet military forces. Despite costly programs of heavy industrialization, which were calculated in part to weaken the opposition of nationalistic agrarian elements and to create a more easily indoctrinated and disciplined class of urban workers, Communism has not taken deep roots in the East European satellites. It was the workers who revolted against the "workers' regimes" of East Germany and Poland. In Hungary, even more importantly, the initiative of October, 1956 was seized by the university students and the young intellectuals, who were quickly joined by workers and soldiers. The complete reorientation of the economies of the satellite countries away from Western Europe toward the U.S.S.R. and Communist China [20] and the quasi-Bolshevization of their culture have not changed permanently the political and spiritual outlook of the East European peoples. Soviet Communism controls the governments but it has not won the minds of the peoples in the "people's democracies." [21]

The Soviets are sensitively aware of how tenuous is their position in Eastern Europe. It is in this region of their empire that the "socialist contradictions"—especially the unmentionable tension between the rulers and the ruled—are painfully obvious. Hence, the Soviet high command has reacted almost neurotically to any Western insinuations that all is not well in Eastern Europe.[22] Psy-

[20] Cf. "Some Aspects of Soviet-Satellite Economic Relations," *World Today*, Vol. II, October, 1955, pp. 431–437.

[21] Hannah Arendt, "Totalitarian Imperialism: Reflections of the Hungarian Revolution," *The Journal of Politics*, Vol. XX, February, 1958.

[22] *Pravda*, for example, on October 28, 1956 condemned the "incendiary 'Christmas messages'" which President Eisenhower and Secretary Dulles had sent to the peoples of Eastern Europe "as provocational calls to action against

chologically, Soviet doings in Eastern Europe have smitten not a few Communist intellectuals inside and outside Russia with a sense of guilt. Indeed, the misgivings of not a few Russians confronted by the evidence of popular revulsion against Soviet brutality were reflected by the low morale of the Russian garrison during the Battle of Budapest (Note 20).

Soviet psychological warfare strategists have sought diligently to distract the West from the weakness of the Soviet position in Eastern Europe. Their objective, since 1947, has been to implant in the West the notion that the Eastern European region has been irrevocably incorporated into the Communist empire—that the Western nations have no recourse other than to respect the *status quo* and to "normalize" relations with the satellite governments. The Communist campaign has been remarkably successful: although governmental or nongovernmental information agencies in the West paid occasional homage to the principle of "liberating" the peoples of the satellite countries, Western policymakers did not seem to take "liberation" seriously. But in 1956, it became obvious that the Western governments had no intention of exploiting the Soviets' deepening dilemma for strategic purposes, or of pressing the Kremlin to seek a more moderate solution of its difficulties in Hungary than brutal repression.[23] The complete policy paralysis of the Western Allies at the height of the Hungarian crisis attested to the success of Soviet psychological warfare efforts to persuade the West that Eastern Europe, far from being the Communists' most vulnerable spot, was in reality their most impregnable redoubt.

For the Soviets, any suggestion of political "settlements" designed to loosen their hold upon Eastern Europe is out of the question. They adamantly refuse to place such a subject on the agenda of any "summit" conference.[24] They appear to fear

the people's democracies." For texts of the messages, cf. *Department of State Bulletin*, Vol. XXXIV, January 16, 1956, p. 85.

[23] Cf. Alvin J. Cottrell and James E. Dougherty, "Hungary and the Soviet Idea of War," *Russian Review*, Vol. XVI, October, 1957, pp. 17–25.

[24] Cf. letter from Khrushchev to President Eisenhower, June 11, 1958. The Tass summary reported: "Khrushchev called attention to the fact that the

that the mere discussion of the problem in an international forum might have explosive repercussions in the satellite capitals. To mask the weakness of its position in Eastern Europe, the Soviet Union has resorted to a variety of techniques: (1) "hush money" —in the wake of the Polish and Hungarian risings, increased economic aid to satellite economies in the form of consumer goods; (2) periodic announcements of negligible withdrawals of Red Army units from Eastern Europe—to foster the impression that the political climate in the satellites is once more "normal"; (3) a return to terrorist tactics of repression against students and intellectuals;[25] (4) the pathetically absurd thesis that the Hungarian uprising was a Fascist counterrevolution; (5) the effort to keep up the façade of Communist bloc solidarity through such fictional devices as the Warsaw Pact; and (6) the public revelation of the struggle, on the level of Communist leadership, among "Stalinists," "Khrushchevists" and "Titoists." The intraparty squabbles which raged during the first half of 1958 were probably quite genuine. But the emphasis which Moscow's official statements placed upon them was obviously designed to obscure real and more embarrassing "contradictions," namely the East European peoples' resentment of Soviet rule.

For several years, and especially since Stalin's death, Communist strategists have attempted to shift the Cold War from Eastern Europe to another battleground—the underdeveloped and uncommitted nations. While the Communists warn the West against proselytizing the subjected peoples of Eastern Europe, they insist that the colonial and erstwhile colonial areas are the battleground where the issue between the West and the Com-

---

Western powers, in their proposals, again raise the so-called question of the situation in East Europe. The head of the Soviet government rejects this new attempt . . . 'to insist on interference in the affairs of other states. . . .' " *New York Times*, June 17, 1958.

[25] Pro-Western youth in Bulgaria, Rumania and Hungary were being sent to concentration camps early in 1958. *A Survey of Recent Developments in Nine Captive Countries October, 1957–March, 1958,* New York: Secretariat of the Assembly of Captive European Nations, pp. 18, 172 and 185. Cf. also "Current Developments," in *East Europe,* Vol. VII, June, 1958, pp. 20–42.

munist system will be decided.

The vital importance of the "gray areas" in the struggle between the two systems is obvious. But the Communists seek to persuade the West that they constitute the one and only arena of conflict. In Africa and Asia, the forces unleashed by the systemic revolution are running against the West. The swelling ideological currents—neutralism, anticolonialism, anti-Westernism, anti-imperialism, anticapitalism, pragmatic socialism and nationalism —are, by their very nature, directed against the West. Thus the Communists have succeeded in reversing the "capital coefficients of strategy" to their advantage. The West, from a large input of effort and resources in the "gray areas," obtains a relatively small strategic output. Conversely, the Communists, with a low cost input in the underdeveloped areas, are able to win allies, stir up trouble for the West and reap handsome strategic profits (Note 21). Several years ago, a Jordanian, referring to Soviet diplomatic support in the U.S. for Cairo's blockade of Israel, summed up the Western dilemma: "One veto by Vishinsky is worth all the aid of America and Britain."[26]

From the West's standpoint, Communist strategy—to distract the West from Eastern Europe and lure it onto the Afro-Asian battleground—is not devoid of irony. First, the industrial potential of Eastern Europe amplifies the Communists' capacity for carrying on protracted conflict in the underdeveloped areas. The satellite countries have figured prominently in the Communist policies of arms shipments to the Middle East and Indonesia; of penetration by cultural and technical missions; and of economic aid to Egypt, Syria, Afghanistan and India.[27] So long as the West passively accepts the *status quo* in Eastern Europe, it can expect to encounter increasing Communist pressure in the "gray areas." Meanwhile, the continued domination of Eastern Europe by the U.S.S.R. will relieve Moscow of a sizable share of

[26] Cited in Robert Strausz-Hupé, Alvin J. Cottrell and James E. Dougherty, *American-Asian Tensions*, p. 158.
[27] "The Soviet Bloc and Under-Developed Countries: An Assessment of Trade and Aid," *The World Today*, Vol. XII, June, 1956, pp. 222–239.

the burden of meeting Communist China's industrial development needs.[28] Secondly, one of the chief underlying assumptions
of the West's policy of "containment" since World War II had
been that the Communist system must substitute expansion for re-
forms; if it were frustrated in this effort for ten or twenty years,
the system would either mellow or disintegrate.[29] This supposes
that the liberalization of Russia, if it ever occurs, will be brought
about by the action of purely indigenous forces. Yet, historically,
Russia has no liberal tradition which could reassert itself.[30]

In 1956, when the riots broke out in Poznań and when the Red
Army intervened in Hungary, the West stood by helplessly, unwilling or unprepared to act. The very precepts of a strategy
which depended on the trigger mechanism of retaliation had
maneuvered the West into a painful dilemma. The West, fearful
lest revolution set off accidentally total war, chose to acquiesce
in the restoration of Soviet control over the countries of Eastern
Europe. In the words of Secretary of State John Foster Dulles,
we were hoping for a "more peaceful" evolution behind the Iron
Curtain. We rationalized our inaction by assuming that the
Soviets, because they could not halt the train of events which
had been set in motion by the risings in Poznań and Budapest,
were in deep and lasting trouble. The rapidity with which the
Soviets moved in putting down the risings and reasserting their
authority should go far in dispelling these wistful hopes.

Eastern Europe remains the weakest link of the Soviet Empire
precisely because it is vulnerable to the impact of the Free
World. The Soviets have sought to shut out the image of the
"Open Society" by ringing down the Iron Curtain and by luring
the West away from Europe onto the Afro-Asian battlefield of
the systemic revolution. There, the West has been at an ideological disadvantage. The image of the "Open Society" does not
evoke a response from peoples who lack the tradition of individual freedoms and whose vision of the West is distorted by the
emotionalism born of bitter historical experience. Thus, the Communists have played to our weakness while we, docilely, have
played to Communist strength.

* See facing page for footnotes 28-30

Success in the pursuit of the protracted conflict strategy is predicated upon keeping the enemy in a defensive and reactive frame of mind and thus preventing him from seizing the initiative.

This is primarily a matter of psychological conditioning. Communist psychological strategy seeks to exploit the enemy's cultural and ideological preconceptions—scientific, economic, political, legal, philosophical and moral—and hardens those assumptions, consciously held or not, which inhibit his ability to counter the devious challenges of the Communists. A prize example is the "war zone, peace zone" notion. Communism defines the rules and the area of the protracted conflict; the West is made to accept them. Through a process of conditioning, the *status quo* power can be induced to respect the boundary of the "peace zone" (i.e., the territory controlled by the revolutionary forces) while implicitly taking it for granted that the battle will be waged solely in the area not yet dominated by the revolutionary power, i.e., the "war zone."

Since 1945, the Communists have marked out the non-Communist territory as the "war zone" and have succeeded in confining the Cold War to this part of the world. World opinion unconsciously accepted the Communist rule of international conduct: under its dispensation the West must condone Communist forays into the non-Communist "war zone" and abstain from

---

[28] Cf. "Trade Between China and the Soviet Bloc," *The World Today*, Vol. II, May, 1955, pp. 202–210.

[29] Cf. "X," George F. Kennan, "The Sources of Soviet Conduct," *Foreign Affairs*, Vol. XXV, July, 1947.

[30] Wlodzimierz Baczkowski, "The Chimera of a Soviet Thermidor," *Orbis*, Vol. I, Fall 1957.

launching counterthrusts into the Communist "peace zone." The Communists, in short, have been allowed to inscribe the territorial limits of the protracted conflict.

The "war zone, peace zone" idea, which has contributed so much to the defensive-mindedness of the West since 1945, can be illustrated abundantly. In fact, the "containment policy," which furnished the official theoretical framework for the Truman Doctrine of aid to Greece and Turkey and subsequent U.S. foreign and security policies, rested on the "war zone, peace zone" assumption. Under the containment theory, the United States was to pursue a reactive policy, by applying counterpressure against the Soviet Empire along "a series of constantly shifting geographical and political points, corresponding to the shifts and maneuvers of Soviet policy." [1] In other words, the sites of the conflict were to be chosen by the Communists.

When the Communists attacked in Korea, they pushed their way deep into the territory of South Korea and fought nearly the entire war on that territory. The West was conditioned to believe that it was not safe to carry the war beyond the Yalu and to interdict the Communist military build-up in Manchuria. After three years of struggle, the West had to settle at the "line of scrimmage"—approximately the Thirty-eighth Parallel. All suggestions for extending the conflict beyond Korea were rejected as fraught with the risk of all-out war with the Sino-Soviet bloc.

The Communists maneuvered the United Nations into accepting their "ground rules." Almost all the debates in the United Nations from 1948 until 1958 over "threats to peace," "intervention," "imperialism" and "rights to self-determination" dealt with problems and tensions arising primarily within the non-Communist world and between the Western powers and the colonial areas. The question of Soviet imperialism or violation of the rights of self-determination of peoples has been

[1] George F. Kennan, *American Diplomacy, 1900–1950,* New York: The New American Library, 1952, p. 113.

raised much less frequently and with a noticeable lack of fervor by the majority of the U.N. membership.

The West's supine acceptance of the "war zone, peace zone" idea encouraged the Communists to send arms to anti-Western governments in the Middle East—Egypt, Syria and Yemen—and to an anti-American government in Guatemala without being called to account by the West. These shipments of military supplies were treated as "purely commercial" arrangements concluded by independent, sovereign governments (Note 22). By contrast, at the time of the Hungarian uprising, it was taken for granted that the West could not extend, even indirectly, military aid to the patriots without triggering a general war in Europe. Although the Soviets could threaten to send "volunteers" to the Middle East at the height of the Suez crisis, Western governments went out of their way to assure the Soviets that Western volunteers would not be allowed to go into Hungary. Indeed, the West even shrank from a purely diplomatic move to recognize the neutrality of Hungary as proclaimed on November 1, 1956, by the legal Hungarian government,[2] lest this should provoke the Soviets into war.

The "war zone, peace zone" assumption is fraught with subtle implications for Western strategy. So long as the West accepts this assumption, the Communists can make substantial gains without incurring losses. Each time the West scores a "victory," as it did, for example, in Jordan in the spring of 1957, it simply preserves temporarily the international *status quo*. Whenever the Soviets make a gain they acquire an additional territorial foothold in areas which have historically been controlled or protected by the Western states.

There is increasing evidence that the Western nations now fear to mount the initiative even along the periphery of the "war zone"—i.e., in the part of the world not directly controlled by the Sino-Soviet Bloc. In Indonesia, for example, an open rebellion broke out during the spring of 1958 against the government of President Sukarno which included pro-Communist elements.

[2] *New York Times,* November 2, 1955.

The United States had the opportunity to deal a severe blow to the prestige of Communism in Asia by supporting effectively the rebels on Sumatra. Although the United States government made it clear that it would pursue a neutral policy in the dispute, the Soviets endowed the Sukarno regime with MIG's and other military equipment, and the Chinese Communists threatened to send further assistance.[3] The Soviet Union felt free to intervene overseas; the United States deemed it prudent to withhold support from the anti-Communist rebels.[4]

While the Communists are reluctant to go to war, they do not hesitate to *threaten* war in order to scotch Western initiative. The use of war threats has assumed, since the Soviet Union obtained nuclear weapons and missiles, added importance in Communist conflict strategy. Given the "balance of terror," the Communists, acting through proxies, can present the West with strategic *faits accomplis* and then invoke the specter of general war in order to prevent the West from taking forceful action in the defense of its legitimate interests. At the same time, the Soviets' display of defiance in the face of Western power serves to convince the weaker nations that the Soviet Union stands ever ready to protect them against the encroachments of "neo-imperialism."

Thus, on November 5, 1956, at the height of the Suez crisis, Soviet Premier Bulganin dispatched a note to the Prime Ministers of Great Britain and France. The day before the official notes were delivered in London and Paris through the diplomatic channels, the substance of the message was made public in a press conference held in Moscow. The announcements which reached the West through the international news services were couched in a much more bellicose language than the official text of the notes, which were made public later. The version broadcast by Radio Moscow conveyed the impression that the Soviet

---

[3] *New York Times,* May 16, 1958.

[4] Ironically enough, a joint communiqué issued at the conclusion of President Nasser's visit to Moscow stated: "Both governments express their profound concern in connection with the acts of interference by governments of foreign countries in the internal affairs of Indonesia." *Ibid.*

government had sent what amounted to an ultimatum to Sir Anthony Eden, ordering him to terminate hostilities immediately or else face Russian rocket retaliation upon Great Britain. Radio Moscow quoted the following sentence from Bulganin's note: "We are fully determined to crush the aggressors and restore peace in the East through the use of force." The news caused considerable apprehension in Western capitals. One day later, the British and the French ordered their forces in Egypt to cease firing. When the official text of the Soviet note was published, it became apparent that the Kremlin had made insinuations, but no unequivocal threat of war.[5] By beaming a distorted version of a diplomatic exchange to the Western peoples over the heads of their statesmen, the Soviet Union, abetted by the sensationalism of the Western press, amplified the psychologic impact of its threat and attempted thus to force the hand of Western policy-makers. The Communist "missile-rattling" was by no means the compelling factor in the Anglo-French decision to withdraw. The Soviets, before they uttered their threat, knew only too well that the position of the two allies had become untenable in the face of the opposition of the United States. But, by ingeniously timing its warning, Moscow was able to claim credit for the liquidation of the Anglo-French military venture in Egypt.

[5] The significant passages in the note read as follows: "In what position would Britain have found herself if she herself had been attacked by more powerful states possessing every kind of modern destructive weapon? And there are countries now which need not have sent a navy or air force to the coasts of Britain, but could have used other means, such as rocket technique. If rocket weapons had been used against Britain and France, they would probably have called this a barbarous action. Yet in what way does the inhuman attack differ from this? . . . War may spread to other countries and become a third world war. The Soviet Government has already approached the United States, submitting a proposal to use naval and air forces, together with other United Nations members, to stop the war in Egypt and to restrain aggression. We are fully determined to crush the aggressors and restore peace in the East through the use of force." Text of note from Premier Bulganin to Prime Minister Sir Anthony Eden, November 5, 1956, in *Middle Eastern Affairs*, Vol. VIII, January, 1957, p. 12. For an excellent discussion of the manipulation of threatening statements by the Soviet Union in the Suez crisis, cf. Hans Speier, "Soviet Atomic Blackmail and the North Atlantic Alliance," *World Politics*, Vol. IX, April, 1957, pp. 318–324.

In May, 1958, the West was the target of an even more subtle threat technique, designed to prevent Western governments from assuming any military initiative in two concurrent conflict situations. "Neutralist" governments, at the obvious behest of Moscow and Peking, lodged with the United States angry protests calculated to inhibit intervention on behalf of the Indonesian rebels or the pro-Chamoun forces in Lebanon. President Sukarno of Indonesia hinted broadly that if the United States should send aid to the rebels in Sumatra, "others" would be sure to intervene in support of the Jakarta government. This, he said, would lead to general war. Later, an Indonesian government spokesman announced that the Chinese Communists had offered to send thousands of volunteers to fight the rebels. "They are only waiting for the signal from us," he added.[6] At approximately the same time, the Soviet news agency Tass issued a dispatch from Moscow which declared that Western intervention in the Lebanese crisis "could have serious consequences throughout the Middle East." A leading Cairo daily, *Al Akhbar*, followed this up with a red banner headline: "War if America intervenes in Lebanese crisis!"[7] In the Indonesian crisis, the veiled warning was intended to prevent the United States from assisting the rebels' effort to alter a situation more or less favorable to the Communists. In the Lebanese crisis, the purpose of the threat was to forestall a concerted Western initiative to preserve a pro-Western *status quo* (Note 23).

Few writers on strategy in this century have described the significance of the initiative in war so trenchantly as Mao Tse-tung. According to the Chinese Communist leader, an army, once it has been forced into a passive position or deprived of its freedom of action, is on the road to defeat.[8] Mao contends that the side which sets out from a position of physical inferiority can seize, through a shrewd exploitation of circumstances the initiative from the superior side and then maintain it.

[6] The Washington *Post and Times-Herald*, May 20, 1958.
[7] *Ibid.*
[8] Mao Tse-tung, *On the Protracted War*, in *The Selected Works of Mao Tse-tung*, Vol. II, p. 215.

The Communists have proven remarkably adept at turning the global network of communications to their advantage. Assume, for example, that the Korean War had been fought under circumstances of nineteenth-century "remoteness," instead of mid-twentieth-century "proximity." In the former hypothesis, the American commander in the field would have been guided almost exclusively by military considerations. Assuming that the American commander held a significant superiority in weapons, he would have been able to seize whatever initiative his own on-the-spot assessment of the situation demanded. Under the actual circumstances in which the Korean War was waged, the American field commander was not a free agent; he was under close supervision by Washington, which, in turn, was buffeted by the prevailing winds from other Western capitals. Hence the Communists were able to exploit a truce offer in Korea by addressing it not to the American military leaders in Korea—who were opposed to a cessation of hostilities until the armistice terms had been agreed upon—but to public opinion in the Western democratic nations.[9] The U.N. military in Korea, just as it was preparing an offensive which might have brought military defeat to the Communist forces, was outflanked and pressured from the rear. It would be difficult to find a better example of the Communists' nimbleness: in danger of forfeiting the military initiative, they secured adroitly their objective by suddenly shifting the conflict from the battle to the conference table (Note 24). By initiating truce talks and bringing about a cease-fire, the Communists prevented the United Nations forces from resuming the military initiative.[10]

[9] *United Nations Bulletin,* Vol. II, July 15, 1951, p. 86.

[10] The use of truce negotiations as a military-political tactic was developed by the Chinese Communists long before the Korean War. The ability of the Chinese Communists to survive and increase their strength as a government within a government for two decades (1928–1949) depended upon a policy of "No war, no peace." During the war with Japan, a truce policy known as the "United Front," ostensibly directed against Japan, recognized the *de facto* partition of China between the Chinese Nationalists and the Communists. As a result of this policy, which was originally proposed by the Communists, Mao was able to carry on 30 per cent of his war effort against the Japanese and 70 per cent against the Nationalists.

The conclusion of the Indochinese War furnishes another instructive example of Communist conference strategy. Negotiation serves to keep the enemy from taking the military initiative. After several years of conflict in Indochina, the Viet Minh was confident of its ability to defeat the French on the battlefield, provided that France would not receive outside assistance in the form of direct military intervention by her major allies, Great Britain and the United States. The Communists obviously reasoned that France's allies, wearied by four years of fighting in Korea, would not come to the active aid of the French in a stepped-up Indochinese action. To forestall Western intervention on the side of France, the Communists, at the Foreign Ministers' Conference at Berlin in February, 1954, induced the Western governments to schedule another conference at Geneva in April, to which the government of Red China would be invited. The problems of peace in Korea and Indochina were placed on the agenda. The scheduling of "peace talks" served to dampen any desire on the part of France's allies to enter the fighting. Three weeks later, on March 13, the Viet Minh launched their attack on Dien Bien Phu. The siege of Dien Bien Phu served to alert some American military leaders—among them Admiral Radford, then Chairman of the Joint Chiefs of Staff—to the seriousness of the situation in Indochina. The British, however, were staunchly opposed to taking any military steps which might jeopardize the success of the Geneva Conference later that month.[11] Prime Minister Winston Churchill made the following statement in the House of Commons:

The timing of the climax of this assault [on Dien Bien Phu] with the opening of the Geneva Conference is not without significance, but it must not be allowed to prejudice the sense of world proportion which should inspire the Conference and be a guide to those who are watching its progress.

Her Majesty's Government are not prepared to give any undertak-

[11] Cf. Richard P. Stebbins, *The United States in World Affairs 1954,* Council on Foreign Relations. New York. Harper & Brothers, 1956, pp. 217–224.

ings about United Kingdom military action in advance of results of Geneva.[12]

The Communists shrewdly invoked the prospects of a peace settlement to stint Western initiative at the same time that they launched an offensive which would enhance their position at the conference table. The switch from military action to the conference table, moreover, enabled the Communists to set the stage for a new strategic offensive in Indochina. After the Geneva talks established a truce line and set plans for national elections in Indochina, they began to infiltrate thousands of their agents into South Vietnam in the guise of "refugees," preparatory to a political take-over of the whole country through the device of unified elections.[13]

While the Kremlin sought frantically to stock its own nuclear-missile arsenal, the Communist leaders cast about for novel methods by which to sustain their offensive in the Cold War without triggering all-out nuclear war. A shift in strategy became all the more imperative when in January, 1954, Secretary of State Dulles announced that all Communist acts of aggression would be met with a policy of "massive retaliation." To circumvent this threat, backed as it was by the increasing superiority of America's nuclear delivery system, the Communists were forced to devise some important tactical innovations. Many of Mr. Dulles' critics were convinced that "massive retaliation" was not a credible policy. The fact remains that, after the policy of "massive retaliation" was announced, the Communists themselves did not start new brushfire wars *à la* Korea or Indochina. They were forced to devise subtler, less overt techniques of penetration than they had employed theretofore. The Soviet Union, hemmed in by NATO on its western flank, shifted its attention to the underdeveloped lands, especially the Arab world.

The new Soviet strategy in the underdeveloped areas, with its

[12] Hansard, *Parliamentary Debates, Commons,* 5th Ser., Vol. DXXVI, April 27, 1954, pp. 1455–1456.
[13] Cf. Roy Jumper, "Communist Challenge to South Viet Nam," *Far Eastern Survey,* Vol XXV, November, 1956, pp. 161–168.

emphasis on stepped-up cultural relations, trade agreements and (in the Middle East) "purely commercial" arms deals, enabled the Communists to vault the Northern Tier and the SEATO defense line, and to exert new pressure on the non-Communist world without furnishing a clear-cut *casus belli.*

In the Far East, the Chinese Communists devised another tactical innovation. The Korean and Indochinese wars and the Formosa Straits crisis had raised the level of American preparedness in Asia sufficiently to make it dangerous for the Peking regime to embark on new military adventures. Having gone as far as they dared in the direction of violent conflict, the Chinese Communist leaders switched the emphasis of their strategy to subversion and political maneuver. The stage had been set by the creation, after 1950, of a number of "autonomous" entities along the border of South China, such as the "free states" of Karen and Kachen along the border of Burma, and the "autonomous" Tai Republic in the southern tip of Yunan, whence Burma, Cambodia and Thailand could be made the targets of "liberation movements." [14] By exploiting the tension-laden minorities problems of Southeast Asia, Peking hoped to lay the foundation for a regional satellite system without risking a head-on collision with the West.

In 1950, the Chinese Communists penetrated the northern part of the little kingdom of Laos, gained control over two northern provinces and set up a "liberation government," known as the Pathet Lao. The Communists sought and obtained permission under the Geneva Agreement of 1954 to retain their position in these "Viet-Minhized" zones, which were contiguous with Viet Minh territory.[15] After the end of the fighting in Indochina, the

[14] Cf. Roger Swearingen, "Techniques of Communist Aggression and the Moscow-Peking Axis," in *Nationalism and Progress in Free Asia,* ed. Philip W. Thayer, Baltimore: The Johns Hopkins Press, 1956, p. 327. During 1957, the Communists extended their influence in the Wa State, along the disputed Burmese border, and in Northern Laos, where an effort was under way to "Viet-Minhize" the country through the agency of the Pathet Lao movement.

[15] Cf. Agreement on the Cessation of Hostilities in Laos, July 20, 1954, Article 11. In *American Foreign Policy, 1950–1955,* Department of State Publication 6446, July, 1957, Vol. I, p. 779.

Pathet Lao, which had fought against the French Army and the French-supported Laotian government, began to press the Royal Laotian government for a place in a coalition cabinet. In December, 1956, the Royal government proclaimed an amnesty, according the Pathet Lao a legal status. Two leaders of the Pathet Lao were admitted to the cabinet a year later. In return, the Pathet Lao gave up administrative control of the two northern provinces and integrated fifteen hundred troops into the Laotian Army, while ostensibly disbanding the remaining six thousand. As it shed its military trappings as a guerrilla force and took on the appearance of a respectable parliamentary party, the Pathet Lao became known as the Neo Lao Hak Xat. In special elections in May, 1958, to fill twenty-one seats, nine Communists and four Communist-backed neutralists were elected.[16] The kingdom of Laos thus served as a proving ground for a refurbished Communist tactic: switching from military operations to parliamentary electoral processes, and thus maintaining the tactical initiative.

16 Tillman Durdin, "Communists in Laos Win Unique Victory," *New York Times,* May 18, 1958. In January, 1959, the Cabinet was reshuffled and the Pathet Lao members were excluded.

CHAPTER 7 ATTRITION

It is axiomatic that the revolutionary side must strive, by graduated and sometimes imperceptible pressures, to weaken the *status quo* forces, strengthen its own forces, and bring about a piecemeal, yet ultimately decisive, shift in the distribution of power.

In the Communist campaign of attrition, the first step is the neutralization of the "intermediate strata."[1] On a global level, the Communists strive to neutralize all the colonial and emergent nations lying between the Sino-Soviet bloc and the West. Within the Atlantic region, they seek to isolate the hard core of the enemy, i.e., the United States, from other allied or friendly states. At the national level, the Communists try to neutralize large political and social segments and influential elites, while isolating those elements that pursue strong anti-Communist policies. Within Europe, Communist objectives are to obtain at least the neutrality of countries which may figure prominently in an effective defense of Western Europe. The purpose of the Soviet neutrality campaign in Europe, waged with increased vehemence and subtlety since Stalin's death, is the dissolution of the Western

---

[1] "Intermediate strata" may be defined as including all those groups which lie between the two principal antagonists and are not directly involved in the struggle, but whose weight could decide the outcome of the conflict should they join either side or even remain uncommitted. These intermediate strata must, at the very least, be prevented from supporting the "capitalist" forces.

system of alliances; secondly, the withdrawal of American and British forces from the European Continent; and finally, the creation of broad demilitarized regions in Central Europe which, exposed to Russian pressure unmatched by countervailing American power, would ultimately succumb to the Soviet Union.

To make the neutrality campaign more plausible, the Soviets have dangled some attractive "bait" before those Europeans who, weary of the Cold War, tend to question the wisdom of their commitments to Western defense. Thus, for example, the Soviets, by agreeing to an Austrian State Treaty in 1955, obviously sought to prevent West Germany's accession to the Atlantic Pact. The establishment of an independent and neutral Austria was intended to spur the hopes of those Germans who believed that only some form of all-German neutrality could induce the Russians to consent to German unification (Note 25).

The major targets of the Soviet neutrality campaign are the "out" parties of Western Europe. Soviet propaganda is only too willing to provide the ammunition for the electoral campaigns of such opposition parties as, for example, the German Social Democrats and British Labour.[2] The West German Socialists, for example, have steadfastly argued that the inclusion of West Germany in NATO would extinguish all hope of national reunification; they professed themselves willing to accept a form of neutrality—or "freedom from alliances" (*Bündnislosigkeit*) as they euphemistically term it—as the price for redeeming East Germany. One Soviet declaration after another has provided the Socialists with fuel for their campaign.[3] By

[2] Nikita Khrushchev said: "If we show persistence—*the people are now beginning to press increasingly on their governments*—with every year and even with every month, the champions of the Cold War will find it harder and harder. . . . Not only the Labourites in Britain, but even part of the Conservatives say 'No, the Russians do not want to wage war and we believe it.'" (Italics added.) "Mr. Khrushchev's World Survey," *Manchester Guardian Weekly*, April 17, 1958.

[3] The case of East Germany as a bargaining pawn in Soviet hands has somewhat of a parallel in Japan. The Soviets, having failed in their efforts to participate in the postwar occupation of Japan (which doubtless would have resulted in territorial division, as in Korea and Germany) gained pos-

thus playing up divergences of opinion within the West, the Soviets seek to rend the moral solidarity of the Western Alliance. Indeed Stalin, in his political testament, reminded Communists everywhere that there were still abundant opportunities for producing divisions within the capitalist West:

> *Some comrades hold that, owing to the development of new international conditions since the second World War, wars between capitalist countries have ceased to be inevitable. They consider that the contradictions between the socialist camp and the capitalist camp are more acute than the contradictions among the capitalist countries; that the United States has brought the other capitalist countries sufficiently under its sway to be able to prevent them from going to war among themselves and weakening one another; that the foremost capitalist minds have been sufficiently taught by the two world wars and the severe damage they caused to the whole capitalist world not to venture to involve the capitalist countries in war with one another again— and that, because of all this, wars between capitalist countries are no longer inevitable. These comrades are wrong.*[4]

The Communists have been fully aware of the fact that their challenges in certain areas of the world at times divided, rather than united, the West. In Malaya, Indochina and Korea, the one Western power which felt its interests to be at stake joined the struggle, while its major allies either abstained from the conflict altogether or extended only halfhearted support. It was not difficult for the Communists to conclude that the Western Alliance lacked global unity of purpose and that they were free to promote divisive conflicts so long as they abstained from challenging the Allies collectively.

Although a basic consensus has reigned in the councils of the Allies over the defense of the NATO area on the European Con-

---

session of certain Japanese islands—notably the Kuriles. They thus hold territorial hostages that may be exploited later to neutralize Japan or to put pressure on the United States to withdraw from its Okinawa base.

[4] J. V. Stalin, *Economic Problems of Socialism in the U.S.S.R.,* Information Services of the U.S.S.R., Embassy of the U.S.S.R., Washington, 1952, p. 15.

tinent, the extra-European efforts of the West have not been distinguished by anything approaching unanimity. Even while the United States was constructing the North Atlantic Alliance in partnership with the United Kingdom, the American Ambassador in Cairo was assisting the Egyptian government in its efforts to dislodge the British from their strategic position in the Nile Valley.[5] The Communists were quick to conclude—as their subsequent actions proved—that Anglo-American solidarity in the Middle East was marred by fundamental divergencies. They were led to make a similar calculation in North Africa, where the anticolonial sentiments of the United States came into conflict with the efforts of the French to salvage their dwindling overseas holdings.[6] The Communists were able to exploit these deep-seated differences among the Western Allies by fanning the flames of both the Suez and the Algerian crises.

Indeed, since World War II, the Communists have missed few opportunities to promote conflicts in order to heighten inter-Allied tensions. They have spurred on the forces of the "systemic revolution" wherever they operate against the West. Although almost every revolutionary conflict contains inherently the seeds of Western discord,[7] the Allies have not been able to agree upon a common approach to the problems of the systemic revolution. The United States, time and again, has been pushed by Communist strategy into the uncomfortable position of "arbiter" between the aspirations of emergent nations and the strategic,

[5] The Egyptians credited the United States with having assisted them in bringing about the Sudan and Suez accords. Cf. *Department of State Bulletin,* Vol. 31, August 16, 1954, p. 234.

[6] The United States, for example, had allowed Habib Bourguiba, while he was fighting for Tunisian independence, to use Voice of America facilities to launch an attack against French colonial rule in North Africa. *Le Monde,* March 8, 1951.

[7] In Cyprus, for example, *enosis* (union with Greece) has emerged as the island's major political issue within the last quarter-century. The local Communist party, the most efficient political organization on the island, has spared no effort to stir up resentment between Cypriotes and British, and between Greek Cypriotes and Turkish Cypriotes, thereby doing their part to worsen NATO relations in the Eastern Mediterranean.

political and commercial interests [8] of the colonial and ex-colonial powers of Western Europe.

Even within the NATO area, the area of maximum consensus among the Western Allies, the Communists have successfully exploited Western differences over the precise nature of the Communist threat and the most effective strategy for countering it. The openness of Western democratic society enables the Communists to discern and exploit subtle shifts of opinion on such issues as foreign aid, arms limitations, suspension of nuclear tests, exchange programs, summit talks and military strategy. Having taken the measure of the basic divisions in the Western outlook, the Communists can easily tailor propaganda declarations and policy proposals to the predilections of opposition parties, pressure groups and disgruntled elements in the Western camp. The Bulganin note of November 17, 1956, for example, which hinted at the possibility of a mutual five-hundred-mile withdrawal of Soviet and American forces from the Iron Curtain, set off, at a time when Russia's demonstrated weakness in this area might have been exploited by a Western policy of concerted pressure, a destructive and bitter debate on the feasibility of "disengagement" in Central Europe. Similarly Soviet proposals for "summit" parleys are "export products" (Note 26).

One of the more subtle methods in the Communist campaign to "neutralize" certain segments of Western society has been to stir, through a process of conditioning, "pangs of conscience" among Western intellectual elites. A noted historian interprets the West's crisis of conscience as follows:

Though the brief period of Western imperialism has witnessed many injustices and cruelties, which however were in no way worse than the

---

[8] The entry of Italy and Japan into the development of Middle East oil during 1957, under agreements with Iran and Saudi Arabia which were widely hailed as being more favorable to the local governments than the existing fifty-fifty arrangements with the United States and Great Britain, introduces into that region an additional source of potential conflict among Free World industrial states. Cf. "New Oil Agreements in the Middle East," *World Today*, Vol. XIV, April, 1958, pp. 135–143.

normal happenings in Asia and Africa before the advent of the white man, it has been on the whole a period of which the West, and especially Britain, has not to be ashamed. It would be wrong to apply twentieth century standards and principles of international law to preceding centuries. By doing that—and it should not be forgotten that these new twentieth century standards were developed by the Western world—the West suffers a bad conscience; the anti-Western propaganda is exploiting these guilt feelings.[9]

Ever since Lenin's time, the charge that colonialism and imperialism are synonomous with the foreign policies of the capitalist states has been a stock-in-trade of Communist propagandists, both in the West and in the colonial areas. This slanderous campaign has been remarkably successful. Liberal and leftist intellectual elites throughout the world take it for granted that "imperialism" is a peculiar vice of the West (Note 27). Socialist states, by definition, are altruistic and pacifist. Capitalist states, by contrast, seek to exploit, to control, to conquer.

According to available accounts of Communist "brainwashing" techniques, it takes weeks until the victim breaks down under the weight of endlessly repeated charges. In the larger dimension, it may take half a century or more for the Communists' international propaganda apparatus to produce an analogous effect upon the elite groups of Western society. There is reason to believe that they have already achieved a remarkable measure of progress.

The obverse of the Communist strategy of *divide et impera* in the non-Communist world is the elaborate effort by the Sino-Soviet bloc to impress the world with the invulnerability of the Communist "monolith." The devices used to contrive this image are founded partly on brute force, partly on clever psychological manipulation. On the one hand, by resorting to purges, banishment and population resettlement, Communism ruthlessly eliminates internal social tensions, rivalries, disputes and dissident movements which might possibly weaken or exhaust the revolu-

[9] Hans Kohn, *Is the Liberal West in Decline?*, London: Pall Mall Press, 1957, pp. 69-70.

tionary bloc.[10] When brute force has failed, the Communists have applied a wide range of subtler techniques and instruments for achieving internal consensus, promoting confidence in their social system, and projecting to the outside world the façade of strength through unity. Among the techniques which they have used toward these ends are: the monopolization of all decision-making power by the Communist party; a rigidly controlled state-party press which is closely geared to Soviet foreign and domestic policy and which insulates the local population against ideas from outside; paper alliances (Warsaw Pact) and trade agreements (Soviet-Polish coal agreement) which mask the unilateral and exploitative character of Soviet policy; citizenship exchanges (e.g., U.S.S.R.–North Korea); and similar devices which convey images of mutual trust, equality and common destiny.

One of the most important means by which the Communists preserve unity of mind within their bloc, shield it from outside influences, and at the same time prevent the West from gaining an accurate assessment of what goes on within the communist system, is the maintenance of the so-called "Curtains," Iron and Bamboo. It is frequently overlooked in the West that these curtains are drawn not only to hinder the West from looking in, but also to prevent the people of the Communist world from looking out and comparing the two systems. The West has generally failed to appreciate the many and real purposes of the Iron Curtain in the Soviet protracted conflict strategy (Note 28).

The Iron and Bamboo Curtains give Moscow and Peking an enormous advantage in the use of psychological warfare. During 1958, the frequently repeated proposals for summit talks proved to be among the most effective divisive instruments in the Communists' arsenal. "They were missiles of propaganda warfare rather than notes of diplomacy and aimed at public opinion out-

[10] The economic and social objectives of Soviet irrigation, hydroelectric and other development schemes are often meshed with a political goal, i.e., breaking up nuclei of resistance by forcibly disrupting the ethnic texture of the population. Cf. H. Frisch, "Hydro-Technical Schemes in the Soviet Union," *Contemporary Review*, No. 1022, February, 1951, p. 110.

side of the communist bloc. Since the communist rulers do not tolerate free discussion at home, their propaganda campaign for a 'summit' conference is being waged—like all 'cold war' battles —upon the territory of the Free World." [11] Given the contrast between a closed and open society, the "Soviet negotiators are free agents; their Western counterparts are not. The Soviets need not worry as to whether the conference will be barren of concrete results. The Western leaders will be loath to return empty-handed and to disappoint the hopes, however ill-founded, of their peoples." [12]

A SUMMARY OF THE OPERATIONAL PRINCIPLES

A recapitulation of the operational principles of protracted conflict described in the last four chapters is now in order. This strategy refuses the frontal, all-out battle with the stronger foe. To seek a direct military engagement under circumstances which would put the outcome in doubt is unpardonable. Whether or not a final, annihilating attack upon the West will be either possible or necessary is a judgment which the Communist conflict managers reserve to the future. If such a choice is ever made, the strategy of protracted conflict will be converted into a strategy of swift, complete decision. But so long as an overwhelming margin of strategic superiority lies beyond the Communists' reach, they have no choice but to postpone the Armageddon.

A clear-cut case of Communist aggression provides the West with that powerful, shocking stimulus of a "new war," to which it is wont to react with high excitement and few inhibitions. A Communist aggressor finds it extremely difficult to condition, in advance of the initial thrust, a Western nation's response to an overt attack. But once a conflict is under way, the Communists are adept at wearing down, through the cumulative effect of many psychopolitical pressures, a democratic society's will to resist. The Communists strive, through a process of conditioning

11 Robert Strausz-Hupé, "The Hoax in the 'Summit' Game," *U.S. News and World Report,* April 11, 1958, p. 76.
12 *Ibid.*

skillfully applied against Western elites, to bring about the demoralization and psychological exhaustion of the Western peoples. Toward this end, they carefully weigh their challenges to
the West. Instead of launching *Blitzkrieg* attacks, they phase
their challenges over relatively long periods of time. Like a
matador asserting his mastery over the bull, the Communist
strategist of protracted conflict grows bolder by slow degrees.

While avoiding the decisive military encounter, the Soviets
have warred upon the West through auxiliaries or proxies—satellite governments, national Communist parties, "neutral" states,
national liberation guerrilla movements, front organizations and
"volunteers." The proxy tactic cloaks the challenge with ambiguities. It enables the Communists to maintain relentless pressure
upon the West without presenting that precise *casus belli* which
historically has provoked the West into casting aside its Ham-
letian doubts and going to war.

Deception is an integral part of the science of war. Both parties to a conflict—the stronger as well as the weaker—often avail
themselves of this tactic; but it is only by deception that the
weaker belligerent can steal a march on the stronger one.

Distraction is one of the most effective plays in the tactical
repertoire of revolutionary Communism, globally deployed
against a superior foe. Lenin gave this advice to the Comintern
in 1921: "The greater the area of the struggle, the greater the
prospect of victory.... The greater the fighting area, the more
must the enemy divide and scatter his forces." [13] The Communists have succeeded to a remarkable degree in diverting the
attention of the West from their weak spot, viz., Eastern Europe,
to the more diffuse "gray areas," where the Communists can bat-
ten upon the anti-Western forces of the systemic revolution.
Within the broader setting of protracted conflict, Western efforts
on the battleground chosen by the Communists—Afro-Asia—can
be little more than *ad hoc* defenses of rapidly deteriorating posi-

[13] *Theses and Resolutions Adopted at the Third World Congress of the
Communist International,* 1921, New York: Contemporary Publishing Association, 1921, p. 59.

tions. These holding operations may serve temporarily to keep the Communists at bay or force them to change their tactics. They do not, however, weaken the power base on which rests the Communists' capability for waging protracted conflict. If the United States, mistaking the place where the issue was met for the place over which it arose, should abandon the primacy of Europe to the expediency of Asiatic strategy, it would play the game of Soviet strategy.

Protracted conflict doctrine calls for the alternate adoption of apparently contrary and ambiguous policies precisely for the purpose of confusing the West and blinding it to the nature of the threat confronting it. Since Lenin's days, the West has been beguiled, as the result of a series of policy zigzags within the Soviet Union, by varying images of Communism-turned-reasonable.

The Communists seek to appear to be more than they really are. By projecting an exaggerated image of their strength, they often inhibit the Western response to their carefully calibrated challenges. The West finds itself the target of an accelerating series of corrosive crises, instigated or aggravated by the Communists. Each crisis is organically related to the next, and all lead up to the strategic climax. The manner in which the West responds to a given crisis may determine its response to future challenges. Hence it is as dangerous to overestimate Communist power as to underestimate it. The penalty for overestimation is invariably the relinquishment of the initiative to the enemy, and the forfeiture of the next tactical round in the protracted war.

The Communists aim to monopolize the strategic initiative for themselves and to keep the West in a defensive and reactive frame of mind. They strive to neutralize the West's tactical superiority and to confine the conflict to those weapons and techniques in which they hold the advantage. The West, inundated with reminders of Soviet nuclear-missile prowess, is made to believe that any effort on its part to seize the tactical initiative at any time will ineluctably lead to general war. If in any given situation the West appears ready to bring superior tactical power to bear, the Communists seek to forestall the move by suddenly shifting the conflict into a new dimension. To this end, they resort to such ruses as truce talks, summit conferences, disarmament negotiations, and threats to send volunteers.

The Communists have succeeded remarkably in their efforts to define the rules of the protracted conflict and to gain general acceptance of those rules within the West: the non-Communist world constitutes the "war zone," in which the Communists are allowed as a matter of course to conduct conflict operations. The West, on the other hand must not, under any circumstances, intervene in the "peace zone," namely, the territory controlled by the Communists. The Communists contend that the West, for the sake of maintaining a safety margin for peace, must be willing to accept compromise settlements whenever the Communists press their offensive into the "peace zone." But it is rarely believed possible that the Communists can be compelled to accept any compromise involving a net military or political setback within their own orbit: the slightest trespass of the Communist frontier is deemed fraught with the risk of all-out war.

The ultimate purpose of the strategy of protracted conflict is to enable the revolutionary side to wear down the enemy while building up its own strength. Vegetius long ago pondered this truism: "It is in the nature of war that what is beneficial to you is detrimental to the enemy and what is of service to him hurts you." The Communists, while carrying on a demoralizing propaganda campaign against the open society of the West, maintain Iron and Bamboo Curtains to insulate their own closed society against the potentially revolutionary impact of the liberal world. While consolidating the socialist "parallel world market" and gradually reorienting the economies of selected underdeveloped economies toward the Communist bloc, they compress the area of the Western market system. These are but two of the many dimensions in which the Communists are waging attritional war against the West.

The strategy of protracted conflict, in sum, is designed to maximize the power gains of the antagonist who matches the

material or technological superiority of his opponent with a pro-
founder understanding of the nature of conflict. This strategy
is calculated to bring about, over a long period of time, a gradual,
yet fundamental shift in the ratio of power between the two contestants. The operational principles of protracted conflict form a
tightly meshed whole and are often interchangeable—a circumstance which, far from disturbing Lenin or Stalin, Khrushchev or
Mao, would have confirmed them in their unitary view of conflict. The principles consist of a few key norms of action which
are intimately related to each other and which can easily be applied pragmatically to the wide range of situations which the
systemic revolution constantly generates—much like a set of
musical chords which, once perfectly mastered, enable one to
play a variety of melodies "by ear" and to learn new tunes
quickly, even if not flawlessly.

The Communist resuscitation, in the fall of 1958, of the
perennial crisis revolving around the conflict center of Berlin,
represented a dramatic application of many of the foregoing principles. The Communists had been deprived temporarily of the
strategic initiative in the Middle East and the Formosa Straits.
Now, they attempted to regain it in Europe by reopening the
question of Berlin. Maneuvering in one of the world's most sensitive areas of confrontation between the Communist bloc and
the West, the Soviets shunned a face-to-face encounter with
NATO military forces. They designated their East German satellite as proxy, charged with the mission of prying loose the West's
hold on Berlin. Thus they sought to accomplish a maneuver that
was certain to involve unacceptable risks if carried out by themselves. Premier Khrushchev, having announced that the U.S.S.R.
intended to lift the occupation of East Germany at an early
date, called upon the Western Allies to withdraw from West
Berlin. Full legal control of East Germany—including the land,
water and air corridors reserved to the West under the Potsdam
Agreement of 1945—was to be turned over to the Pankow régime.
The Soviet plan, in short, was to test by proxy the West's policy
of firmness.

At the same time, the Soviets sought to force the West into according recognition to East Germany, the most artificial among the Soviet satellites. Recognition of the Pankow regime would not only block the reunification of Germany by democratic means but also dampen the rebellious spirit of the satellite peoples. When the Western Allies appeared to maintain a united front against this sudden Soviet move, Soviet strategy displayed a familiar resiliency. Premier Khrushchev announced that the proposed change in occupation controls would be deferred for six months. Khrushchev, in taking this ostensibly reasonable step, was counting upon another debilitating debate between the governments and the out-parties of Western Europe, and between the United States and its allies, over the feasibility of disengagement on the Continent. The six-month period was designed to soften up opinion in the West, both official and public, so that the next stage of the recurring Berlin crisis would find the West less united and less determined to stand firm.

The case of Khrushchev's Berlin gambit, together with the accompanying campaign of psychonuclear warfare, furnishes a rich example of protracted conflict strategy in action. This particular case should not be mistaken for a unique manifestation of Communist strategic prowess. We may presume that the scene will shift and that other actors will act out the play at other places. Yet the plot will remain the same, and each of its twists and each of its turns weaves a pattern that is an organic whole.

CHAPTER **8** IMPLICATIONS—A SITUATION

REPORT

The Communists have always held that war is indeed a continuation of policy "by other means." Communist doctrine is a doctrine of irreconcilable and protracted conflict between classes and between the capitalist and socialist states. This conflict is an "organic whole." For the Communist there is only one war, namely, the war to the finish. As to the finish, Mr. Khrushchev asserts, "We will bury you."

For the West, the irreconcilable conflict with Communism has not been an "organic whole." It is this circumstance which explains a series of Western reverses which, had they been viewed as so many defeats in one and the same recognizable campaign, would have alerted the free people to the catastrophic decline of their fortunes and aroused them to a vast effort of common defense.

The Communists are likely to win World War III because they know they are in it. The Third World War was not openly declared by the Communists in 1946. Nor was a state of war recognized by the West. If it had been, probably none of the Free World positions forfeited since World War II would have been abandoned without determined resistance. More important still, the decision of whether to hold or to abandon those positions would have been made by an Allied council of war and not by the individual members of the Western Alliance, nor would the question as to what weapons to use and what strategy to pursue have been left to the discretion of any one government. There would have been one plan of action, one strategy and one combined command—one "organic whole" of political, military and economic effort.

From 1946 to 1958, the world was nominally at peace. There was no atomic war. Yet future historians may well reach the conclusion that, in these twelve crucial years, a crucial world war was fought and largely lost by the Western Allies.

In the light of the sustained Communist onslaught, perhaps the most costly among the many illusions that have bemused us since the end of World War II is that we have been living in a kind of peace. Admittedly most everyone, except the most determined Pollyannas, is agreed that for some years we have lived in a state of conflict with the Soviet Union. This state of conflict has been called the "Cold War." Yet, somehow, local wars, far-off rebellions and the recurring clashes with the Soviet Union or Communist China are being taken as deviations from the norm. That nostalgic norm is peace. So persistent has been this illusion in the United States and other democratic countries that even the most massive evidence to the contrary has failed to shake it. This never has been the belief of the Communists.

That we are still not conscious of being defeated, except perhaps momentarily in the technological race, or of having been involved in a mortal struggle, does not make our appalling defeats less real. On the contrary, the measure of success of Communist protracted conflict principles is that the Communists have gained control of regions heretofore firmly held by the Western powers without provoking a counterattack by the Western coalition.

The Communists, ever since they started upon their march to power, have operated from an inferior position. At the outset, they could not begin to match the military and economic power of their opponents. They were inferior in all respects—except in the determination to win a power monopoly and the skill of exploiting the irresolution of those whom they proposed to conquer. Broadly speaking, as of 1959, they are still inferior to the combined power of the West.

International Communism, while striving to achieve a decisive margin of military-technological superiority over the West, will continue to feed parasitically upon the global systemic revolution. Despite the fact that this revolution is not of their making, the Communists will claim it as their own. It is precisely this usurpation which has made their protracted conflict strategy so successful. Confident of the superiority of their understanding of the revolutionary processes of history, the Communists can be expected—barring a clear threat to the security of their home base —to shun a direct, decisive encounter with the West so long as the victorious survival of Communism would hang in doubt. More likely than not, they will continue to rely upon indirect, irregular and ambiguous challenges and utilize tactical innovation to deceive the West as to their method and purpose. Obviously, it will fit their plans to overawe the people of the West with their strategic capabilities—or at least with the image of those capabilities which they themselves project. They will attempt to paralyze the decision-makers of the Western nations. To this purpose, they will increasingly exploit a variety of communications channels to produce conditioned guilt complexes, schizoid attitudes toward the Communist threat, an excessively defensive mentality and diverse social neuroses among Western elites. Needless to say, they will go on masking the serious internal weaknesses of the Soviet Empire while working steadily to divide the West and drain it of its strength.

The general expansion of Soviet power continues. Its internal goal has been the creation of an industrial base which will support a diversified major military machine. This base has grown, and the Soviet military machine has grown with it. The U.S.S.R has attained the full spectrum of the latest weapons. Whatever disturbances have rent the Communist world (and, admittedly, some of these imposed taut strains on Soviet society) have not seriously impaired the fundaments of Communist power in Rus-

sia, Eastern Europe and Red China. The combined juggernaut of
Russia and Red China remains a formidable tool ready to do the
bidding of the Communist leaders.

The West's view of Communism tend to polarize at the extremes of optimism and despair. On the optimistic side are
ranged those who believe that the revolutionary fervor of Communism has been exhausted. Further, we are told, Communism,
as an active dynamic force, is not transferable and that, for example, it cannot shift from Moscow to Red China. More important still, according to this diagnosis, the Communist system is
dissolving and its harsher features are being absorbed into the
more "liberal" society of post-Stalinist Russia.

Many arguments are adduced in support of this view. First,
the Soviet leaders, being completely rational men by our standards, recognize the inherent threat implied in nuclear developments not only to their own survival but to the survival of humanity as a whole, and, therefore, have voluntarily renounced their
ambitious program of world domination since its pursuit would
set off a chain reaction that will bring about their own undoing.
Secondly, the managerial group arising in Russia, displaying pronounced middle-class characteristics, has already placed a severe
brake upon the ideological drives of the Communist party members. This group will grow in numbers and political power and,
indeed, has already become the most potent domestic force
within the Soviet Union. Since these Communist industrial managers as well as their counterparts in the administrative, military
and academic bureaucracy are presumably motivated by the
same life goals which beckon their opposites in the United States,
they will wave aside the revolutionary appeals of the Communist experiment and settle down to the pursuit and enjoyment of
solid, unideological rewards very much like the members of
any country club in the United States. With these people, therefore, we can do business.

Those who hold to this view, namely, that the Soviet Union is
already well on the way to transformation into the mellow image

of the West, deem the over-all performance of the Free World in the Cold War to have been as successful as it has been prudent. They, in fact, begin to see victory in sight and light at the end of the long tunnel of the Cold War.

By the contrary and pessimistic view of the confrontation of the Free World with the Communist bloc, Communist power has grown at an unprecedented rate notwithstanding many serious, albeit foreseeable, reverses.

This conclusion can be verified by a comparison of positions already won and lost by the Free World and the Communist respectively; it need not be based upon estimates of future and hence presently unverifiable trends.

In sum, to say the least, an analysis of the relative power position of the Communist bloc and the Free World warrants as readily a pessimistic as an optimistic interpretation of the events of the last twelve years. Under these circumstances, we cannot agree, as a matter of prudence, to base our policies exclusively on the most favorable assumptions as to the state, here and now, of Communist society and the intentions of its rulers. Even were the most hopeful prognosis about the future correct *at present,* the Communists are still cleaving to their characteristic doctrines and practices. Even were we to concede—as we do not—that Communist strategy now obeys a conditioned reflex rather than consciously held ideological beliefs, its progression impinges massively upon the remaining domain of freedom and demands our appropriate response.

Unfortunately, at this late hour the citizens of the United States—now the citadel which guards the survival of Western civilization—are still divided as to whether or not rising Communist power really represents a mere irritation rather than a deadly threat to their existence.

In general, two alternative lines of policy correspond to the two alternative assumptions as to the evolution of Communism and our achievements and prospects in the Cold War.

Those who believe that the processes of disintegration within the Communist bloc are already well under way are not only convinced of the correctness of the policies which the United States has pursued in the past, but are also unwilling to counter any Soviet moves by substantial, direct and challenging action. They advocate a policy of seduction, designed to "let the steam out" of the Communist bloc by proving to the Communist leaders, time and time again, that the West has no real desire to tangle with the fundamental concepts on which the Communist system is based.

On the other hand, those who believe that the Soviet power position is improving steadily are of the opinion that de-Stalinization was not tantamount to de-Leninization, that the lines of dogma are as rigid as ever—and that for us and the cause of freedom the worst is yet to come. In consequence, they, in general, advocate a strategy of bringing pressure to bear against the weak points of the Communist bloc and of checking it wherever it tries to make a foray into the Free World. Adherents of this school of thought are finding their views increasingly less popular not only in the United States but also in practically every country along the Soviet periphery. The spirit of appeasement is again abroad in the councils of the Atlantic democracies. This state of mind, hostile to the simultaneous application of pressure and containment against the Communists, can itself be considered as an instrument of Communist power, for the Communists do not relax *their* pressures upon the Free World, nor do *they* harbor any illusions about the fundamental antagonism of their system and ours. In other words, the adherents of the "convergence theory"—the theory that Communism is growing more "liberal" and "democratic" and thus promises to approximate social democracy, if not the American "way of life"—are all on this side of the Iron and the Bamboo Curtains.

The inability to respond promptly and energetically to obvious threats is a characteristic symptom of a declining society. Only rarely has a great nation been destroyed by one dramatic blow. Defeat was preceded nearly always by a slow erosion of the will to resist aggression from without, followed by a weakening of its own people's sense of common purpose.

The Western Allies, more often than not, have conceded needlessly the initiative to the Communists. Their policies have been essentially reactive; actions were taken too late. Western statesmanship has failed to anticipate incipient crises and to prevent the Communists from building up the anti-Western forces to such proportions as render effective counteraction either extremely difficult or impossible. When military action is necessary, it is best begun and ended swiftly. Prolongation of a conflict, such as occurred in Korea, invariably redounds to the advantage of the Communists since the Western peoples, as a result of their own cultural tradition, are loath to engage in protracted conflict. The worst policy conceivable for the Western nations when faced with a crisis is to fight a delaying action with half-measures. Time has proved to be the Communists' invaluable ally.

Whatever cohesion the Free World has achieved has been wrought by fears intermittently aroused. It has countered fitfully specific acts of Communist aggression; it has not made a pondered and steady response to the totality of the Communist challenge to all free peoples and institutions.

The advantages of the Sino-Soviet bloc are compounded, for their foreign policies, consisting mainly of unique strategic and political acts, are much less predictable and much harder to parry than ponderous American programs. So long as the United States neglects strategic political moves, the Communist orbit can maintain the initiative with a minimum of effort. Meanwhile, there is the real danger that, unless the United States registers more spectacular successes against creeping Communist expansion, the American people, discouraged by the "boomerang effect" of many of their liberal international programs, will lapse again into isolationism, the old-fashioned kind or the new model: "Citadel America."

It is no exaggeration to say that in recent years the Western governments have shown neither enthusiasm for, nor skill in, the conduct of their official "information programs," which are a poor substitute for ideological-political warfare. Western peoples, in general, are hardly exercised about the future of the free way of life. So defensive has the Western mentality become that many intellectuals devote most of their time to apologizing for the institutions and the processes of liberal society. Paradoxically, even those intellectuals who are most dedicated to the cause of individual freedom within their own nations do not manifest as profound a concern over the threat which Communist expansion poses to human freedom. Neo-isolationists in a sense, they are often ready to write off one area of the world after another to Communist penetration rather than run the risks entailed by a policy of prevention through intervention. They take it for granted that if contests do occur between the Communists and the West, they must take place on the soil of the non-Communist world.

At this moment, we are not "containing" the Communists: they are containing us—behind a constantly shrinking perimeter of Free World defenses. Behind the Iron Curtain, the Communist "peace zone" is closed to our "interference"; the Free World is the "war zone" in which the Communists can, with impunity, bring all of their implements of conflict to bear.

In this "war zone" we hold, if we are lucky, the ground which the Communists have not yet captured—or we give way. Unless we change the peculiar rules of this strange game, the Communists, even were they much less adroit than they have proved themselves to be, cannot help but win. That the enemy is confident of victory is clear. The highest-ranking official journal of Communist China has trumpeted:

Today the last bastions of imperialism are being shaken violently by the irresistible popular revolutionary forces. The billion people of the socialist camp now have at their side in the struggle against imperialism the more than 700 million people of the former colonial countries which have already won national independence. In addition, there are the 600 million people in the countries which are still fighting for independence or full independence. . . .

In human history, the forces of the new always defeat the forces of decay. New, emergent forces, though seemingly weak, always prevail over the old, moribund forces which are still seemingly strong. What is decaying will inevitably be replaced by the newborn—such is the law of development and in society.[1]

[1] Yu Chao-li in the *Red Flag*, August 16, 1958 cited in the *New Leader*, October 20, 1958, p. 23.

CHAPTER 9 THE CONDUCT OF CONFLICT

The realignment of forces and nations which has emerged since 1945 attests to the inadequacy of American policy during the first dozen years of the Cold War. The shift in the distribution of power, on the whole, weighted the scales in favor of the Communists, although many of the policies developed in Washington, taken singly, were both imaginative and constructive. American actions suffered from certain serious shortcomings. Nearly every policy, even though conceived as a pondered response to the Communist threat, can be seen on close analysis to have been an *ad hoc* one, unrelated to the others in an integral scheme.

This shortcoming is traceable, in part, to the very structure of the government bureaucracy in a democracy. The various departments and agencies which are charged with responsibility in the realm of foreign affairs have not thus far been able to mesh the different strands of military, economic, diplomatic, political and psychological policy into a meaningful pattern. Our conceptual framework does not accommodate the idea of conflict as an organic whole. We labor under the disadvantage of having to consider each conflict situation in a vacuum, as it were. Using empirical methods, we try to arrive at an independent solution for each problem as it arises.

The Communists, by contrast, possess a doctrine which provides the guide lines for planning and implementing a long-range program of expansion. Thus equipped, they are able to stage tactical shifts without losing sight of their ultimate objective.

We lack such a doctrine because, chiefly, we are what we are. American society is a pluralistic society. Although the great majority of Americans are agreed, in the abstract, that Communism is evil, they are divided—as they are on every other major national issue—on what to think and do about Communism and its manifestations. In America, the doctrines of national action which vie for recognition and acceptance are as varied as the interpretations of Communist purpose on which they are based. Neither our people nor our government nor, for that matter, the Free World in general have agreed on the basic nature of the Communist threat; lacking this consensus, they cannot agree on a common plan of action for meeting it.

The tested Communist doctrine of conflict is the only universal conflict doctrine presently in existence. It synthesizes all operational techniques which history has proved workable, from nonviolent persuasion and coercion to the most modern forms of technological warfare. The Communists, their achievements in missiles notwithstanding, do not have a "master weapon" on which they place sole reliance. Their skill lies, rather, in their ability to vary tactical combinations. "Political technology" takes precedence over military technology. All the various facets of foreign operations—political, diplomatic, economic, psychological or military—are carefully phased in the Communists' policy decisions. Byron Dexter describes this operational co-ordination as follows:

There is in train today a development without parallel in history— a war which has as its frank objective the overthrow of all the parliamentary governments of the world and their replacement by communist dictatorships centrally controlled in Moscow. The distinguishing characteristic of the campaign is the interchangeability of political and military weapons. A "peace offensive" in Moscow, a cultural conference in Warsaw, a strike in France, an armed insurrection in Czechoslovakia, the invasion of Greece and Korea by fully equipped troops —all are instruments of one war, turned on and turned off from a central tap as a gardener plays a hose up and down a piece of land on which he is nurturing a crop, watering some plants lightly, some heavily.[1]

At the root of, and basic to, the Communists' success has been their organizational skill. The Communists deem organization the most important single element of their strength. Continuous and irreconcilable conflict requires an organizational capacity comparable to that which democratic states institute only in times of war and dire crisis.

The Communists' success has not been achieved because we could not match their intelligence apparatus but, rather, because they developed a superior technique for conflict management. The Kremlin, for decades, has refined the implements of political strategy, propaganda and organization. If the various parts of our government are to move in unison in exploiting Soviet vulnerabilities, its top policy advisers, planners and decision-makers must work from commonly accepted premises. At a minimum, effective operational co-ordination between our governmental departments and agencies concerned with waging the Cold War entails agreement on methods for the evaluation of Communist strategy.

One major shortcoming that besets our present system for arriving at and implementing effective national security policy is inherent in our national heritage. The republic, since its establishment, has been blessed with individual opportunity and material security unparalleled in history. In such an environment there is a premium on action. Traditionally, in our society, the doer rather than the thinker has been the man who counts. Secure within their continental frontiers and absorbed by practical tasks, Americans did not feel the need for a philosophy of history, not to speak of a national strategic doctrine.

But the world has changed. The balance of power maintained for so long by the European powers and European rule over

[1] Byron Dexter, "Clausewitz and Soviet Strategy," *Foreign Affairs*, Vol. XXIX, October, 1950, p. 41.

Asia and Africa has been overturned. The systemic world revolution of our times exceeds in magnitude and velocity the revolution which attended the breakdown of the feudal system and the emergence of the nation-state. Now, the courses of action we should pursue are not so readily discernible as they once were. Communism did not plant the seeds of the new revolution—they were sown centuries ago when the West first reached out into the far corners of the earth. But the Communists are now bidding for the leadership of this revolution. The forces of systemic change, were they harnessed to the chariot of Communist power, would engulf us. The choice is no longer between going to war to obliterate a clearly defined force of evil or of remaining at home in comfortable isolation. Because Soviet Communism is pursuing a policy of the gradual, cumulative erosion of our bases of strength, we may never be faced with a situation that appears to justify the kind of uninhibited military crusade which we were able to wage so successfully in the past.[2]

In the face of the protracted strategy of the Communists, something more than instinctive, pragmatic action is required. Acute discernment, the ability to project isolated and obscure facts into meaningful patterns, is a faculty essential to our needs. Our policy should be devised at least in part by those who have the training and ability to generalize from many complex particulars—in short, by those who have the ability to think conceptually.

No machinery for countering Communist conflict techniques can be designed and operated without the guidance of national purpose firmly agreed upon and clearly defined. Strategic doc-

---

[2] Henry A. Kissinger said: "The key to the Soviet policy can be perhaps expressed in the phrase that it is a strategy of insuring that we will never get a pure case of aggression. Either they will present a problem in which the risk seems too great in terms of the objective to be achieved or in which they seem to have a legitimate grievance, so that there will always be a block of powers that will advocate giving in on this particular issue in order to placate them." *Eighth Student Conference of United States Affairs: The National Security Policy of the United States,* West Point, New York: United States Military Academy, December 5–8, 1956, pp. 39–40, 41.

trine and the mechanisms set up for its implementation are but the handmaidens of defined and accepted national objectives toward which strategy can be purposefully directed. In the last resort, our national objectives cannot be stated—this side of sonorous platitudes—except by giving an unambiguous answer to the question: can we live with Communism or must we fight it? Our answer to this question will be found in the final chapter of this book. Meanwhile, it will be profitable to discuss in broad terms how we might improve on what we have been trying to do.

We have lost ground in our conflict with Communism for many reasons. For one, the penchant of the American governmental bureaucracy for piecemeal interdepartmental planning has opened disastrous gaps in our political, economic, psychological and military programs. Only a central, eclectic intelligence can co-ordinate a global war which is fought as bitterly in the realms of ideas and economics and in the "underground" as it is in open battle. The development of the broader strategic view requires that we give far more attention to leadership and "theory" than our pragmatically bent society is wont to do.

The Western and Soviet systems of selecting leaders have little in common. The potential leaders of the individualistic West are largely the products of a milieu in which personal success and individual well-being are the highest values. Leaders in the Communist world are motivated not only by a ferocious desire for power and the advantages that accrue from its possession but also by a jealous ideology which condemns the individual and elevates collective power to the highest social good. Regardless of periodic changes in the Communist hierarchy, the credentials of Communist leaders remain the same: intimate knowledge of the nature of power and adherence to a simple theory of conflict.

That democratic leaders are amateurs in the art of conflict management is due in part to the characteristics of our political system based as it is upon compromise. Democratic leaders rotate frequently in office because of party rivalry and shifting public opinion. To stay in office they must often preoccupy themselves with secondary, parochial problems—to the neglect of crucial issues. It has been almost impossible to interest democratic leaders in the development of a comprehensive strategy designed to frustrate Soviet ambitions.

Another obstacle to the development of such a strategy is the vague notion that it would be immoral to use the instruments of political warfare against the past masters of political warfare. Political warfare, the weapons *par excellence* in the nuclear age, has been permitted to remain the almost exclusive tool of the Communists. Yet, it is impossible to conceive a positive strategy against the Communist bloc that does not envisage the employment of political warfare.

Perhaps more fundamental, our leaders are inhibited in their actions by the omnipresence of elite opposition groups. No matter what the issue, there is always at least one vociferous interest group which will rise in opposition to any given proposal for action. In our political system, decisions are often dominated by minorities. This happens in every case where a small group feels strongly about an issue and the majority takes no interest. Hence, more often than not, the Executive is left to face the monolithic challenges of the Communists with one or both hands tied behind its back.

This handicap stems from one of the most admirable features of the American democratic system—freedom of expression, which makes inevitable a virtually uninhibited partisan debate over foreign policy. The "great debates" which are sources of strength in the internal affairs of a democracy serve in many cases only to vitiate our foreign policy by reducing the flexibility of the Executive. They also provide the enemy with invaluable clues to the general mood of American policy-making bodies and to the future direction which policy is likely to take in specific areas of the world. The Communists are able to capitalize upon this liberality and to make shrewd estimates of the likely American reactions to new challenges as they are hurled down. The United States, on the other hand, even though its intelligence services may succeed, at substantial cost, in amassing considerable data about *conditions* in the the Communist world, gleans precious little information about Communist intentions in the realm of foreign policy, since the decision-making process in the Communist bloc is esoteric.

The answer to our problems does not—and, indeed, cannot—lie in institutional modifications. We cannot cease being what we are. What we can try for, however, is to advance to political maturity. Responsible American elites should be able to act as intelligent critics without depriving the government of all freedom of choice in the conduct of American diplomacy.

In times of war, we generally halt politics at "the water's edge." It is the burden of this book that we are at war with the Communists, for whom the military engagement is but one aspect of a unified theory of conflict. Our political leaders and publicists, were they to grasp this transcending fact, would certainly conduct themselves with greater discretion.

A unified strategic policy requires efficient co-ordination of the various arms of government charged with the implementation of American foreign policy. Such a unified policy can be formed without surrendering to a monolithic ideology. It will never be elaborated without the development of an adequate machinery within the government. We cannot play at the game of multi-dimensional war with the devices of prerevolutionary diplomacy.

We cannot exploit Soviet vulnerabilities and weaknesses without an accurate understanding of the basic forces and factors which pertain to a particular situation; nor can we anticipate Soviet strategy without being able to gauge accurately the relative importance of seemingly isolated Communist moves. We need, therefore, an evaluation apparatus which can project a total and integrated picture of our relative strengths and weaknesses vis-à-vis the Communist bloc. Only on the basis of such a comprehensive and continuing balance sheet can we assess the weight and impact of "new factors," such as technological innovations or political developments.

Military-technological power has become the crucial pivot upon which the fortunes of the conflict turn. The Soviet Union might someday attempt to gain its objectives through surprise nuclear assault; the United States, if it is to remain true to its ethos, cannot. Hence, the counterstrategy of the West must be a strategy of deterrence, designed to discourage any Communist notion of launching a successful surprise attack. This is the philosophical framework within which the West must struggle for victory.

In many quarters, the achievement of terminal firepower (in the form of the H-bomb) by three nations has been interpreted to mean that the technological race has come to an end and that the contestants are stalemated militarily. Because of this "stalemate," it is argued, the so-called "balance of terror" is a relatively stable balance. Such an assumption is dangerous, given the reality of the continuing race for weapons superiority. The concept of continued mutual deterrence, based on existing strategic capabilities, is put in doubt by the phenomenon of incessant technological change. "The rapidly accelerating technological race is the essence of the conflict. . . ." [3]

For a few years to come, the Western nations—provided they bring their moral and psychological capabilities abreast of their technical capabilities—could enjoy a greater actual freedom of strategic maneuver than the Soviets.

Undoubtedly, Soviet efforts to paralyze the West and to disrupt its policy apparatus through bluff, bluster and blackmail will increase with advances in Soviet weapons technology. In fact, judging by past Soviet behavior, their daring probably will outpace their actual capabilities. The conflict, in other words, will be carried on at two distinct levels: objective-technical and subjective-psychological. The rate of progress need not be the same at each level. It is possible that the Communists might achieve their desired political victory at the psychological level before they ever attain a decisive margin of technical superiority. On the other hand, the United States and its allies have it in their power to win the global psychological-political battle even if the

[3] Stefan T. Possony, "Review of Nuclear Weapons and Foreign Policy by Henry A. Kissinger," *Annals of the American Academy of Political and Social Science,* Vol. CCCXVI, March, 1958, p. 141.

technical power balance should begin to shift in the Soviet's favor. The Western nations are still capable of making carefully calculated strategic and tactical moves against which the Soviet leaders would fear to risk decisive counteraction, precisely because they deem the security of their home base more important than the strategic value of a peripheral position. But the West can do this only if it stops brooding neurotically on "survival" every time the international situation becomes tense. If the American and British actions in Lebanon and Jordan in the summer of 1958, as well as the firm U.S. stand over Quemoy several months later, accomplished nothing else, they cleared the atmosphere of the pernicious notion that the development of Soviet missiles had robbed the Western nations of all freedom of military action in world politics.

The next ten years of the protracted conflict may prove to be the most momentous in human history. The Communists will try to exploit this period to disarm and divide the West; to complete their military build-up; and to win the technological race. The Communists recognize that they must strive for a *decisive* margin of superiority in the realm of military-technological weapons— a margin which would enable them to attack with impunity or to pose to the West the choice between surrender and total defeat. In the event of such a decisive "breakthrough" in the weapons race, the protracted conflict could be terminated by a strategic knockout blow. In the absence of a *decisive* breakthrough, however, any *marginal* superiority in the weapons race can serve to enhance the effectiveness of other conflict means— political, psychological, organizational or economic.

The Russians, their frequent aberrations of doctrine notwithstanding, remain convinced Marxists. According to Marxists dialectical doctrine, technology (i.e., the means of production) is the key to the revolutionary process in history. But in the post-Lenin view, technology does more than merely transform the class structure of society: it transforms, also, the international power situation by gradually replacing one socio-economic system with another. This, indeed, is the new meaning of the dialectic in the global setting of the protracted conflict. Marx taught that the industrial proletariat would assume one day complete control of those technological instruments which form the *Unterbau* of social power. Lenin substituted the conflict of state systems (socialist versus capitalist) for the conflict of social classes (proletarian versus capitalist). The West's historical position of global supremacy has rested upon its virtual monopoly of technological power. To achieve hegemony for themselves, the Communists realize that they must not only break the West's technological monopoly but also outdistance the West in those technological capabilities which will form the future *Unterbau* of international power.

In addition to superior weapons, technological reserves are also needed to compensate for the possibility of successful hostile surprise. Communist strategists are well aware that the Western Alliance will not launch preventive war. Since the Western nations extend to the Communists the option of striking the first blow, the former must be ready to absorb the heavy cost which their defensive posture entails. This is primarily a matter of maintaining adequate levels of reserve forces. If the offensive and defensive capabilities of the two sides, at a given time, should balance out quantitatively and qualitatively, and should a surprise attack be technologically feasible, the Communists can count upon a sizable strategic margin in their favor, simply by virtue of their assured ability to make the first move. This factor points up the difficulty of calculating a "safe" margin of Western deterrence. The Communists are able to measure margins of deterrence differently from Western strategists because they may hope to destroy a substantial portion of the West's offensive capability before it can be put into operation. For this reason, the concept of global dispersion of strategic capabilities takes on added significance for the Western nations.[4]

---

[4] The concept of geographic dispersion of strategic capabilities, which served to deter Soviet aggression in the bomber age, will retain validity in the missile age. The greater the dispersion—through a global network (on land, underground, on sea and undersea, and in the air) of missile-launching

Technology is not merely a matter of "hardware." Politics, psychology and other social sciences are interwoven with developments in the technological order. The term "psychotechnology" indicates a broad and as yet unexplored area, the significance of which may be illustrated by citing the possibility of posing nuclear threats either physically or psychologically. No doubt, the technological race between the Atlantic Allies and the Soviets forms a backdrop for many apparently unrelated international disturbances. The dramatic technological advances announced by Moscow in recent years have spurred the Afro-Asian systemic revolution. Soviet backing has emboldened anti-Western nationalist leaders—in the Middle East, for example— to challenge the West under the shield of Soviet "nuclear blackmail." By thus supporting the forces of anti-Western nationalism with veiled nuclear threats, the Soviets hope to effect a gradual rollback of the West's overseas strategic bases upon which the West's nuclear delivery capabilities largely rest.

The military technology of a nation or of a bloc of nations depends upon a number of broad factors. Many of these determining factors lie beyond the ability of the Communists to control or influence outside of their own sphere. But the Communists can be expected to do whatever they can to hamper weapons-system development in the Western countries. By stressing, in their propaganda, the potential devastation of nuclear conflict, they play upon the guilt feelings of Western scientists and thus attempt to make them reluctant to participate in military programs. By proposing suspension of nuclear weapons tests, they seek either to reduce the Western lead or to increase their own. The Communists also try, through nuclear blackmail and pacifist propaganda, to turn the peoples of the world against Western bases on their soil.

---

capabilities—the more *technically difficult* will be an attempted knockout. Moreover, as geographic dispersion increases, the *political feasibility* of an attempted knockout decreases, for the Soviet Union, in order to strike at the sources of Western power, must aim its weapons of mass destruction at nearly every people on the earth's surface.

In the face of this calculated Communist campaign to win technological dominance there are some potentially dangerous gaps in our military establishment. Among these our inadequate capability for fighting certain kinds of limited war, with or without atomic weapons, may well be one, although there is wide disagreement among the professionals as well as laymen on the limits of limited war and on where and when such a war might or should be fought. But the central military problem is to stand up against the Soviets' military-scientific blackmail and to meet, in the last resort, a Communist all-out nuclear attack: The West's extended strategy must rest upon the psychological as well as the objective acceptance of the risk of total conflict. Anchored in that resolution the West's extended strategy must seek to make all-out war an extreme risk for the Soviets, to unhinge the Communist system and thus bring Soviet expansion to a halt.

It is rather in the psychological arena than in its technological workshop that the West has displayed its most alarming shortcomings. Objectively, Western strategy has been far more effective than the sensational charges of its critics will have it. No doubt, our military posture is susceptible to a great deal of improvement. But an exaggerated zeal for improvement, especially when it is triggered by pained surprise at the latest ploy of Communist psychological warfare or considerations of domestic political advantage, might prove to be "counterproductive" in developing our real range of power.

There is a considerable gap between the launching of a Sputnik and the zeroing in, with Soviet intercontinental missiles, of all the West's farflung strategic installations. It is the responsibility of the Free World scientists to scrutinize the significance of sensational Soviet technological achievements, especially those which are announced by Communist political news agencies, and not take Communist claims at face value. It is the responsibility of Western journalists to place those achievements in their proper perspective. As the world moves into an era of accelerating technological development, there is a greater need than ever for the exercise of a critical faculty by Western elites. If the latter drop their intellectual defenses, the Communists are certain to take advantage of the breach. We can, if we choose, expand and utilize our superior technology to foreclose any possibility of the Soviets seeking to resolve the conflict by force. This choice will be costly, but in all prudence it must be made.

Much has been said and written about the battle for the minds, hearts and stomachs of the "uncommitted" world. To many, this struggle is tantamount to the battle for the world itself. Few would doubt that the hunger, poverty and disease which are the continuing lot of millions of people living in the Free World are a source of danger in the protracted conflict.

The key problem is not only to develop the appropriate economic techniques but also to change the cultural and social ideas of the so-called backward peoples in order to bring them from their sunken civilizations into the twentieth century. As Western technical culture has become universalized, the peoples in the dependent lands are reaching eagerly for the material benefits symbolic of Western culture even while they reject the sociopolitical ideals upon which this culture was built.

Most Western plans for coping with the understandable aspirations of these peoples completely overlook the psychological gulf which divides East and West and which only time—rather than increased communications—can bridge. In the wide areas of Asia and Africa, the economic, political and ideological revolution in progress represents the fragmentation of the organic Oriental society under the impact of the industrial West. If this revolution is anti-Western, this is due at least in part to the simple psychological fact that man instinctively resents change and the agencies that would bring about this change in the ways of his life.

The Communists have demonstrated that they understand only too well the forces at work in the systemic revolution. While the United States is attempting to solve the problem of the underdeveloped areas by working from the top down—i.e., through the existing government—the Communists are working from the bottom up, that is, by gearing their policies to the emotions of the people. U.S. policy is predicated upon the maintenance of existing order; the Communists' upon the creation of chaos. The foreign-aid programs of the West are guided largely by objective economic criteria; the Communists are interested only in the conflict and propaganda potential of a given foreign-aid gambit—be it a steel mill in India or pavement on the streets of Kabul.

For two-thirds of the world, the process of economic growth is just in its inception. It is essential in the early phases of this process that the most powerful economic power on earth exercise prudence in laying the philosophical and strategic guidelines of its aid program.

Most of the emphasis of the programs tendered thus far has been on the economic aspects of the problem. But even our economic hopes can be realized only in an environment free from the threat of Communist penetration. Foreign economic-aid programs cannot be carried out in a vacuum, divorced from political considerations. True enough, in view of all the complaints uttered in many recipient countries about aid with political strings attached, we might be tempted to think that such a separation can and must be made. In fact, this is neither feasible nor desirable. It is possible, albeit sometimes difficult, to separate private foreign investment from foreign-policy considerations. It is patently impossible, however, to draw any firm line between a government-aid program and international politics. No matter how much the West is willing and able to invest in the development of the "uncommitted" countries, there will always be a gap between the Western contribution and rising native expectations. The Communists need only move into this gap, be it even with the most modest resources, in order to divert to themselves whatever credit the recipient peoples might have been willing to accord a foreign giver. We cannot afford the luxury of succumbing to the demands of so-called neutralist nations to satisfy their hyperbolic economic demands lest they drift into the Communist orbit. We must never lose sight of the fact that much of the fashionable "neutralism" which abounds in the "gray areas" depends, for its *raison d'être*, upon the continued bipolarity of the world. These countries cannot embrace categorically one or the other side of the global conflict without forfeiting their unique bargaining position. If many of the new nationalist leaders have not realized it before, they are beginning to learn by hard experience that Communism is even less capable than we of meeting their economic needs. To ungracious demands from these quarters that we supply the aid they seek or see them go Communist, we may well heed George F. Kennan's advice and bluntly tell them: "Go!"

The current phase of the protracted conflict will not be settled by the battle for the uncommitted areas however vital the outcome of this battle may subsequently become. Instead, the crucial decisions will be made in the hearts of the opposing camps —in the Western Alliance and within the Communist bloc which stretches from the Elbe to China's Yellow Sea. In the underdeveloped world, the West's strategy for the decade ahead cannot be more than a holding action. There, the task must be to gain time, to avoid fixed commitments, to improvise and to abstain from action for action's sake. The contention, often heard in our midst, that the underdeveloped world represents increasingly the desisive battlefield of the Cold War bespeaks the success of Communist strategy in distracting our attack from the most vulnerable sector of the protracted conflict—the Communist system itself.

Communism, in the mid-twentieth century, poses a vexing paradox: while the "flow" of Communist conflict doctrine continues unabated into areas traditionally under the sway of the West, the citadel of the Communist system is subject to increasing internal stress and deterioration. Victory, in the protracted conflict, will indeed go to the side able to preserve its position longest.

At the present juncture of the conflict, however, paralysis of the will is increasing faster in the West than is the rate of decay within the Communist orbit. While the Communists are taking every precaution to insulate the masses they control, their subversive operation against free countries continues almost unhampered. The conflict, in its essence, is the clash between two social systems: the "Open" and the "Closed" society. The most feasible way to restore some logic to the West's efforts in this struggle would be to project the image of the "Open Society" to those millions behind the Iron or Bamboo Curtains who have been prevented from making a meaningful comparison between the two systems and drawing the obvious conclusion.

The "Open Society" is, by definition, open to the inspection of all and everyone. There are now, on our side, no insuperable obstacles preventing the average citizen of the Communist bloc from observing at first hand our way of life and, for that matter, from seeing whatever our average citizen can or cares to see. Formally, the bars are down. As long as some basic rules of reciprocity are being observed, exchanges of persons and of cultural goods should work out to the advantage of all parties. The accumulated evidence, however, does not justify the expectation that the democratic peoples can rely upon visitors from the Communist bloc to bear the message of the Open Society to the millions at home. To begin with, the Communist governments' choice of those who are permitted to travel abroad and to draw the requisite amount of foreign exchange is, to say the least, selective. With few and mostly involuntary exceptions, Communist governments have issued visas and travel funds only to true and tried servants of the regime.

Indeed, there has been a rising stream of Soviet tourism to the West. Even so, the Soviets have not filled the quota set aside by Western educational institutions for exchange students from the Soviet Union, nor have they relaxed that close supervision which apparently keeps the average Soviet tourist group on its prescribed path—and closely bunched. Most everywhere in the world, including Red China, Soviet residents abroad are confined to compounds and denied the privilege of solitary and spontaneous exit. In sum, we cannot put our faith on these carefully chosen and guarded strangers in our midst as the apostles in their own lands of the Open Society.

No doubt, our projected image has filtered into the awareness of the peoples under Communist rule in various ways: the very existence of the Open Society confounds a hundred years of angry Marxist prophecy, and the men and women behind the Iron Curtain are no less sophisticated politically than are we. On the other hand, the Communists control all domestic media of communications, and no great tyranny has ever been brought to fall by the mere presence somewhere of free institutions.

Intimate and unhampered communications between peoples are the *sine qua non* of a stable world order. The Open Society invites comparison—and can stand it. The dynamic exposure of our society is not the least effective response that we can make to the conflict strategy of the Communists. But the response will be muffled and weak if we accept the rules laid down by the Communists: their "peace zone" closed to the flow of our ideas; the "war zone" open to their propaganda, disseminated by scores of Communist parties and myriads of affiliated organizations.

We should invite the Soviets to join in exchange programs that maximize contacts between persons: let us, for example, "exchange" ten thousand American students for the equal number of Soviet students, each quota to be absorbed for one academic year by the largest possible number of colleges and universities. This experiment would not be without risks. We can and should accept them, for the Open Society places its trust in individual judgment. For the Soviets the question will be as to whether the new Soviet man can share freely the daily chores and pleasures of his contemporaries in our community—and return, ideologically intact, to the collective fold. We should insist that the Soviets answer this question. If the Soviets will not agree to broad programs that assure a free flow of persons and communications and persist in playing the game as is their wont, namely with the cards stacked against us, then we must employ every possible method to perforate the Iron Curtain and to educate the peoples under Communism to the facts of life under freedom. For this purpose, we should deploy every means available, including the most powerful electronic devices placed along the

periphery of the Communist bloc, and join vigorously the ideological debate. To pussyfoot on ideological issues is to accept
defeat at the hands of the Communists in the most crucial sector
of the conflict spectrum. We must appeal tirelessly and persua-
sively to the peoples under Communist rule to break down the
Closed and raise the Open Society. That they cannot hear our
call today and that their masters will be displeased by our message should not deter us from our missionary effort.

The world political events of 1958 portended a steady acceleration of the pace of conflict. Virtually in every sector of the East-
West struggle—military, technology, international trade and alliance politics—increasing pressures converged upon the United
States.

The statistical facts of Soviet-U.S. power relationships are
plain. Our setbacks in the Middle East and the Far East tell an
unambiguous story of Western vacillation and indecision. Any
realistic assessment of the past record and our present predica-
ment should trigger, as a matter of course, an all-out effort by
the American people. The most formidable obstacle to purposeful
action is the uncertainties that pervade the American public
mood. Only if this barrier is broken and our ideological resources, as well as our industrial might, are brought fully to
bear in the conflict, can we hope to exploit the patent weaknesses
of our opponent.

The intellectual and ideological bankruptcy of the Communist
regimes has been increasingly and conspicuously attested. Yet, the
Western world has done hardly anything to take advantage of the
internal contradictions of Communism. There has not been a major
statement of Communist doctrine in Russian since the publication of Stalin's *Foundations of Leninism* over thirty years ago;
even Mao Tse-tung's ideological forays have been addressed
more to the problems of conflict than to the issues of modern society. The contents of Russian publications and the statements
of Soviet leaders mirror increasingly the shortcomings and in-
adequacies of Communist totalitarian society. A potent force of
suppressed opposition lies latent within the Communist bloc.

The risings in Eastern Europe during 1956 attested unequivocally to the explosive potential of this force.

In October, 1956, the workers and students of Hungary rose against the Communist state. To be sure, that state was Soviet-dominated. But a movement that started as a national protest against foreign rule soon turned into an ideological revolution. That revolution was directed against Communism or, to use the Communists' own terminology, against socialism. For this development, not only the Soviets but also most Western statesmen and expert observers, bemused by the charms of "national Communism," were totally unprepared.

For the first time in history, the myth of dialectic materialism exploded with a bang that was audible everywhere. For once, Communist propaganda could not plausibly claim that a "counter-revolution" had been launched by reactionary bourgeois and feudal landlords, for these had been shot or driven out years ago. What the critics not only of Communism but of all collectivist philosophies had always suspected but were never able to prove conclusively was suddenly revealed as a demonstrable truth: There is no such thing as collective freedom, and the vaunted freedoms of "popular democracy" are shams. The urge to individual freedom burst to the surface in the Hungarian Revolution.

During the crucial days of the Hungarian rising, the West appeared to stand transfixed before the very brazenness of the Soviets' intervention in the affairs of a country which, according to their own claims, enjoyed complete sovereignty. Again, the West accepted meekly the Soviets' extraordinary thesis according to which the world is divided into two zones: theirs, the "peace zone"; ours, the "war zone." The Western powers wrung their hands when the Hungarian freedom fighters were being crushed by Soviet armor, inveighed against the Soviets in passionate addresses to the United Nations—and abstained from any concrete action whatsoever. They recoiled from challenging the Soviets in Hungary because they feared war. Yet, they could have made a graduated response to Soviet military intervention without incurring a risk of unleashing general war greater than the Soviets took in, let us say, blockading Berlin or arming the Egyptians or threatening to send "volunteers" to the Middle East or addressing nuclear blackmail notes to various members of the Western alliance. Among the steps that the United States could have taken were the diplomatic recognition of the government of Premier Imry Nagy that for a few days controlled effectively the city of Budapest and, probably, most of Hungary; the explicit offer of asylum to the thousands of Soviet soldiers who either refused to fight the Hungarian revolutionaries or actively co-operated with them; the delivery of food, medical supplies and miscellaneous equipment to the Hungarian rebels by such well-known and tried methods as parachute drops; and the proffer of airborne Red Cross assistance to the inhabitants of Budapest. Such moves would have forced upon the Soviets the choice of either acquiescing to them or increasing the violence of their intervention. Would the Soviets have met these limited forays into their "peace zone" by unleashing general war? This was, to say the least, a highly unlikely contingency, particularly since, at the time of the Hungarian rising, Poland and Eastern Germany were seething with unrest and the Kremlin had good reason to distrust the reliability of its own garrison troops in Eastern Europe.

Undoubtedly, the question of counterintervention in Hungary was examined—agonizingly, we must presume—in the secret councils of the United States and the Western Alliance. It was answered negatively. Hungary's spontaneous sacrifice on the altar of the Open Society was in vain, for the Western powers were not prepared to match the tremendous risks taken by the Hungarians with more modest risks of their own. Yet, if we insist upon furthering riskless policies and will not join the issue with the Communists except on our own territory, then, as this study has shown, the Open Society stands to lose the ground which it still holds, and stands to lose, together with its power and possessions, its belief in itself.

The fact that the leading elites of the Free World were caught just as unaware by the unfolding developments as were their

Communist opposites, and to this day have failed to acknowledge the deeper significance of the Hungarian Revolution, reflects not so much poor intelligence as the fuzziness of their own ideological position. Suffice it to say that Western policies toward Titoism and various forms of "national Communism" are fraught with ambiguities which, although they might pass for clever diplomatic tactics, cannot but cast doubt into the hearts of the peoples under Communist rule and weaken the resolution of the West itself. It was this moral failure rather than the lack of practical means for exploiting the momentary embarrassment of the Communists which denied to the West a signal opportunity for spoiling the reconsolidation of the Communist system. The West thus missed its greatest chance of taking the initiative in the Cold War at a time when the Communists were in the midst of reorganizing their unsteady forces. This verdict is unaffected by the West's apparent belief that the Cold War had ended or entered into a less virulent phase.

Soviet leadership and the leadership of the Communist parties in Europe are still off balance. However, in order to bring about a fundamental change in the power relationship between Communism and the Free World, these opportunities have to be exploited. Assuming even that Communism is falling, we will have to push what is falling. The extent to which Moscow has reasserted its authority since 1956 demonstrates that the Communists, left to their own devices, will consolidate their position. They will be able to execute the present maneuver, difficult as it is, just as Stalin managed to complete, in the 1930's, the perhaps ever more difficult reorganization-by-purges of the Communist movement in Russia and abroad.

The weight of Communist power still presses upon Europe; the cadres of the Communist parties in France and Italy are still virtually intact; and the shift of Soviet diplomacy, reinforced by military threats, to the Middle East and North Africa has diverted the forces of the West from their primary targets, namely Communist power in Europe, and put the West once again on the defensive.

At the very moment when Communism passed through a severe ideological crisis, the United States' policy of discriminating between, on one hand, undeserving (because Russian) Communism and, on the other hand, deserving (because Titoist or "national") Communism, robbed the Western position of persuasiveness as well as dignity. The United States appears caught in its own preconceptions, which assign to the right of national self-determination the highest of all international values.

The United States has many policies, each more or less sensible, for coping with the Communists. Sensible or not, they do not total up to a coherent over-all strategy. The United States' wooing of the diverse forces of nationalism which allegedly threaten the Communist empire, while de-emphasizing the ideological issue, plays into the hands of the Communists who are concerned first and foremost with mending their ideological fences. The enemy is still Communism, no matter the brand. Whether it be called "polycentric" or "multigroup" or even "neutralist" Communism will not alter the fact that it points in the direction of the permanent revolution. The West, unless it tempers its paralyzing fear of global war and brings the full impact of the Open Society to bear against the Iron Curtain, will find that it has lost not only some of its most valuable natural allies—the peoples under Communist rule—but also the potentially decisive battle in the protracted conflict.

There is no reason, as far as the objective situation is concerned, why the West cannot still thwart the Communist maneuver and fight the protracted conflict on the enemy's territory rather than—as heretofore—on its own. The sands have not yet run out. But if the precious time that still remains shall not be lost, the West must rouse itself from its wish-dreams, face up to the new danger and resolutely join the issue.

CHAPTER **10** THE APPROACHING CRISIS

During the next decade, the protracted conflict between the Communists and the Western Alliance will be waged —as it has been waged since its inception—against a background of the systemic revolution. Neither side will be able to control always the forces that transmute in the crucible of the systemic revolution the elements of the world order. The emergence of centers of political power and the tremendous increase of population in Asia and Africa together with the "revolution of rising expectations" in all underdeveloped countries will slowly yet profoundly alter the existing international and regional balances of power. Developments in Communist China alone are fraught with incalculable consequences for all of mankind. Certainly, the sparks of new conflicts will fly, and beyond the formidable problems of today loom problems that will be even more formidable and promise to keep the international community in a state of chronic and perilous instability. At first, future conflicts may arise as indigenous disputes in out-of-the-way places, but the Communist conflict managers can be relied upon to weave sooner or later the strands of local conflict into the global pattern of Communist strategy. Generally speaking, the new Afro-Asian states are politically unstable, socially fragile and economically weak, and they are likely to remain so for decades. Most of them are "nation-states" by international courtesy rather than by virtue of any ethnic or cultural homogeneity. In nearly all of them, international tensions, generated by religious and racial frictions, are aggravated by problems of mere economic survival. Their traditional social structures are crumbling under the impact of Western ideas and techniques. Unless massive forces are brought to bear from outside, most of these new states will either break apart or else will be integrated more or less violently into wider unities which coincide with "civilization areas." Either development will unleash revolutionary movements more devastating than those which now beat upon the contemporary order.

In this age of universal transformation there are then two important factors of international change which, in the Communist scheme of things, reinforce one another in a most dangerous manner. First, there are genuine stresses and strains due to technological, social and industrial progress, which require major institutional, economic and political changes. Second, while great parts of the world population still live in preindustrial cultures and traditional social and political attitudes clash with the exigencies of universal technological and economic change, major issues are likely to be settled by conflict, i.e., settled as they have always been because men simply lacked the wisdom and forbearance to settle them by peaceful means.

Of no nation are these remarks more pertinent than with respect to Communist China. China is ruled by enthusiastically dedicated and doctrinaire Communists—true believers—who are attempting to solve immense problems with terrifying speed and deadly seriousness. Peking is determined to catapult China, within a decade, into the ranks of such modern industrial powers as, for example, Britain and Germany. Meanwhile, the increase in China's population will add several times as many millions as comprise the total population of Britain to the teeming masses already under the iron grip of militant Chinese Communism. It is folly to expect that these enormous pressures will not erupt in some form and in several possible directions. Expansion into Southeast Asia, continued conflict with America's allies in Asia and even a murderous clash with the Soviet Union—all these are possible future developments. "Will a militarily strong China, with a powerful heavy industry, be satisfied with the present unequal distribution of land and other resources as between its own vast population and the much smaller population in the Soviet Union and Eastern Europe? There would seem to be much to think about in these developments, not only for us, but also for those who make policy in Warsaw, Prague, Bucharest, Budapest and, especially, Moscow." [1] In short, Communist China looms as a future storm center of the systemic revolution.

Wherein lie the great weaknesses of the Communists? Their hostility has been so aggressive, fanatical and unprincipled, and so freely turned against all, including themselves, that much of the world, even where conflict is endemic to the society and politics, has been repelled by the disgusting spectacle of Communist practice. The domestic economic policies of the Soviets, so bent on military power and so contemptuous of the aspirations of the average man and woman, belie the promises of Communist ideology and challenge comparison—nearly all of it unfavorable —with the performance of the Western economic system. To the ruling clique of Communism, all of mankind is a mere means to an end, and the end is its own triumph in a power struggle. All-consuming lust for power is the logical consequence of a doctrine which makes conflict its primary assumption. In the long run and despite the fact that conflict is rife in many places, the ultimate response everywhere to the very inhumanity of Communism— the real thing and not the propaganda version for export—must be inevitably fear and revulsion. Communism has lost attraction for all but the most embittered power seekers and anti-Western fanatics to whom the very indifference of Communism to human values is its most persuasive recommendation.

Thus far, power struggles within the Communist clique ruling Peking have been far less frequent. Yet the monolith of Communist rule rests upon the precarious base of ruthless, albeit increasingly sophisticated, repression. The image which Commu-

[1] *New York Times*, October 22, 1958.

nist China presents to the world is truly terrifying.[2] It is not at all clear how long Chinese Communist leadership can contain the tremendous tensions which the pedantic imposition of Communist doctrine and the violence done to traditional culture have engendered. In Russia, deep-seated popular resentments released by the death of Stalin set in motion internecine conflicts on the highest level of Communist leadership. In China, the death of Mao may well touch off a struggle by the aspirants for supreme power, a struggle all the more violent because behind each of the contending factions will be arrayed popular pressures even more formidable than those latent in Stalinist Russia.

The gap between the Soviet and Chinese tyrannies, on one hand, and democracy in the United States, is unbridgeable. The American people today are far more than merely the descendants of the American people of 1800. They are the product of continuous ethnic and cultural transformation in the long stream of Western culture whose sources lay in Greece and Rome, refreshed and swelled by Christianity. The very essence of the American system is that it is always in the making, incomplete and open. It accommodates all men, ideas and things. It is tolerant and generous, which is precisely what Soviet Communism is not. American tolerance is not so much the disciplined forbearance practiced by the most mellow nation-states such as

[2] "A Chinese scientist educated in this country, but who had returned to the mainland and then gone to Taiwan, reports, 'The whole country is built on the sufferings of the people. It is hell.'

"Our Warsaw correspondent reports that Eastern European Communists have been stunned by the Chinese communes, a system of social organization which is regimenting and militarizing the Chinese people with a tightness and severity that has no modern precedent. . . . A Yugoslav writer has perhaps characterized the Chinese communes best by describing them as a combination of Stalinism and feudalism, hardly a prescription for Utopia.

". . . The tremendous exertions now being extorted from the Chinese people are being demanded for the purpose of increasing Communist China's military-economic strength as rapidly as possible. It must be assumed that the work of China's more than half billion people, even done under the lash, will be productive and that Communist China's military-economic power will grow, perhaps even grow rapidly." Editorial, *New York Times,* October 22, 1958.

the British, the Dutch and the Scandinavians, but an easy and, sometimes, bland acceptance of the evident variety of the human species.

America awaits another De Tocqueville to assess judiciously the factors which have given the United States its unique character and strength. Nearly all the attempted portraits of the U.S. are marked by bias toward either what is called liberal or, contrariwise, the conservative interpretation.

The United States is the most nearly classless society of history. To be sure, groups and individuals still remain divided by economic and social barriers. Because so large an expanse of the American scene is bright, the shadows of poverty, disease, crime and intolerance are all the darker. Conversely, waste and crudeness mar the countenance which the affluent society turns to the peoples of backward countries so perilously close to the mere subsistence level. The very weight of material plenty now threatens to smother the flame of idealism that illuminates the first pages of American history. Paradoxically, the materialist philosophy of Communism evokes sacrificial zeal. Paradoxically, America's high-minded dedication to moral principle is blurred by much that is gross in practice. But, measured by the slow, grudging pace of more rigid societies in Europe and Asia, the forward thrust of American society has been sure and powerful. Each advance gives rise to new problems; inequities, taken for granted only yesterday, today agitate mightily the public conscience. The American dream has not yet come true, perhaps because it keeps on changing all the time. But its realization has become plausible, more plausible perhaps to peoples elsewhere than to some Americans obsessed with their country's shortcomings and impatient with its progress. It is this promise which America places on the scales of the systemic revolution.

American society is humanist. Its ruling philosophy, pragmatism, is not a mere intellectual coating but a common way of thinking. It accords admirably with the American's gregarious temperament and bent for solving problems not so much by pure and solitary reasoning as by experimentation and teamwork.

Wary of ideological involvement and informal in procedure, Americans have advanced much further on the path toward a classless society than any other people. The New Middle Class is, socially, all-inclusive. All this makes American society remarkably cohesive and well adjusted. The enormous influence of women, culturally as well as economically, is naturally directed in a conservative direction. Americans, precisely because their society is so well attuned to gradual change, are loath to contemplate international strife—and the contingency of American involvement. Yet the naïve illusion that international conflict can be exorcised by dismissing it from the collective mind is not the stuff from which victories in revolutionary conflict are fashioned. Consequently, the triumph of the United States is by no means certain.

The Western peoples derive strength from the free interplay of various points of view. From the conflict of many ideas emerges eventually a greater truth. Yet, the Western peoples, absorbed as they are by the competitive search for ultimate objectives and ultimate truths, are unable to communicate to other peoples their own vision of the future, their own intentions and their own concept of the universal good. By contrast, the Communist bloc can be likened to an organism seeking to respond to individual situations on behalf of the entire organism rather than of its individual parts and capable of speaking with a single voice.

It is unlikely that, here and now, the United States can find a common denominator for its optimal objectives and those of the other democracies, not to speak of those of its allies that are not governed by democratic institutions. Hence, the United States must seek to work out a compromise that allows latitude for different national points of view and yet maintains a firm agreement on a few essential principles. This feat calls for flexibility of policy and tolerant urbanity which thus far have not distinguished notably the conduct of American relations with other peoples. Sometimes, a little indifference will go a long way.

Not so surprisingly, the American people, like any prosperous democracy, are reluctant to risk what they have so richly wrought on ventures into the unknown. Foreign policy is a venture into the unknown. Perhaps the most ideal state of things for a great and prosperous democracy would be to have no foreign policy at all. Yet the United States cannot escape the challenge of protracted conflict. In this conflict each single alternative is fraught with terrifying risks. The question that faces the United States is how to reconcile the ethos of a society that has come to take its possessions for granted and has elevated individual security to its principal goal with the necessity to take risks in order to safeguard the security of the nation as a whole.

Whether they recognize it or not, the United States and the Communist bloc are accelerating the systemic revolution by projecting to all peoples two contrasting images of a future world. Both the United States and the Soviet Union are concerned with the problem of attaining mastery over the forces that generate conflict. Each envisages a future harmony. For Americans, the new world to come is the community that rests upon the consensus of all men; for the Communists, the ultimate state of human progress follows upon the extermination of all their enemies.

In both Moscow and Peking, the realities of history are accounted for by postulating two kinds of man: the Communist who, having received the light of Marxist-Leninist doctrine, is thereafter objectively rational, and the capitalist who is eternally barred from the truth. The rest of mankind is but an inert mass waiting to be shaped in the mold of Communist doctrine.

The American people believe nothing more deeply than that conflict can be brought under rational control. The means of doing so is the democratic process. Admittedly, there will be conflicts of interests, attitudes and opinions, and vigorous debate is the salt of democratic life. But mutual self-restraint and deference to law keep the conflicts within bounds. Conflict as much as co-operation spurs progress, but democracy rejects the extremes of class war and class dictatorship—as it rejects all extremes—as the dialectic steps of social evolution.

Americans conceive of men as equal; the Communists conceive

of them as being divided into two classes. For Americans absolute mastery or absolute rationality is a fiction. Problems are solved through the working together of many minds because "many minds are better than one." The great majority of all men can take part in this unending quest. None is barred from it by class, none is "the elect." Marxism attributes to man a split personality, so to speak, and translates this split into the social mechanics of class war. Americans do not attribute perfect rationality to any man or group, nor do they turn their backs on any man or group as incurably stupid or depraved. Communist doctrine vests the Party with perfect rationality. Hence the Party can and must dictate the course of human progress. Americans assign omniscience to no one, and the interactions of many people possessed of many different elements of truth, experience and perception, lead onward to a higher synthesis.

For forty years, the Communists have presided over the industrialization of Russia. The economic and technological growth of Russia has been prodigious. But the Communists, whatever satisfaction they may have drawn from their achievements in a backward country, could not blink the fact that developments in the highly industrialized countries of the West had rendered Marxian theory irrelevant. Against the massive evidence that exposes the absurdity of their doctrine, the Communists have brought to bear but one argument: power and the politics of power. The march of Soviet power has served to conceal the bankruptcy of their ideology.

Because they must eliminate this dichotomy, the Soviet leaders, their propaganda notwithstanding, long have realized that permanent, genuine coexistence between their system and ours is nonsense. The logic of the emerging world conveys an inescapable conflict between Communism and the Free World—a conflict which inheres in the basic principles on which each system is founded. A struggle was and remains inescapable. Conceivably, the resolution of the struggle in total war may also be inescapable. This is a question that remains to be determined by experience and not by preconception. The compelling reasons why total war should be prevented need no reiteration. Indeed, the prevention of war, within states, between states, and on the grand scale of global confrontation is the object of United States policy. This is not a static policy aimed at preserving a frozen *status quo:* it is a dynamic policy founded upon reform and international change wrought without recourse to war. Any tendency on the part of Communism to avoid all-out nuclear war in no way contradicts the fact that Communism assumes the necessity for continued conflict. The duel between the United States and the Soviet Union resolves itself, in the long run, into a contest between two social systems. In this arena, the United States as protagonist of the Western world should win, for its social system suits not only the American people but also beckons— an ideal, perhaps remote yet still attainable—all peoples, including those of the Soviet Union.

In crucial respects, the American people are ill equipped for the task of promoting a modern world order. The United States, alone among the great nations of our times, never suffered invasion or defeat. No remembrance of major discord at home, except for the fading memory of the Civil War, mars American history. Contemplating the domestic scene, the American people cannot help being optimistic: the boldest dreams of preceding generations have been redeemed beyond all expectations. America is fabulously rich; on the whole, America is happy; and America is optimistic about her future and about the future of the race. Such generic optimism does not foster a sense of the tragic.

Nevertheless, history has cast the United States in the inevitable and unenviable role of leader of the Free World. Against the pseudo-universal and long-range goals of Communism, the United States must proclaim unabashedly its genuine universal goals and unveil a sustained program for attaining them. Our first task—to give spiritual and political content to the many specific actions we must take—requires that we unfurl a banner to which the just aspirations of all peoples can rally. Only the vision of a new world order—a new universal system capping the systemic revolution of our times—will have the power to draw diverse humanity to our cause.

It is often said that, in order to win out in protracted conflict with Communism, we need but the determination to win. A vast conflict between two vast systems of power cannot be won by a display of semantic prowess. Evidently, most people confronted by a challenge to their survival propose to meet it. Yet, in order to win, the determination to win is the mere preface to the determination to pay the price of victory. The determination to pay the price is much more difficult to sustain than the happy resolution to get the better of one's opponent, especially in a protracted conflict where the costs of waging it as well as its future outcome are indeterminate. Little in their history has prepared the American people for a protracted conflict with a remote terminal point and an indeterminate outcome.

Whether the American people can muster the requisite determination and preparedness will depend upon their recognition of the basic facts of the world today: We are in the midst of a world revolution; we are locked in a mortal conflict with the Communist system for mastery of that revolution. The prospects of either contestant in this struggle can only be expressed paradoxically. As we approach the seventh decade of the twentieth century, the rushing tides of history appear to favor the Communists. Up until now, the Communist leaders have understood far better than the leaders of the West the revolutionary character of this era. Furthermore, by utilizing the principles of protracted conflict the Communists have been able to capitalize on their superior insight and make far greater inroads into the Western system than would have been likely in the light of any objective analysis of the real power positions of the opposing camps.

Notwithstanding all this, the long-range prospects for the West are infinitely superior to those of Soviet or Chinese Communism. While short-range trends may favor the Communists, the Western concept of man and Western institutions correspond far more closely to reality than does that pseudo-scientific residue of the nineteenth century called Communism.

The establishment of a universal political-legal order under Western leadership stands as the only alternative to the culmination of the global systemic revolution in conflagration. The United States, which alone among the great nations was founded upon a rational set of political and legal ideals, must bear the prime responsibility for the creation of such an order, compatible with the requirements of the Good Society. The order America seeks does not demand a world state; it may be achieved through the evolution of a voluntary federalism whose form is as yet undiscerned. Irrespective of the formal means, the essential end of American policy must be the construction of an international order in which the rule of liberty under law enters into the possession of the great majority of mankind, instead of remaining the exclusive heritage of the Western peoples.

This goal will be blocked by an all-encompassing Communist bid for power which will continue and be accelerated within the next decade. By now, it appears that the more prescient among the Communist leaders recognize that the long-range, sociological forces of history will run against them. Boris Pasternak will not be the last voice of conscience that will rise to speak in Russia. Consequently, the Communist leaders must either press forward and win the protracted conflict within the next one or two decades or forfeit their power. If by coercion and deviousness they should remold the world into the Communist image, the all-pervading tyranny which masquerades as Communism would degrade the human race to puppets of the "New Class" described so pungently by Djilas.

Such a bleak outcome is not inevitable, once the West in general and the United States in particular understand the principles of protracted conflict so largely responsible for the past successes of our enemy. From such an understanding can be forged the tools of victory. No one can doubt that the action which should flow from a realistic grasp of the methods and aims of professional revolutionaries working toward the destruction of our "decadent bourgeois civilization" is long overdue. Whether Western civilization is sinking into its final twilight or will survive to erect the modern world order which only the West can build—this question will be answered by victories and defeats in varied battles of the protracted conflict still to be fought.

EPILOGUE

Approximately four years have passed since the analysis of Communist strategy contained in the foregoing chapters was made. It has often been noted that in the highly fluid field of international strategic affairs, most books enjoy a "half life" of about two years. During this brief period, they are sufficiently in tune with the times to exert at least a temporary influence upon the attitudes of the reading public and perhaps upon the thinking of men who are responsible for shaping public policy. But after a fleeting existence, they no longer seem relevant to the contemporary course of world events. Publication of a soft-cover edition of *Protracted Conflict* four years after, therefore, may prompt some to ask: Why bother? This is an appropriate occasion to reassess the value of the insights originally presented and to estimate their continuing validity.

The purpose of this short epilogue, then, is to examine unfolding Communist strategy within the last four years and to reflect upon the relatively consistent operational code which is discussed in this book. Through the application of the protracted conflict strategy (the only strategy available to the Sino-Soviet bloc), Communism has continued to make incursions into the Free World, not only in the more familiar theaters of conflict but also into regions that seemed less susceptible to Communist penetration at the time the book first appeared. But in the meantime, im-

portant changes have occurred within the target societies at which
Communist efforts have been directed—especially the Atlantic
Community. No less significant are the changes occurring within
the bloc itself; the relations of the two major Communist powers
have been marked of late by conspicuous frictions. It is against
a shifting background of developments in the Communist, Western and "in-between" worlds that the Communists' policy objectives must be assessed.

Generally speaking, the Soviet Union in pursuing its protracted
conflict strategy continues to operate from an overall economic
base which is substantially inferior to that of the United States.
The disparity becomes even more pronounced when the industrial-
technological capabilities of the allies are added to each side. So
far as sheer economic prowess is concerned, the international
Communist bloc is still waging an uphill battle against the industrial nations of the Free World.

During the early years of the Khrushchev era, say from 1955 to
1959, the Soviet Union's economic performance seemed rather
impressive, quantitatively as well as qualitatively. Those were the
years of annual growth rates approximating perhaps seven to
eight percent, of expanding foreign assistance, of the Sputniks,
and of a noticeable improvement in the position of the Russian
consumer. In 1959, Allen W. Dulles, then Director of the Central
Intelligence Agency, estimated that the Soviet gross national product (GNP) had risen from 38 percent of the United States GNP
in 1955 to 45 percent in 1959.[1] Although some economists took
issue with his statistical analysis, Mr. Dulles' evaluation was a
fairly typical one toward the close of the 1950's. At that time, when
the debate over comparative growth rates was reaching its peak
of intensity, the American rate was reckoned at just about half
that of the Soviet Union. The latter's prospects for "catching up"
sometime in the 1970's seemed quite good. Not a few Western observers, taking the boasts of Communist propagandists virtually
at face value, voiced alarm at the productive onrush of the socialist

[1] Statement before the Subcommittee on Economic Statistics of the Joint
Economic Committee of the United States Congress, November, 1959.

camp. Such apprehensiveness lent superficial plausibility to the claim that "the wave of the future" was running inevitably in favor of Communism.

Indications are not lacking, however, that Soviet central planners have hit some snags in the early 1960's. The years 1960 and 1961 were years of declining agricultural production and, in some regions, of crop failure. Considering the fact that Russia and the Eastern European countries were, historically, grain-exporting countries, the difficulties that they have encountered in the way of feeding their own peoples would suggest that the ideologically inspired Communist experiment in the collectivization of agriculture has led to abysmal failure, undoubtedly chronic and perhaps irreversible. Premier Khrushchev himself has admitted that the Soviet planned goals for mechanizing agriculture have not been met. Hence the future transfer of manpower from the farms to industry, on which contingency the success of Soviet industrial planning hinges, will be fraught with complex problems. Furthermore, the reduction of Soviet ground forces, announced with considerable fanfare two years ago, has been postponed. These factors, combined with the entry into the labor force of the "lean" age groups (a result of the lower birth rate of the World War II period), have culminated in a shortage of labor, one which may very well warrant the conclusion that so far as the Soviets are concerned the recent phase of most rapid economic growth has reached its peak.[2]

Premier Khrushchev, then, has been walking a tightrope in his efforts to woo the Soviet masses with promises of not only an increase in consumer goods but also a shorter work week. When the Soviets look east and west, they perceive both rising expectations and mounting frustrations within the Communist domain. Economic aid for the industrialization of China has not kept pace with the much-vaunted Soviet growth. In the satellite countries of Eastern Europe, where the peoples enjoy a close-up view of the transformation of Western Europe, popular aspirations for a higher

[2] Robert Strausz-Hupé, "Can the Soviet Union 'Catch Up' with the United States?" Foreign Policy Research Institute Study Paper No. 16, May 1962.

standard of living are perhaps even stronger than they are in the more insulated U.S.S.R. In other words, Communist central planners are feeling mounting demands upon limited resources more acutely than do Western policy-makers. Indeed, there is reason to believe that henceforth the Soviets will experience an increasing pinch in the cost of carrying on an international competition in the race for space and over the full and varied spectrum of weapons technology. It is not at all surprising that the so-called "Soviet economic offensive" into the underdeveloped areas has been modulated somewhat during the last two years, nor that the steep rise in the price of butter and meat in Russian stores reflects the failure of Khrushchev's farm program.

Nevertheless, in spite of intra-bloc economic difficulties, the Communists have not relented in their efforts at the strategic penetration of the Free World. If anything, the official pronouncements of the leaders of international Communism have within recent years become more militant and more confident than ever. The statement issued by 81 Communist parties meeting at Moscow in November 1960—a document which is in many respects comparable to the classic formulation of Communist strategy laid down at the Sixth World Congress in 1928—eloquently reflects a conviction that the historical conflict of systems is approaching a climactic phase:

Our time, whose main content is the transition from capitalism to socialism initiated by the great October Revolution, is a time of struggle between the two social systems, a time of socialistic revolutions and nationalistic-liberalistic revolutions, a time of the breakdown of imperialism, of the abolition of the colonial system, a time of transition of more peoples to the socialistic position, of the triumph of socialism and communism on a world-wide scale....

The strength and invincibility of socialism have been demonstrated in recent decades in titanic battles between the new and old worlds. Attempts by the imperialists and their shock forces— fascism—to check the course of historical development by force of arms ended in failure. Imperialism proved powerless to stop the socialist revolutions in Europe and Asia. Socialism became a world system. The imperialists tried to hamper the economic progress of the socialist countries, but their schemes were foiled. The imperialists did all in their power to preserve the system of colonial slavery, but that system is falling apart. . . .

Today it is the world socialist system and the forces fighting against imperialism, for a socialist transformation of society, that determine the main content, main trend and main features of the historical development of society. Whatever efforts imperialism makes, it cannot stop the advance of history. . . . The complete triumph of socialism is inevitable.[3]

Premier Khrushchev's address to a meeting of Communist organizations on January 6, 1961,[4] was based on the 81-nation declaration and spelled out in greater detail the strategic and tactical lines to be pursued for the coming decade. As might be expected, the Soviet leader singled out the United States as "the chief bulwark of world reaction," author of a militaristic and imperialistic policy of strengthening aggressive blocs which make it the enemy of peoples everywhere. (What this really means is that the defense posture and coalition diplomacy of the United States have slowed down the process of the historical dialectic and forced the Communist leaders to move with consummate caution.) Khrushchev's speech signalled the intensification of the worldwide propaganda campaign against "the rebirth of German militarism," that foe of peaceful co-existence, disarmament and relaxation of tension with which, Khrushchev asserted, the United States had made a "crimi-

[3] Quoted from *Two Communist Manifestoes,* with introduction and commentary by Charles Burton Marshall, published by the Washington Center of Foreign Policy Research, 1961, pp. 11-12.

[4] In his Introduction and Commentary, *ibid.,* pp. 1-5, Mr. Marshall discusses the importance of the 81-Nation Statement and the Speech of January 6, 1961 "for what they convey of Communist outlook, assumptions, expectations, interests and purposes in the contemporary world. . . . What is clear is that it would be imprudent in the extreme to form our expectations and resolve our policies in disregard of what these documents say."

nal deal." (Notably in Great Britain and the United States, the anti-German campaign has borne a certain amount of strategic fruit during the last two years.)

From the operational standpoint, perhaps the most significant part of Khrushchev's speech dealt with the now famous distinction among three types of war: 1) global nuclear war; 2) local, limited war, either conventional or nuclear; and 3) wars of national liberation. Reiterating those classical principles of the protracted conflict strategy which are dealt with in Chapter 4 of this book, Khrushchev specifically warned Communist strategists against creating situations which would provoke general military hostilities with the United States or bring on limited wars (e.g., through aggression of the Korean type) which might escalate into general war.

Khrushchev's thesis that war between capitalism and socialism is not inevitable should be translated to read that, at least until the Soviet Union can achieve a decisive superiority in military technology, military adventurism must be avoided at all costs; a frontal military encounter with the United States at this time would represent a cataclysmic disaster for Communist strategy. (While war might also destroy the capitalist system, the Communists can derive no comfort from such a prospect.)

The Soviet announcement on August 31, 1961, of the decision to resume nuclear weapons tests, followed by Marshal Malinovsky's references, in the fall of 1961, to the importance of the pre-emptive strike and, early in 1962, to the anti-missile missile reveals a great deal more than the Soviets' opaque prose on "peace and coexistence" and "total disarmament." The Soviets hope, it appears, to achieve within the foreseeable future a margin of technological superiority which would render a first-strike option thinkable. This would constitute, in the eyes of Communist strategists, a strategic bonanza—a favorable condition which, up until now, has never prevailed. One other possible interpretation of the Soviets' military development program cannot be overlooked: they might have felt sufficiently inferior to the United States to justify an urgent effort to improve their weapons system.

The Communists seem confident that with or without a sudden spurt well ahead of the West's military technology, they will eventually triumph. According to Khrushchev's doctrine of January 6, 1961, the key to the "safe" conduct of an international conflict strategy designed to weaken and envelop the West is the "national liberation movement." Nationalist revolts against the West might culminate—and, according to Khrushchev, should culminate—in war, namely that third and permissible type of war in the nuclear age: the war of national liberation.

Wars of national liberation, such as revolutionary struggles carried on by "the people" (i.e., forces under the control or influence of Communism, or whose objectives happen to coincide with those of Communism) are both "just" and "inevitable." These uprisings, which break out when the "cup of popular patience" overflows against "reactionary regimes," deserve (and will receive) the wholehearted support of the Communist world. In fact, the Soviet leader declared, it is "the sacred duty of the Communists to support such wars." In other words, orthodox Communist strategy still calls for an assault against the West through a variety of proxies and auxiliaries: satellites; conspiratorial parties; guerrilla armies; neutralist, nationalist, anti-colonialist and pacifist movements (whether in underdeveloped or bourgeois societies); and all manner of front organizations. The purpose of the present strategy is still to compound the gradual defeat of the West over a relatively long period by piecemeal conquests, feints, maneuvers, political zig-zags, ambiguous negotiations, imperceptible social penetrations, psychological manipulations and various forms of violence, provided that these fall below the threshold of provoking the West into decisive counteraction. Indeed, if one merely substitutes the word "safe" for the word "just" in connection with wars of national liberation, one can readily see that the prescriptions spelled out by Khrushchev on January 6, 1961, constitute a ratification of the *Protracted Conflict* thesis: the Communists have always preferred to avoid the general encounter and rely upon an indirect approach to the acquisition of power, influence and territorial positions.

The Soviet leadership is undoubtedly aware of the need for proceeding with great caution even in support of "national liberation" wars, for even in the underdeveloped regions of the world the direct military embroilment of Soviet and Western forces would be accompanied by the possibility, albeit remote, of escalation. (There is some reason to believe that the Soviet intervention in Laos since late 1960 has been designed at least in part to take over the management of the conflict in that region from the Chinese Communists who, in the Soviet view, did not sufficiently appreciate the risk of escalation.) Today more than ever, it is a fundamental tenet of the Communists' protracted conflict strategy that the prospective gains be greater than the potential risks in any given encounter. Even a small risk of escalation provides some deterrence against direct Soviet military involvement. Hence Khrushchev was extremely careful in defining what he meant by "wars of national liberation." These are internal wars—not interstate conflicts which might catalyze war between the two superpowers. The Premier's dialectical discourse on modern war reflected his earnest purpose to make absolutely certain that Communists around the world understood their instructions. From the Soviet point of view, any war is just if it represents a safe and controllable method for the advancement of Soviet objectives; if it generates dangerous risks it is unjust in the extreme.

One caveat on the subject of national liberation warfare is in order. During the last fifteen years, Western strategic analysts have concentrated their attention upon the phenomenon of national liberation movements in the erstwhile colonial areas of Asia and Africa. But it is clear from the context of Khrushchev's utterances that he is speaking of something broader than struggles against Western colonialism in the strict sense of the term. Khrushchev himself concedes that old-fashioned European colonialism has almost disappeared. Interestingly enough, among the examples of national liberation warfare he mentioned not only Vietnam and Algeria but also Cuba, which was already an independent state at the time of the struggle. It is clear that the concept of national liberation warfare is applicable to every weak or unstable country which is linked to the West through treaty, military assistance, economic aid or investment, and where class, ethnic or other resentments can be aroused to a critical pitch against an incumbent pro-Western government. In the Communist lexicon, any link whatsoever with the United States, the leader of world militarism, reaction and capitalism, constitutes imperialism and violates a country's sovereignty and deprives it of its national independence. Not until a country has severed all links with the United States and adopts a "neutralist" orientation toward the socialist camp can it be called—in Khrushchev's parlance—"free."

Within the last four years, Communism has sought to push forward along several geographical fronts, carefully tailoring its tactics to the specific regional environment, alternately building up and easing pressure, weighing the assets and liabilities of various moves. The conflict methodology, which has always been characterized by innovation and shifts of emphasis, has within recent years exhibited greater variety, subtlety and ambiguity than ever. In Western Europe, the most sensitive and potentially most volatile region in the world for probing operations, the Soviets have been forced to maneuver with circumspection. But Europe is so potentially rewarding a field as to entice recurring Soviet probes. Indeed, the Soviets must strive to bring about a liquidation of the North Atlantic Alliance; this is a prerequisite to the achievement of their other global goals.

Berlin has continued to serve as a handy "crisis lever." When the Soviets have wished to promote talk of summit meetings, Western recognition of East Germany, the denuclearization of Central Europe and sundry proposals designed to chip away at NATO unity and strength, they have found it convenient to apply political pressure against Berlin, hinting at the possibility of unilateral changes in the city's status which might bring military force into play. The Soviets have issued five threats and ultimatums since the fall of 1958, seeking to divide the Atlantic allies on the question of how to deal with the Berlin problem. The deadlines have come and gone without either decisive concessions on the part of the Western governments or any serious effort on the part of the Soviets to back up the ultimatums with dangerous showdown maneuvers. Nothing has happened to alter the basic estimate of the situation made on page 53 *infra:* "Until such a time as they are ready for total war, they cannot launch a direct attack in Europe —in fact, in Europe even a graduated challenge would run the almost immediate risk of all-out war."

Although no decisive change has occurred in the status of West Berlin, the Soviets have tried to bring about the slow erosion of the city's position. After the Kennedy Administration, in July 1961, had made it clear that it would resist by armed force if necessary Communist efforts to interfere with allied access rights to West Berlin, the Communists devised new and unexpected moves to symbolize a changing situation, and to extricate themselves from mounting embarrassment. The building of the wall through Berlin in the summer of 1961—a move which found the West unprepared —effectively cut off the flow of refugees from Ulbricht's domain. The Communists have had to calculate the consequences of their Berlin policy in terms of losses and gains. On the liability side, from their point of view, the wall stands as a monument to penitentiary society, and the persistent efforts of "counterrevolutionaries" to escape from the "workers' paradise" at the risk of their lives prove to be a constant irritant. Furthermore, the increased pressure on Berlin prompted the United States to reinforce its military commitments to Europe. The calling up of reservists and the instigation of a nationwide civil defense debate in the United States were a warning to Premier Khrushchev not to push too hard in Berlin. On the asset side, the Soviets succeeded in driving, at least temporarily, a diplomatic wedge between the Anglo-American and the Franco-German partners; advancing the campaign for unilateral nuclear disarmament (not to mention the "red or dead" nonsense) among the British and American publics; raising the pressure for international summit meetings at which the "relaxation of tensions" could be discussed; and compounding the political problems inherent in the task of revising NATO military strategy. In sum, the indirect methodology described on pages 107-108 *infra* has been continued and refined: the purpose today, as in late

1958, is still to use the Berlin crisis as a cutting tool for disfiguring NATO.

In other regions of the world outside the zone of immediate NATO protection, the Communists have been able to pursue a bolder course for two related reasons: 1) the stakes are lower than in Western Europe; 2) so, too, are the risks of general war. Southeast Asia furnishes an excellent case in point. From a purely military standpoint, the area had become relatively stable after the Geneva Conference of 1954. Faced with a declaratory United States policy of "massive retaliation," Communist strategists had decided to shift over from overt violence to political and psychological warfare, e.g., by boring their way into South Vietnam and by employing economic means to gain a foothold in Cambodia. The kingdom of Laos, as the authors pointed out in the book, page 95, "served as a proving ground for a refurbished Communist tactic: switching from military operations to parliamentary electoral processes. . . . "

But Southeast Asia became a region of renewed Communist guerrilla penetration during the period of transition from the Eisenhower to the Kennedy Administration. The Communist strategists sought to take advantage of the partial policy paralysis which besets quadrennially the United States Executive from the time of the nominating conventions until inauguration or some months thereafter. In this case, they stepped up their pressure to obtain control of the strategically located area of Laos, thereby setting the stage for the subsequent subversion of South Vietnam and Thailand. The United States, following a Laotian coup in August 1960, did not give wholehearted political and military aid to anti-Communist elements. But in December, the Soviets openly shipped planeloads of military equipment to the Communist Pathet Lao forces while accusing SEATO and the United States of "imperialist aggression."

The intensified Communist offensive in Southeast Asia testified to years of careful preparation for the resumption of violent conflict. It also revealed that the strategy of "massive retaliation" had lost much of its credibility (as a result of Soviet missile progress and Western policy shifts) before Western conventional and counterguerrilla capabilities had been built up to adequate deterrent strength. President Kennedy in March 1961 warned the Communists against a military takeover of Laos, but the warning was not followed up with a timely marshalling of power on the local scene. The ensuing year witnessed frenzied United States diplomatic efforts to create a neutral coalition government in Laos, while the Communists continued to nibble away at the tiny country.[5]

When the allies of the United States in Asia began to display signs of nervousness at Washington's intentions in the spring of 1962, United States marines were landed in Thailand to prevent the demoralization of SEATO. This action, like the U. S. troop reinforcement in Europe, put the Soviets on notice that there were limits as to how far they could push. Apparently, the Communist strategists decided that, since any dangers of direct military embroilment with the United States seemed remote, it would be prudent to consolidate their position and communize the area via the political route. The U.S.S.R. and the United States finally achieved in June 1962 the establishment of "a neutralist coalition" of three. The Premiership (together with the key Ministries of Defense and Interior) went to Prince Souvanna Phouma, who had been disposed to cooperate closely with the Communist Pathet Lao and with the U.S.S.R.;[6] the Pathet Lao leader, Prince Souphanouvong, was named Deputy Premier and Administrator of Economy and Planning; the other Deputy Premiership was allotted to pro-Western General Phoumi Nosavan. Officially, each of the three could exercise the veto over decisions. But with the Pathet Lao in physical control of two-thirds of the country, it could be

[5] Bill Mauldin portrayed the essence of the strategy in a cartoon showing President Kennedy and Premier Khrushchev seated at a dinner table with Laos as the entrée on the latter's plate. The caption was a polite question by Khrushchev: "Do you mind if I eat while we're talking?"

[6] Cf. Richard P. Stebbins, *The United States in World Affairs 1960*, published for the Council on Foreign Relations, New York: Harper & Brothers, 1961, pp. 270-283. Also the series of articles by Ronald Stead in *The Christian Science Monitor*, March 21, 23 and 24 and April 2, 1962.

expected that Nosavan would be hard pressed to exercise any real influence in this coalition. The "neutralization" of Laos at this time (a little over a year after President Kennedy and Premier Khrushchev agreed to it at Vienna) can serve Communist strategy in various ways: 1) It can free resources for campaigns to improve the Communist position in neighboring countries (Vietnam, Thailand, Cambodia and Burma). 2) So long as the Communists choose to make "neutralism" work in Southeast Asia, they will be able to point to a model for the "solution" of other critical problems such as Berlin and the concomitant reduction of Cold War tensions, thereby facilitating the phase of global consolidation. 3) "Neutralism" in an area such as Southeast Asia derives its complexion primarily from the Communist-Western power ratio which prevails locally. Laos, therefore, is ripe for Communist plucking at a time convenient to the phasing schedule of Communist strategists. Not a few Western and Asian observers were of the opinion that the Communists in Laos can dominate the entire country. In fact, the Communists were probably strong enough to ensure their victory in "free elections," if they wished to tip their hand and score the kind of respectable electoral triumph they have been vainly seeking for decades. A too obvious takeover might spoil the efficient execution of the protracted conflict strategy in other critical zones of the Cold War, particularly in the NATO area. The United States sought the agreement to put a good face on a bad situation. It is not a very comforting thought that the 1962 outcome of Laos might have been still worse.

Communist strategic gains in the Middle East and Africa during the last four years have been less spectacular. Communist penetration of the Arab world was most evident during the years 1955-1958—a period of maximum instability. But after the American military intervention in the Lebanon in mid-1958, the anti-Westernism of Arab nationalists became somewhat less vehement. The Communists, in spite of their crucial support of Nasser at the height of the Suez crisis, their military aid to Syria, their immediate backing of the Kassem government following the coup which removed Iraq from the Baghdad Pact, and their technical assistance to Egypt in the construction of the Aswan High Dam, have not yet been able to establish an impregnable base in any Arab state.

As might have been expected, the Sino-Soviet bloc has done its best to prolong and exacerbate the exhausting Algerian conflict, and to amplify its tensions throughout the African Continent, where a prime Communist objective has been to cut off the dialogue between Africans and the West. The statement which appears on page 63 of the book has not lost its strategic significance: "At the pith of the Algerian conflict was a paradox: The rebels fought in the cause of Arab nationalism and yet advanced, wittingly or unwittingly, the cause of Moscow in a gigantic maneuver directed against the Western Alliance and at the domination of the Middle East and Africa." In supporting the "national liberation" struggle of the FLN, the Communists undoubtedly sought to weaken NATO by forcing France out of her position of strategic influence on the southern littoral of the Mediterranean. This could pave the way for the subsequent construction of Soviet bloc bases in North Africa, and expose the members of the French Community in West Africa to penetrative pressure from the north. As a result of the Evian Accord of March 1962, Algeria was to achieve self-determination, with France maintaining certain vaguely defined responsibilities in the realm of defense and foreign affairs. The fact that not a few of the leading figures in the Algerian Government received their revolutionary training in the Soviet Union, Czechoslovakia and East Germany raises the specter that Algeria might gradually become a "neutralist" state which would align itself via the Belgrade-Cairo Axis with Soviet bloc objectives. Much will depend upon the combination of political, economic and military policies which France pursues vis-à-vis the new state. But in the background looms the ominous promise of aid from Peking tendered as the new state entered upon the "new phase" of its struggle against French "imperialism."

The Communists made their bid for power in the heart of Africa when they supported first Lumumba and then Gizenga in the Congo crisis. They have been rebuffed. For the time being, at least, they must devise other approaches. Perhaps the chief benefit which they initially reaped from the Congo affair was the rise of political tempers in the United States and some allied countries in Europe over the role to be played by the United Nations in the process of decolonization. On top of their Congo setback, the Soviets suffered an embarrassing political reversal in Guinea, when the Russian Ambassador was summarily expelled and the U.S.S.R. was roundly criticized for sending goods of inferior quality.

Communism as a doctrine of social organization cannot yet boast many converts in Africa: the patterns of African culture and personality dampen the appeals of totalitarian discipline. Moreover, as Western Europe grows in political and economic vigor, its *presence* in Africa will probably become increasingly attractive to the governing groups of emergent African states in need of outside economic and technical help. As this happens, the Communists' operational problems in many parts of the continent will be further compounded. Nevertheless, the Communists can be expected to continue their efforts to work out an effective strategy for Africa. In their propaganda, they will strive to monopolize the credit for the wane of European colonialism. Through selected assistance programming, cultural exchanges, and unrelenting political flattery, they will try to win the permanent allegiance of the new nations to a brand of neutralism which, they surmise, will prove increasingly useful to Communist diplomats in the United Nations. Most serious of all, through agitation, penetration of social structures and the supply of both conflict training and weapons, they can be counted upon to fan tensions and disputes (e.g., in South Africa, Angola and Algeria) where these will drain or confound the West without boomeranging upon the Communists themselves.

Perhaps the most remarkable success scored by the international Communist movement in the last four years has been in Latin America—a region the Communists have been cultivating for over thirty years. There is reason to believe that the Communists, having failed for the time being to find the right strategic key to Africa, are now concentrating more of their attention on the "soft underbelly" of the Western Hemisphere. It is true that the Communists have never managed to convert many Latin American urban industrial workers into shock-troops of revolution. But given the great chasm which divides rural and urban areas in Latin America, it would seem that the strategy for that region will consist of a unique amalgam of Leninist methodology and the "Yenan Way" of Mao. Among the intellectuals, students, journalists, civil servants and nationalistic businessmen in the cities, anti-Yanquismo furnishes the Communists with their most effective rallying cry, while in the countryside Communist sloganeers have exploited peasant discontent with demands for radical "land reform." The case of Cuba provides a classic example of how the partisan warfare campaign, which begins as a movement to liberate the nation from the yoke of a predatory militaristic regime and which is originally supported by the urban intelligentsia and middle class, ends in the creation of a full-fledged Communist state, convertible into a Soviet forward military base when the Kremlin chooses to make it so.

Che Guevara's mode of guerrilla warfare bids fair to solve one of the Communists' most difficult problems in Latin America, namely how to defeat an incumbent government backed by a United States-equipped army. The future spread of guerrilla movements to other Latin American countries is likely to confront the United States with an increasingly unhappy choice: to intervene or not to intervene, both alternatives being equally awkward. It is not likely, however, that the Communists will, within the immediate future, rely exclusively on guerrilla warfare. If other Latin American states fall under Communist control, the take-over process need not necessarily follow the precise course of Castro's revolution. First of all, American policy-makers are likely to be on guard against the same kind of plot. This circumstance alone counsels the Communists to abide by the principle of tactical innovation which they have applied so imaginatively to a variety of situations. Moreover, the Latin American environment does not call in every instance for the particular strategy of violence employed in Cuba. Despite the tremendous diversity of Latin

America, many countries suffer so acutely from ethnic cleavages, socio-economic frustrations, traditionalist-reformist tensions, institutional weaknesses and general political instability that they offer opportunities for either the violent or the non-violent displacement of incumbent governments. Thus far, it does not appear that the Alliance for Progress is informed by a sense of strategic realities. Yet only a comprehensive understanding of Communist strategic concepts and methods will enable the United States to counter ambiguous power shifts in which the Communist role has been cleverly camouflaged.

The advent to power of the Kennedy Administration has ushered in a new phase of American foreign policy in the protracted conflict and, in a sense, a new foreign policy style. The President appears to be willing to exploit postures of power in international affairs, even while going beyond President Eisenhower in devising concessions to entice the Soviets into a more conciliatory frame of mind. The tactic of leaning over backward to demonstrate reasonableness has, in other times and places, reaped political benefits; but it can also prove a risky course to pursue in terms of the security of the United States and the allies who depend upon this country for *their* security.

The Kennedy Administration has increased the defense budget in order to achieve greater strategic flexibility, especially in the realm of non-nuclear and unconventional warfare capabilities.

During 1962, the United States, benefiting from programs launched in the late fifties, substantially narrowed whatever lead the Soviets had enjoyed in missile development and space exploration activities. The Kennedy Administration also made a courageous decision, in the face of mounting adverse propaganda, to resume nuclear tests in the atmosphere (with all possible precautions for human health) for the purpose of reinsuring United States nuclear superiority against the possibility of a Soviet technological breakthrough. Finally, the year following the abortive Cuban invasion—a piece of mismanagement which was generally recognized as the President's gravest strategic failure in his first year of office—saw the United States striving to achieve within the Organization of American States a more cohesive policy for the security of the Western Hemisphere. But whether the United States will be persuaded that it is barred from meaningful initiatives toward Cuba, or whether it will muster the political ingenuity and will required, in the face of a Latin American phobia over "intervention," to reduce the Communist salient in the Western Hemisphere, time alone can tell. One prediction appears fairly safe: Communist propagandists, bent on protecting *their* most exposed and "undefendable" position in the world, will spare no effort in a frantic campaign to demonstrate that the United States must resign itself humbly to "peaceful coexistence" with the Havana regime.

The Cuban debacle, the failure of the neutrals at the Belgrade Conference to censure the Soviet Union for resuming nuclear tests, the Indian takeover of Goa—these and other developments have helped to bring about within the United States a reassessment of the international environment in which it must carry out its defense and foreign policies. There seems to have been a marked decline in the compulsive yearning, so noticeable a few years ago, to placate the chimera of "world public opinion" as articulated by a half dozen neutralist tribunes. Now that the Europeans have almost completed the most rapid, the most benign and the most radical process of liquidating overseas empires in the history of the human race, the guilt complexes which have long afflicted many Americans on questions of European colonial policy have begun to wear off. At the same time, some of the old idealist illusions which used to hover over the United Nations, confusing its deliberations and impeding its mission, are now evaporating in the astringent climate of international organization politics. There is a growing recognition that the advanced industrial nations of the free world, from whose legal traditions the Charter of the United Nations developed, have a special responsibility to expand their power base and reassert their prime political influence upon the course of world history.

The notion of Communist invincibility is not implicit in the concept of protracted conflict. The authors do not attribute superhuman intelligence and infallibility to the Communist conflict managers, nor monolithic efficiency to the bloc. Perhaps it was unavoidable that a study focused upon the operational principles by which Communist leadership seeks to envelop the West should seem to interpret contemporary history as a series of cumulative triumphs for the Leninists and of unmitigated disasters for the West. Nothing could be farther from the truth, unless it be the contrary proposition.

Communist strategists have, at times, blundered badly. The Iron Curtain and the secretive nature of a conspiratorial party hide many of their errors; their worst mistakes can be discerned only by themselves. But it is plain to the outside world that Communist plans, far from always reaching their mark, sometimes boomerang. It would seem, for example, that Peking's decision to apply military pressures along the northeast border of India, whatever other purposes it may have served, has produced certain adverse consequences. The Chinese have alienated throughout India elite groups which not many years ago were quite friendly toward the Mao regime. Within the last two years, many Indians have felt constrained to curb their criticism of SEATO, the Mutual Security Program in Pakistan, and the United States policy of supporting the Nationalists on Formosa. (They realize that the nearness of the Seventh Fleet to China's coasts compels the People's Republic of China to orient a large part of its military power toward the southeast, away from India's borders.) This is not to suggest that all the consequences of the Sino-Indian dispute can be counted as gains for the West. International strategic affairs are rarely attended by unambiguous consequences. One of the results of the Sino-Indian dispute is the fact that the Soviets' political stock has risen steadily in India and Indians are trying harder than ever to persuade Western governments that the latter should offer widening concessions to the Soviets in the interest of accommodation.

In other areas, too, it can be shown that the Communists have worked assiduously to gain certain objectives but that their efforts have not yet paid off. In Iran, they have long sought an opportunity to overturn the pro-Western government of the Shah, but to no avail; although social discontent in Iran invites exploitation by Communist propagandists, the Persians have lived under the Russian shadow long enough to know that they can expect no improvement in their national situation by being absorbed into the Soviet empire. On the other side of Asia, Communist efforts to galvanize popular sentiment against the Kishi Government contributed toward the humiliating cancellation of President Eisenhower's visit to that country in the summer of 1960. Thus far, however, the Communists have been able to manipulate neither the lure of China trade nor the fear of nuclear detonations to convince the Japanese that they should sever their economic, political and defense ties with the United States.

The Communists, in brief, cannot arrange matters thus that *all* the complex forces now operating in the international environment will help rather than hinder them. In the past, they have reaped handsome gains from relatively modest strategic investments. Nevertheless, they have not been able to repeal the basic laws of strategic costs. In fact, the law of diminishing returns may be setting in. During the "flow period" of Communism which marked the close of World War II and its immediate aftermath, the Communists found in various regions of the world power voids which attracted penetration. The years 1945-1960 witnessed the strategic retreat of the European imperial powers from South and Southeast Asia, from the Nile Valley and from most other parts of Africa. But the power vacuums are being gradually filled, thanks to nationalism, development aid, cultural pride, regional integration movements and other factors, by growing new autonomous power centers. It is commonplace to note that the changing nature of the international community poses multifarious new problems for Western diplomacy—in the United Nations, for instance. But the obverse of the Western problematics should not be forgotten. The growing complexity of world politics forces the Communists to increase steadily the amount of the resources which must be poured into the protracted conflict. True, the bloc today commands greater total resources than four years ago. But one might well ask whether the Communists' global ambitions have not, for the time being, outpaced the rate of growth of their power base. The Soviets seem to be in need of a period of consolidation to nurture their strength, to restore full managerial control over their entire system, and to acquire new dialectical insights into the international situation before they can embark upon another "flow period" as they so confidently expect. The major strategic question confronting the West in the years ahead will be whether it will relax its posture, grant the Soviets the kind of temporary accommodation which they would find advantageous, and facilitate the process of Communist consolidation—or whether it will gear its policies to compounding the difficulties which face the Communist planners.

In this respect, the issue of maintaining an adequate military defense in the face of mounting disarmament demands will be crucial. The Soviet campaign for general and complete disarmament began to undergo marked intensification with Premier Khrushchev's address to the United Nations General Assembly in September 1959. The outcome of the nuclear test ban negotiations and the first round of talks in the seventeen-nation disarmament conference at Geneva suggest the conclusion that the Soviet appeal for the dissolution of all national military establishments still represents a propaganda position rather than a realistic statement of intent. If the leaders of international Communism believe, as Premier Khrushchev has frequently averred, that only Soviet military power holds the "forces of capitalist aggression" at bay, then it seems most unlikely that they would be willing to dismantle that power before their international strategic objectives have been achieved. As long as the world is divided into rival ideological-social systems, the Communist hierarchy, when it waxes eloquent about general and complete disarmament, holds forth but a vision of a disarmed *Communist* world. Most certainly, they will not settle for a disarmed world in which the final outcome of the power contest remains in doubt. Under the principles of Marxism-Leninism, any Communist leader who negotiated away the bases of military-technological power on which the security of the entire socialist camp rests would stand guilty of the most flagrant criminal revolutionary negligence.

The campaign for general and complete disarmament, viewed in the framework of the protracted conflict, creates an international psychopolitical climate favorable to the advancement of Communist rather than Western strategic objectives. To begin with, it helps slacken the pace at which the United States carries on international competition in the realm of sophisticated weapons technology. This in turn may either bring about a form of unilateral qualitative reduction by the United States in certain segments of the weapons spectrum, or ease the economic pressure of sustained arms competition upon the U.S.S.R. at a time when the latter encounters mounting allocation difficulties. Secondly, it causes the delay or indefinite postponement of steps required to strengthen and update NATO defenses in Europe. Thirdly, it raises many more problems of political misunderstanding and suspicion for an open, liberal coalition than it does for a closed, totalitarian bloc (even allowing for the differences between the U.S.S.R. and China). Fourth, it helps to obscure the continued use of violence by the Communists in relatively "safe" regions. And lastly, it strengthens pacifist tendencies within the Western world, compounds the guilt complexes of elite groups over defense expenditures, military establishments and further weapons development, and inhibits Western policy-makers from undertaking counter-interventions in the protracted conflict which might spoil the chances for that perennial will-o-the-wisp known as a Soviet-American accommodation.

One of the most baffling developments within the Communist world, and certainly one of the most difficult for the West to evaluate properly, has been the evolving pattern of Sino-Soviet relations since 1958. The schools-of-thought on this subject are many. At one extreme are those who believe that there are no differences whatsoever between the two major Communist powers and that all talk of a Sino-Soviet "rift" serves only to dupe and confuse Western governments. This "skeptical school" would even be reluctant to concede that Peking, anxious to receive all the industrialization aid it can obtain from Moscow, has been unhappy over Soviet aid shipments to "bourgeois nationalist" movements in the underdeveloped world. At the other extreme is the "sanguine school," which believes that jealous nationalism is proving stronger than the universalist ideology of Communism in China and Russia and that, sooner or later, an open split between a militantly revolutionary China and a relatively conservative, *status quo* Soviet society is inevitable. The "skeptical school" would discourage Western policy-makers from banking on differences within the bloc, while the "sanguine school" would encourage an essentially passive policy of "watchful waiting" (a policy which, incidentally, always appeals to a large segment of Western officialdom) until the Communist system falls apart at the seams.

Steering a sensible course between the skeptics and the sanguine—this, as in most things, seems the wisest United States policy toward the Communist bloc. Undoubtedly disagreements exist between Russia and China, running deeper than the personal rivalry of Mao and Khrushchev. The Chinese, with their traditional sense of cultural superiority, have sought to lay claim to ideological leadership of the bloc. At times they have criticized Soviet policies; at other times they have boasted that China, despite her lower productive level, has reached a more advanced stage of social development along the road to Communism. The disparity of economic-technological potential between the two countries leads to jealousy, demands for industrialization aid, and frustration when the wealthier partner either fails to deliver all that he might, or wastes his resources on nationalist movements in underdeveloped countries which might tomorrow turn against him. Chinese Communism, moveover, looks back to different revolutionary experiences from those of Lenin, Stalin and Khrushchev, and hence entertains different ideas about how to accomplish strategic objectives. Within recent years, it has generally been identified with a more militant attitude toward the international promotion of revolution. Lacking nuclear weapons, Peking has nevertheless preached a "harder" ideological line than Moscow. (Some strategists have suggested that it is the non-nuclear character of China's military machine which makes it possible for the People's Republic of China to pursue the more intransigent line.) The Chinese have insisted publicly that war between Communism and Capitalism is, if not inevitable, at least likely and that certain aspects of the Soviet policy of seeking "peaceful coexistence" may prove dangerous to the success of the movement.

Throughout their history, Communists have often exhibited a proneness to express their arguments over strategy and tactics in the broadest dialectical terms. It is very likely that the vaunted Sino-Soviet ideological dispute of recent years has really involved a disagreement over strategic priorities and over the optimum political and military tactics to be adopted at the current phase of the protracted conflict. In which area can the greatest gains now be made: in Europe or in Asia? By which methods are they to be made: by negotiating, by resorting to violence, or by a "mix" of these? The Soviets, quite naturally, are interested in liquidating the Berlin problem on terms favorable to themselves; similarly, the Chinese Communists are anxious to absorb Formosa. But it would not be wise for both powers to push eastward and westward simultaneously, for this might well arouse the Western powers to a sense of strategic urgency. In the nuclear age, strategic blackmail would seem to be most effective and safest when focused upon one critical area at a time. One thoughtful observer has warned that if, "in a few years, the Russians gain their Berlin objective through intimidation, the Chinese will then be in a position to point to Quemoy and Taiwan as 'abnormal' situations and reasonably suggest to Moscow that it is now 'their turn.'" [7] At least up until now, the Chinese Communists have been reluctant to embark upon a final solution of the Formosa question without military backing from the U.S.S.R., and the latter has been unwilling to extend such backing before weakening NATO, perhaps by forcing the kind of Berlin settlement which would drive a wedge between West Germany and the Western alliance.

The Sino-Soviet tangle is fraught with some disturbing am-

[7] Alice Langley Hsieh, *Communist China's Strategy in the Nuclear Era,* New York: Prentice-Hall, 1962, p. 185.

biguities, so far as its implications for United States policy-making are concerned:

> *In certain areas where Soviet and Red Chinese strategy operate in close proximity as, for example, in Southeast Asia, it is not at all clear whether they conflict or reinforce one another. In any case, the real or alleged tensions within the communist bloc have not resulted in a palpable diminution of communist initiatives abroad. . . .*
>
> *In sum, the ruling groups within the Soviet Union and the leaders of other communist states are still united on one overarching objective, namely to expand communism. They are—and it would be surprising if they were not—disagreed on specific strategies and tactics, on the where and the how much. Even here, the tenor of their* public *controversies might be deceptive: the Chinese communists, despite their insistence on an aggressive strategy, have been more pacific in their Far Eastern bailiwick than has Khrushchev, notwithstanding his digressions on "peaceful co-existence," in his dealings in Western Europe.*[8]

Donald S. Zagoria of the RAND Corporation underscores the need for caution in analyzing Sino-Soviet relations. The two powers, he points out, have much more in common with each other than with the Western world; this basic fact circumscribes rational limits to whatever conflict may go on between them. "One obvious such limit is that the two Communist powers cannot change partners in the world struggle."[9] Zagoria concludes with the salutary warning that conflict between the two leading Communist nations need not, in the long run, benefit the West at all.

United States policy-makers cannot but take into account whatever difficulties may arise to mar smooth relations between the U.S.S.R. and Communist China. This is an elementary requirement of sound strategy. Indeed, there is even a legitimate place

---

[8] Robert Strausz-Hupé, "The Sino-Soviet Tangle and U.S. Policy," *Orbis*, Vol. VI, Spring 1962, pp. 28 and 34.

[9] Donald S. Zagoria, *The Sino-Soviet Conflict 1959-1961*, Princeton: Princeton University Press, 1962, p. 22.

for a policy of "watchful waiting." But what is dangerous in the
present situation is the possibility that exaggeration of the Sino-
Soviet rift might engender Western lassitude—a willingness to
temporize, hope for the best and forego courses of action which
place the Communist bloc under pressure. While the Communist
empire is passing through a "time of troubles," the West is ill-
advised to relax its vigilance and, even more preposterously, sym-
pathize with Premier Khrushchev in his "China Problem." We
can be sure that both the Soviets and the Red Chinese will continue to take full advantage of the slightest indecision or wishful
thinking to which their public mutual recriminations have given
rise in Western circles. So long as both of these powers are fundamentally committed to the political (if not the physical) annihilation of the West as a viable cultural system, it will in the long
run be less dangerous to err on the side of underestimating rather
than overestimating the significance of the rift. It is the fissures
inside the Western alliance, rather than the obscure intrigues
within the Communist ranks, that should command the attention
of Western policy-makers.

Developments within the Atlantic Community, and especially
in Europe, since the late 1950's constitute perhaps the most significant of all the recent changes in the substructure of international
relations. The European countries are experiencing a remarkable
rate of sustained economic growth at a time when their old empires in Asia and Africa have almost completely broken up. At the
same time, the decline of jealous nationalism in the heart of
Europe makes the achievement of some degree of closer political
integration appear to be a feasible objective for the 1960's. Both
the formation of the European Economic Community and the
movement toward a European *political* community give the lie to
Communist "scientific" predictions. As a result of this regional
renaissance, the U.S.S.R., in the words of Walter Lippmann, "has
lost the power to intervene effectively in the internal affairs of
Western Europe." [10] To be sure, a number of nettlesome problems
continue to confront the North Atlantic Treaty Organization—

[10] New York *Herald Tribune*, May 26, 1962.

such as nuclear sharing and the relationship between the United States and the E.E.C.

The dominant motif within the Atlantic Community is a confident feeling that NATO is being slowly transformed from a treaty organization into an enduring partnership. Up until now, NATO has ensured the defense of Europe and slowed down considerably the "inevitable march of history" charted by Marx and Lenin. Under a forceful leadership, NATO can continue to do this indefinitely, while employing its expanding economic power to project onto a global scale those ideals of Western culture which have been the true revolutionary forces of history. If the Atlantic countries realize to the full their potential as the world's premier cultural, political, economic, scientific-technological and military community, the preservation, development and extension of liberal, humane values will be assured. The Soviets realize this. They also realize that the Atlantic nations at the present time possess a much larger production and trade base with which to carry out the process of international development. This is why the Communists, in the spring of 1962, began to turn their propaganda guns at the Common Market, calling it a "state monopoly agreement of the financial oligarchy of Western Europe," an instrument of the arms race and a threat to the economic independence of the underdeveloped countries. As Communism in the Soviet Union approaches the half-century mark, the signs are multiplying that it has passed the peak of its economic dynamism, while Western productivity gains seem to know no limits. Hence the prime objective of Soviet strategy must be the dissolution of the Atlantic alliance, lest the full panoply of the West's resources and intelligence be brought to bear upon the task of organizing the international order. In brief, the Communist Utopia has derived its lustre from the West's past failures and its promise pales before the concrete achievements of the Atlantic peoples who have become aware of their common danger and their common destiny.

NOTES

1. The relationship between Soviet strategy and Pavlovian psychology merits further study than it has thus far received. The following passage from one of Pavlov's most important works appears highly relevant to Communist conflict doctrine: "We all know how associations, once established and acquired between definite stimuli and our responses, are persistently and, so to speak, automatically reproduced, sometimes even though we fight against them. . . . Again, experience has taught us that a difficult task should be approached by gradual stages. We know also how different extra stimuli inhibit and discoordinate a well-established routine of activity. . . . Again, we know how weak and monotonous stimuli render us languid and drowsy, and very often lead to sleep. . . . In the dog two conditions were found to produce pathological disturbance by functional interference, namely, an unusually acute clashing of the excitatory and inhibitory processes, and the influence of strong and extraordinary stimuli. In man precisely similar conditions constitute the usual causes of nervous and psychic disturbances." I. P. Pavlov, *Conditioned Reflexes* trans. by G. V. Anrep, New York: International Publishers, 1927, pp. 395–397. The form of psychological disturbance produced depends upon the organism's nervous system. Excitation predominates in the more resistant nervous system, inhibition in the less resistant. The more resistant nervous system, marked by "exaggeration of the excitatory

and weakness of the inhibitory process . . . is able to perform a large amount of coordinated activity." *Ibid.*, p. 398.

2. Mao has openly acknowledged his debt to the ancient Chinese strategist Sun Tzu, who wrote one of the world's oldest military treatises, *The Art of War*, about 500 B.C. Sun Tzu's most notable aphorisms include the following: "All warfare is based on deception. Hence . . . when we are near, we must make the enemy believe that we are far away; when far away, we must make him believe that we are near." "To fight and conquer in all your battles is not supreme excellence; supreme excellence consists in breaking the enemy's resistance without fighting." "In all fighting, the direct method may be used for joining battle, but indirect methods will be needed to insure victory." "Force the enemy to reveal himself, so as to find out his vulnerable spots." (All of these are from the translation by Lionel Giles.) Mao Tse-tung quotes several of Sun Tzu's statements: "Avoid the enemy when he is full of dash, and strike him when he withdraws exhausted." "Make a noise in the east, but strike in the west." *Strategic Problems of China's Revolutionary War*, in *Selected Works of Mao Tse-tung*, London: Lawrence & Wishart, Ltd., 1954. 5 vols., Vol. I, pp. 217 and 218. To the ancient Chinese tradition Mao owes his keen appreciation of the psychopolitical factors in warfare and the role of human intelligence in the manipulation of violence. Mao's strategy shuns a head-on clash with the enemy so long as the latter enjoys a clear advantage. It is a strategy of ruses, designed to bluff the antagonist out of fighting and to induce him to retreat rather than seek a major engagement. Mao is a master in the art of using truce negotiations to outflank the enemy, sap the morale of his forces, and prevent him from seizing the tactical initiative. In his most important piece of military writing, *On Protracted War*, he spells out the central theme of his strategy: At all times strategic action must be kept under perfect control. Mao warns especially against military adventurism. The Communist commander, "swimming in an ocean of war," must "make sure of reaching the opposite shore

with measured strokes." While the enemy is strong, Communist strategy should be "to avoid great decisive battles in the early stages of the war, and gradually to break the morale, the fighting spirit and the military efficiency" of the foe. Cf. *Selected Works,* Vol. II, pp. 188, 201 and 202.

3. According to Lenin, an intimate relation exists between the economic structure of the capitalist world and that of the "colonial" territories. Cf. V. I. Lenin, *Imperialism:The Last Stage of Capitalism,* New York: Vanguard, 1927. The Communists, in their assault-by-attrition on the West, attempt to disrupt this vital relationship. Initially, they overemphasized the economic dependence of the capitalist system upon the colonial areas. With the passage of time they became aware of political and strategic reasons, just as compelling as the economic, for bringing the "nonsovereign" territories within the scope of their conflict strategy. The Communists saw their task: to aggravate the problems which invariably accompany profound social change, and thus convert the systemic revolution of Africa and Asia into a weapon against the West. Even while the Western colonial powers were becoming more responsive to the aspirations of their wards, Communist propagandists conditioned the native elites to believe that imperialism, far from being liquidated by the West, was actually being expanded by new and subtler methods. Communists infiltrated the Western-created universities in the newly emerging regions to inculcate into future nationalist leaders a pathological hatred of the West. Cf. Walter Z. Laqueur, *Communism and Nationalism in the Middle East,* New York: Praeger, 1956, pp. 13–18. The interwar decades were a time of preparation for the "anticolonial flow period" which was ushered in by the Second World War. Since 1945, the Communists fomented and abetted exhausting ideological, economic, military and semimilitary conflicts between the West and the peoples of the colonial areas. "Liberation" wars in Indochina, Korea, Malaya and Algeria drained off the West's military and economic resources while building up a stockpile of anti-West-

ern hatred. The Communists, risking little, were able to turn these conflicts to their own profit.

4. The Soviets have always subordinated military operations to politics. In 1939, the Soviet Union, facing the threat of war in Europe, was already embroiled in a two-year-old undeclared war with the Japanese in the Far East. This war, although it had attracted little world attention, was fought on a relatively large scale. In the battle of Nomanhan, between May 4 and September 16, the Japanese alone lost eighteen thousand troops. While this battle was going on, the Russian Ambassador in Berlin was already involved in the devious negotiations which culminated in the Nazi-Soviet Pact. Despite the strategic significance of the territory which was at stake, the Soviet leaders subordinated the struggle to the dictates of the larger political situation developing in Europe. The Soviets, as Clark W. Tinch has pointed out, sought patiently and skillfully to remove the German threat by joining it. "A war with Hitler's ally, Japan, at this time—that is, a *formal, proclaimed* war—could only bring ruin to Soviet plans. If, on the other hand, the negotiations with Germany would be nursed into bloom, then the Japanese question would take care of itself. To gain a basic understanding with Germany would be perhaps to stagger and immobilize Japan's designs on Russia." "Quasi-War Between Japan and the U.S.S.R., 1937–1939," *World Politics*, Vol. III, January, 1951, p. 184. A ceasefire between the U.S.S.R. and Japan was reached three weeks after the signing of the Molotov-Ribbentrop Pact. In April, 1941, Japan and Russia concluded a neutrality pact which protected Russia's rear as she prepared to concentrate her resources on the Western front against the expected German assault. It also left Japan free to make war on the United States.

5. Winston Churchill gives this account of the origin of the Warsaw uprising: "On July 29, three days before the rising began, the Moscow radio station broadcast an appeal from the Polish Communists to the people of Warsaw, saying that the

guns of liberation were now within hearing, and calling upon them as in 1939 to join battle with the Germans, this time for decisive action. 'For Warsaw, which did not yield but fought on, the hour of action has already arrived.'" *The Second World War: Triumph and Tragedy*, Boston: Houghton Mifflin, 1953, p. 129. Arthur Bliss Lane, former U.S. Ambassador to Poland, quotes another portion of the July 29 broadcast from Moscow: "Poles, the time of liberation is at hand! Poles, to arms! Make every Polish home a stronghold in the fight against the invader! There is not a moment to lose!" *I Saw Poland Betrayed*, New York: Bobbs-Merrill Company, 1948, p. 43. On July 31, when Soviet forces were within ten kilometers of Warsaw and the Polish underground heard that Soviet tanks had already penetrated German defenses east of the city, General Bor, the Home Army Commander, gave orders for a general uprising to begin at 5 P.M. on the following day. On August 2, when it became known in the outside world that the insurrection, involving some forty thousand men, had actually been launched, the radio broadcasts from Moscow suddenly stopped. The Soviet air force, which had attacked German positions in Warsaw almost every night for the ten nights previous to the rising, immediately ceased operations over the city. At the same time, the Soviet ground offensive came to a halt. According to Edward Rozek, the Red Army was already in the outskirts of Warsaw before receiving the order to withdraw. *Allied Wartime Diplomacy: A Pattern in Poland*, London: John Wiley, 1958, p. 236. Stefan Korbonski, last head of the Polish underground, has given this description of the situation: "Ever since the outbreak of the Rising, the peoples of Warsaw had been living by listening, listening to hear the Soviet guns. When these ceased firing, and a dead silence ensued, our people hoped that this was due only to some momentary difficulties, and went on listening. They all remembered the July broadcasts of the Soviet 'Kosciuszko' station, appealing to the population of Warsaw to rise. . . . During the initial period it never even occurred to anyone that the Soviets might deliberately stop their offensive so as to enable the Germans to

destroy the city of Warsaw." *Fighting Warsaw: The Story of the
Polish Underground State 1939–1945,* London: George Allen &
Unwin, 1956, pp. 385–386. It was clear that General Bor's army,
which had planned to co-ordinate its insurrection with the Soviet
offensive, could not by itself defeat the Germans. Without assistance from the outside, the Home Army could not even survive
for more than a week or ten days. General Bor sent urgent
appeals to London for aid. Churchill pointed out to Stalin that
although Soviet planes would have to fly only one hundred miles
to drop guns and ammunition to the beleaguered rebels, the
British would have to fly seven hundred miles from Italy in an
effort to render aid. Stalin answered brusquely that the information which the British had received concerning the extent of the
insurrection was "greatly exaggerated." *Triumph and Tragedy,*
p. 132. The United States government, wishing to aid the Home
Army, requested Soviet permission for American planes, flying
from France, to land behind Soviet battle lines at airfields which
were already in use by the Americans for shuttle bombing missions. Herbert Feis, *Churchill, Roosevelt, Stalin: The War They
Waged and the Peace They Sought,* Princeton: Princeton University Press, 1957, p. 385. Andrei Vishinsky replied to Ambassador Harriman's request as follows: "The Soviet Government
cannot, of course, object to English or American aircraft dropping arms in the region of Warsaw, since this is an American
and British affair. But they decidedly object to American or
British aircraft, after dropping arms in the region of Warsaw,
landing on Soviet territory, since the Soviet Government do not
wish to associate themselves either directly or indirectly with the
adventure in Warsaw." Stalin sought to justify his position in a
message to Churchill and Roosevelt on August 22, 1944: "Sooner
or later the truth about the group of criminals who have embarked on the Warsaw adventure in order to seize power will
become known to everybody. These people have exploited the
good faith of the inhabitants of Warsaw, throwing many almost
unarmed people against German guns, tanks and aircraft." *Triumph and Tragedy,* p. 136.

6. The Japanese, according to Hanson W. Baldwin, "in February 1945 had approached the Russians with a request that they act as intermediary in arranging a peace with the Western powers. The Russian Ambassador, Malik, in Tokyo, was the channel of the approach. . . . The United States was not officially informed of this approach until after the end of the war." *Great Mistakes of the War,* New York: Harper & Brothers, 1950, p. 96. It was only at the Potsdam Conference that the United States learned that the Japanese were seeking peace. Stalin told President Truman that the Japanese had wished to send an envoy to Moscow. A communication from the Japanese Ambassador to the U.S.S.R. read in part as follows: "On July 13, the Ambassador had had the honor to submit a proposal of the Japanese Government to send Prince Konoye to Moscow. . . . The mission of Prince Konoye was to ask the Soviet Government to take part in mediation to end the present war and to transmit the complete Japanese case in this respect. He would also be empowered to negotiate with respect to Soviet-Japanese relations during the war and after the war." Quoted in Harry S. Truman, *Memoirs,* Vol. I, *Year of Decision,* Garden City: Doubleday and Co., 1955, p. 396. Cf. also Winston Churchill, *Triumph and Tragedy,* pp. 641–642. During this crucial period, Stalin played a double game. On the one hand, he sustained Japanese hopes for a Soviet intercession which would ameliorate the Allies' harsh demand for unconditional surrender. On the other hand, Stalin appeared before the Western Allies at Potsdam as the champion of unconditional surrender. He explained his rejection of the Japanese peace feelers on that ground that he did not wish to compromise Allied war aims in the Pacific. By this stratagem, Stalin forestalled the opening of negotiations, either directly or through third parties, between Japan and the United States. The Potsdam Declaration, which was based to a certain extent on Stalin's evaluation of the situation, expressly ruled out any bargaining with Japan. As Paul Kecskemeti has shown, "there could be only one conceivable reason for a Japanese failure to surrender without delay on the terms proclaimed at

Potsdam, namely, Japan's hope that prolonged resistance would force the allies to make further concessions. The Allies ruled out the possibility that the Japanese might refrain from bowing to the Potsdam ultimatum for a different reason. Actually, such a reason did exist: the Japanese expected last-minute diplomatic help from Soviet Russia." *Strategic Surrender,* Stanford: Stanford University Press, 1958, pp. 187–188. The Soviets had it in their power to bring the war in the Far East to an end before the first A-bomb fell on Japan. They chose instead to prolong the war until they could enter it and thus gain a voice in the Far East postwar settlement. Not a few of the concessions granted to Stalin at Yalta were contingent upon a major Soviet contribution to the defeat of Japan. If, for example, the Japanese Kwantung Army had surrendered to the United States, the way would have been prepared for American rather than Soviet occupation of Manchuria. Although Stalin has insisted that the Soviet Union would not enter the Pacific War until the conclusion of a favorable agreement with Chiang Kai-shek's government, he decided, within forty-eight hours of the dropping of the atomic bomb on Hiroshima, to move against Japan. "Russia had to buy her ticket to the Pacific peace conference, but she had to hurry or the show would have started and the seats would all be taken. . . ." John R. Deane, *The Strange Alliance,* New York: Viking Press, 1947, p. 275. One of the best summary interpretations of the closing days of the Pacific War has been given by Edwin O. Reischauer: "After desperate soul searching and frantic intrigues, the Japanese government naïvely decided to seek peace through Soviet mediation, but the Russian authorities . . . were the last people in the world to desire the war to end before they had a chance to enter it. Thus the summer of 1945 witnessed one of the strangest races in history, a race between the Japanese trying to get out of the war and the Russians trying to get in, but, since only the Russians fully realized that a race was on, they of course won." *The United States and Japan,* Harvard Foreign Policy Library Series, Cambridge: Harvard University Press, 1950, p. 240.

7. Tsarist governments rarely resorted to military aggression to achieve their foreign policy objectives. Russia has enjoyed her greatest military successes in defensive rather than offensive wars. Because of her vast territories, Russia has been able to wage attritional war against two invaders—Napoleon and Hitler—and, by trading space for time, to emerge victorious. By contrast, Russia's experience in wars waged abroad or along her own borderlands has been bitter: the Crimean War, the Russo-Japanese War, World War I and the Finnish War. In this type of peripheral warfare, the Russians were beset by logistic and organizational difficulties. Although these latter problems have been rendered much less acute in the last fifteen years, they left a deep imprint upon Russian strategic thought. The Soviet leaders still follow their tsarist predecessors in preferring to rely upon indirect methods of achieving foreign policy objectives— infiltration, propaganda, subversion, diplomatic maneuvering, etc.

8. "Nothing would suit him better," said Isaac Deutscher of Stalin, "than to be first a spectator and then an arbiter in the contest to come. This ambition he could satisfy only by a deal with Hitler: an alliance with the West would have obliged Russia to fight from the first day of the war." *Stalin: A Political Biography*, New York: Oxford University Press, 1949, p. 435. George F. Kennan has observed that the Western democracies in 1939 were confronted by three dictatorial foes: Germany, Japan and the Soviet Union. Of these three, Japan was the only one which the Western democracies could have defeated without the aid of another world power. Since the two remaining world powers (i.e., Germany and the Soviet Union) were both enemies of the democratic West, it was inevitable that the West, in order to defeat one of these enemies, would have to ally itself with the other. It was this situation which allowed Stalin to play the role of the "holder of the balance." *American Diplomacy 1900–1950*, New York: New American Library, 1952, p. 74. Cf. also Chester Wilmot, *The Struggle for Europe*, New York: Harper & Broth-

ers, 1952, p. 709; N. S. Timasheff, *The Great Retreat,* p. 162; and Winston Churchill, *The Second World War: The Gathering Storm,* Boston: Houghton Mifflin Co., 1948, pp. 363 and 367.

9. It has been said that the Soviets, at the time of the Korean conflict, had no wish to be drawn into a general war with the United States on such unfavorable strategic terms as then confronted them in the Far East and globally. "In retrospect, it seems extremely doubtful that the Russians—especially before they had acquired great air-atomic capabilities—would have taken anything less than a direct attack upon their immediate sphere of control as the occasion for deliberately precipitating a total war." Robert E. Osgood, *Limited War: The Challenge to American Strategy,* Chicago: University of Chicago Press, 1957, p. 180. "It was perhaps true that the U.S.S.R. would not permit an unambiguous defeat of China in an all-out war. . . . But it does not follow that the U.S.S.R. would risk everything in order to forestall *any* transformation in our favor, all the more so as our nuclear superiority was still very pronounced." Henry A. Kissinger, *Nuclear Weapons and Foreign Policy,* Council on Foreign Relations, New York: Harper & Brothers, 1957. p. 49.

10. Heretofore, Western military writers have considered guerrilla warfare almost exclusively in purely military terms. They have been concerned primarily with the effectiveness of guerrilla tactics when employed against conventional armies. There is no question that valuable lessons can be gleaned from such a military study, for the modes of guerrilla organization and operation may come to have increasing significance in an age when technological developments make decentralization, flexibility and mobility of regular ground forces more necessary than ever. The future importance of guerrilla warfare is assured, for it is now clearly recognized as the safest method of waging open conflict within the restraints of the "balance of terror." But guerrilla warfare, during the last quarter of a century, has undergone an important transformation from a type of warfare

the objectives of which were chiefly military to a mode of conflict the objectives of which are conceived in a larger political
dimension. The Western nations are confronted today with the
new challenge of guerrilla warfare posed by the strategists of
international Communism and national liberation movements in
the "gray areas." It matters little whether this or that liberation
movement is linked with Communism: inasmuch as it places a
heavy drain on the West's conventional military strength and
seeks to dislodge a Western power from an established position of
strength on the periphery of Eurasia, its immediate strategic objectives will parallel those of the Sino-Soviet bloc. Modern guerrilla
movements are armed with elaborate psychopolitical weapons.
Guerrilla wars waged against colonial rule have wrought havoc
upon Western coalition diplomacy. Guerrilla leaders today operate
in a world linked by mass communications: every action in a remote area of the globe is instantaneously transmitted to the nerve
centers of world opinion. The daily and detailed coverage which
the Western press gave to the small-scale irregular uprising of mid-
1957 in Oman, for example, was in sharp contrast to the world's almost total lack of awareness of previous outbreaks in this remote
region before the advent of the airplane, the wire services and
the mass-circulation dailies. It is the communications network,
more than anything else, which enables the contemporary guerrilla to amplify the political effects of his terroristic methods.
The deep-rooted cultural tradition of the West renders it an easy
prey to blackmail by protracted guerrilla terror. Unlike the average citizen of a democratic country, the guerrilla does not feel
ill at ease in the presence of conflict. Since he regards conflict as
the best—indeed, the sole—means of achieving his objectives, he
is able to come to terms with terror, violence and abiding insecurity. By fomenting conflict and instability, the guerrilla levies
blackmail upon the humanitarian West's longing for peace and
thereby enhances his political bargaining power: the *quid pro
quo* is the granting of territorial independence in return for the
termination of the exhausting conflict. Jacques Soustelle, the
former Governor General of Algeria, summed up trenchantly the

dilemma of the West: "As stated by Mao Tse-tung, one of its masters, this method of war is not new in principle. It is the Spanish guerrilla against the armies of Napoleon, the fight of the Russian partisans during the Nazi invasion. But in the present world it takes on a special importance, first because the weapons for total destruction make a return to it necessary, but more because any democratic state is automatically at a disadvantage in a conflict of this nature. The extent to which public authority is divided and limited in democratic regimes, the slowness of parliamentary procedures, the restrictions on police action— all are grave impediments in counteracting terrorism. Moreover, the Western armies have adapted themselves with difficulty to the requirements of scientific war in its perfectionized form. They will have still more difficulty in reconverting themselves in order to fight a dispersed and elusive enemy who uses simple weapons, such as rifles and grenades, and vanishes into wild country or goes underground in cities and suburbs." "France Looks at Her Alliances," *Foreign Affairs*, Vol. XXXV, October, 1956, p. 124.

11. Moscow Radio spoke as follows: "A clear expression of the warm sympathy of the Soviet people for the Egyptian people . . . are the numerous statements by Soviet citizens, among whom there are great numbers of pilots, tank men, artillery men, and officers who took part in the great fatherland war and are now in reserve, asking to be allowed to go to Egypt as volunteers. . . . In leading Soviet circles it has been stated that if Britain, France and Israel do not withdraw all their troops from the territory of Egypt . . . then the appropriate authorities of the U.S.S.R. will not hinder the departure of Soviet citizen volunteers who wish to take part in the struggle of the Egyptian people for their independence." Text in Department of State Publication No. 6505, August, 1957, pp. 215–216.

12. "*Ad hoc*" proxies are those groups, parties or governments which, at a given stage of the protracted conflict, let themselves be used, wittingly or not, as vehicles of Sino-

Soviet strategy. They are linked with Moscow and Peking not by lines of command or even by formal alliances, but by the bond of immediate interests. In the countries controlled by the West, Moscow's *"ad hoc"* proxies are popular front movements, fellow-traveling organizations, and left-wing socialists of the Nenni variety; they form tactical complements to the local Communist parties and help to condition opinion in a direction favorable to Moscow. In the vast stretches of the underdeveloped world, the *"ad hoc"* proxies are the forces of radical nationalism and anti-Western extremism.

13. The first and abortive Algerian national rising occurred shortly after the First World War and was carried out under the direction of Messali Hadj, who had been trained in Moscow. The methods of the rebellion which broke out in 1954 bore a striking resemblance to the terrorist guerrilla tactics refined by the Communists in China, Malaya and Indochina. Manuals found on captured Algerian *fellaghas* prescribed what were essentially Communist-style terrorist tactics. Jacques Soustelle, "External Influences in the Algerian Rebellion," paper prepared in May 1957 for the Foreign Policy Research Institute. Apparently the Algerian rebels hoped to establish their rule over certain parts of the countryside, much as Mao Tse-tung had done in Yenan during the 1930's and Ho Chi Minh in the Tonkin Delta around 1950. In the spring of 1957, the rebels planned to capture the town of Tlemcen on the Moroccan-Algerian border and make it the provisional capital for those parts of the country which they controlled. Reto Caratsch, *The Swiss Review of World Affairs,* April, 1957. For a discussion of FLN strategy, cf. C. L. Sulzberger, "The Nationalist Strategy of Terror in Algeria," *New York Times,* June 5, 1957.

14. The Soviet effort to penetrate Syria in 1957 and to make it a satellite represented an attempt to convert an *"ad hoc"* into a controlled proxy. In the likely contingency of limited military engagements, or of political maneuvering influenced

by threats of limited military action, a satellite Syria could be of the utmost significance. It could enable the Russians to escape from the position they were formerly in, in which any military move on their side would involve action by Russia herself, and therefore a high probability of initiating World War III. " . . . [By consolidating their hold upon the government of Syria, they would be better able] to maneuver, to threaten, and even, if necessary, to attack, while preserving a high degree of security for Russia itself." Paul H. Nitze, Commentary on Vice Admiral Ruthven E. Libby, U.S.N., "Strategic Military Importance of the Middle East," in Philip W. Thayer, *Tensions in the Middle East*, Baltimore: Johns Hopkins Press, 1958, p. 46.

15. The idea of nationalization was by no means new. Back in the early 1920's, the Egyptian Socialist Communist Party had included it in its published program of objectives. Cf. Laqueur, *op cit.*, p. 34. Nationalization had also appealed to certain social reform planners following the revolution of July, 1952. Cf., e.g., Mahmoud Kamel, *Tomorrow's Egypt*, Cairo: Eastern Press, 1953, pp. 110–111. President Nasser declared at a press conference on August 12, 1956 that the actual decision was not made until *after* the United States had retracted its offer of aid for the Aswan High Dam on July 19. He was apparently anxious to allay suspicion that the subject of nationalization had been discussed at the time of Soviet Foreign Minister Shepilov's visit to Cairo during the previous June. In the postnationalization crisis, however, Nasser conferred daily with the Soviet Ambassador.

16. Western "realists" who are prone to disparage the importance of international law in modern world politics may dismiss the problem of legal responsibility as a trivial one. But the Communists, although they may be contemptuous of Western legalisms, nevertheless recognize such concepts as "ideological quirks" of the Western mind which they must take into account in plotting their strategic moves.

17. "The so-called counterinformational measures for the deception of the enemy include the dissemination of false information, demonstration attacks, diversion, dummy means and works, and various other ruses. All of these measures have as their objective the presentation of a false picture of one's own situation or possibilities to the enemy in order to cause him to react in a predetermined manner. The importance the Germans attached to deception during World War II is to be seen from the fact that they created a general staff in 1942 'for the delusion and deception of the enemy.' Misinformation—false rumors and data skillfully passed on to the enemy—has the objective of convincing the enemy of the existence of certain circumstances which possess no reality." Lieutenant Colonel Miloje Sekulich in *Vojno Delo* (Yugoslavia), NR, 4–5, 1957. Cited in *Military Review*, Fort Leavenworth, Kansas, Vol. XXXVIII, November, 1958, p. 93.

18. Russian history abounds in examples of skillful deception. One of the most famous and most amusing of these relates to the chief minister of Catherine the Great. Potemkin, anxious to impress his empress with the rate of progress made by the nation under his administration, took her on a river voyage past several "stage-prop" villages which had been constructed in South Russia especially for her journey. In recent decades, owing to the effectiveness of the Iron Curtain, the West has often been victimized by a similar deception. The Iron Curtain serves to shield from the view of the outside world the great disparity between the weaknesses of the Soviet system and the image of strength which the Communists have projected abroad. Yuri A. Rastvorov, former colonel of the MVD, has given an account of Soviet "elaborately planned deceptions" on the occasion of visits by Wendell Willkie and Henry A. Wallace to the U.S.S.R. In 1942, Rastvorov was in charge of a brigade ordered to "stage a proper welcome" for Willkie on his trip to a *sovkhoz* (state farm). After cleaning up stables and repairing roads, the brigade unloaded "a fantastic array of provisions—caviar, seafood, whisky

and champagne—all apparently for the purpose of making our visitor believe that such items were commonplace around a *sovkhoz*." "Red Fraud and Intrigue in the Far East," *Life*, December 6, 1954, p. 180. "The falsification perpetrated on Vice President Henry Wallace during his 1944 visit to Magadan in northeastern Siberia was more serious," he adds. Along the route mapped out for Henry Wallace and his party, all slave laborers and barbed-wire prison compounds were removed from sight. A special intelligence officer was assigned to Wallace to make sure that he did not wander off the chosen paths. Wallace visited the Kolyma mines which superintendent General Nikishov had once described to Rastvorov as "an arctic purgatory where men perished by the tens of thousands." "As a result of Soviet stagecraft," concludes Rastvorov, "Wallace in his book, *Soviet Asia Mission*, favorably described General Nikishov as the director of 'a combination TVA and Hudson's Bay Company.'" *Ibid.*, p. 182.

19. Soviet Academician Blagonravov, who is also a lieutenant general of artillery, admitted in an N.B.C. interview that the first Sputnik had not been launched as part of the Soviet participation in the IGY, but he gave assurances that the second one would be, and that Western scientists would be notified in advance so that they could carry out tracking operations. But Sputnik II was also launched without any prior notice. Academician Blagonravov declared on Moscow Radio: "I remember how surprised the Americans were when we launched the first sputnik. One can imagine how much more they are surprised now in learning about this new, much larger sputnik." *New York Times*, November 4, 1957.

20. "A crowd of about 2,000 people, on their way to the Parliament building to demand Gerö's removal and the withdrawal of the Soviet forces, met four Soviet tanks guarding the approaches to the Parliament building. At the sight of the unarmed crowd the tank crews reacted in a surprising manner. Instead of shooting at the demonstrators, they allowed them to

hoist the Hungarian flag on the vehicles, and then proceeded with them toward the Parliament building. As the demonstrators arrived in the large open square . . . together with the Soviet tanks, the A.V.H. formations, established in the surrounding buildings, opened fire. Hundreds of people fell dead on the ground. This frightful slaughter was stopped by the Soviet tank crews, who turned their guns on the A.V.H. men on the rooftops." George Fisher, "Twelve Days of Freedom," in *Hungary, October 1956,* Bulletin of the Committee on Science and Freedom, No. 8, April, 1957, p. 34.

21. Within the last decade, the Communists, at relatively low cost to themselves, have carried out a series of offensives in the peripheral areas, including: (1) attritional guerrilla wars in Malaya and Vietnam; (2) attritional ground war in Korea; (3) military or political support of anti-Western guerrilla movements in Algeria, Lebanon, Aden and Cyprus; (4) infiltrations and partial occupation of Burmese and Cambodian territory; (5) virtual annexation of Tibet; (6) paramilitary-political infiltration of Laos; (7) political infiltration into the governments of Indonesia, Syria and Iraq; (8) assumption of power via the ballot box in Kerala, India; (9) significant economic inroads into Burma, Afghanistan, Egypt and Syria; (10) arms shipments to anti-Western Arab governments and diplomatic support for Egypt in the Suez Canal crisis.

22. The legal concept of freedom of the seas which has prevailed in the Western state system since the end of the Napoleonic period now operates to the strategic advantage of the Communists. The Western powers have traditionally been the leading sea powers of the world. When Great Britain ruled the seas, she pursued a policy of keeping them open for the peaceful commerce of all nations. Naval hegemony passed to the United States during World War II under circumstances which made it difficult for Americans to recognize the long-range responsibility which rests with the world's leading oceanic power.

The Soviets, during the decade following the war, gradually built up a large submarine fleet, and can now, with impunity, penetrate the seas which comprise much of the strategic defense in depth of the Free World. Soviet submarines can transit the Straits of the Dardanelles, move into the Mediterranean and thus drive a naval salient into the Western defense system based in Europe and North Africa. Under existing concepts of freedom of the seas, the United States would not seriously consider lodging a protest in the U.N. against Soviet submarine activity. But at the Geneva Conference on the Law of the Seas, held in the spring of 1958, the Soviets attempted to gain acceptance for the idea that the area of the high seas should be declared "off limits" for the conduct of nuclear weapons tests and for the "aggressive movement" of surface war vessels. Later they protested vigorously against hydrogen-bomb flights over open seas.

23. Communist "missile blackmail" threats, up to the end of 1958, did not take the form of ultimata. Instead they were ambiguously worded in such a way as to raise the specter of nuclear war without ever committing the Soviets to a specific course of action. The warning delivered to the Greek government eight days before the parliamentary elections in the spring of 1958 was typical. In an interview for an independent liberal Greek newspaper, Khrushchev declared that the installation of missile and nuclear bases on Greek soil "could, in the event of the outbreak of war, attract over Greece atomic reprisals with all the tragic consequences," *New York Times,* May 4, 1958.

24. The Communists employed the same tactic, with less success, in Malaya. By 1954, it was apparent that the guerrilla war was turning against the Communist Malayan Races Liberation Army, which was being forced deeper into the jungle and further isolated from the civilian community on which it depended for support. The Communists, to reduce the military pressure against them and to cut down the growing number of defections, shifted to political maneuvers. They realized, how-

ever, that a "truce campaign" would make little headway among the authorities of the Malayan Federation who had been fighting them for six years and who were wise to their ways. Consequently, the Communists by-passed the local commanders in Malaya and raised their "trial balloon" where they thought it would do more good, namely in Great Britain. Communist delegates to the Trades Unions Congress called for a cease-fire in Malaya in September, 1954. The British, however, saw through the Communist stratagem and ignored the truce overture. Cf. "The Emergency in Malaya," *World Today*, Vol. X, November, 1954; *New York Times*, September 11, 1954; and "Election Year in Malaya," *The Economist*, January 15, 1955.

25. There is widespread belief in both Finland and Sweden that Finnish "independence" is intimately linked with continued Swedish neutrality. If Sweden, so runs the argument, were to join NATO or a pro-Western Scandinavian defense pact, the Soviet Union would retaliate by occupying Finland. Thus Soviet respect for the "independence" of Finland is considered to be the *quid pro quo* of Swedish neutrality. Cf. Samuel Abrahamsen, *Sweden's Foreign Policy*, Washington: Public Affairs Press, 1957, p. 91.

26. The letters addressed by Nikolai Bulganin (then Premier and spokesman for Nikita Khrushchev, but recently demoted) to President Eisenhower and the heads of Allied governments in 1957 were not confidential documents. They were intended for publication. They were missiles of propaganda warfare rather than notes of diplomacy and aimed at public opinion outside of the Communist bloc. Since the Communist rulers do not tolerate free discussion at home, their propaganda campaign for a "summit" conference is being waged— like all "Cold War" battles—upon the territory of the Free World.

27. By dint of constant repetition, the Marxist view of the West saturated the leading universities of the Western

world during the early decades of the twentieth century, whence
they influenced the thinking of not a few Asian students who
later led their countries' struggle for independence. These leaders, drawing upon the history of their own countries, eloquently
reinforced the facile assumption that "colonial empires are established by sea powers, whereas expansion into contiguous
land masses does not produce 'empires' or colonialism." Hans
Kohn, "Reflections on Colonialism," in *The Idea of Colonialism*,
ed. by Robert Strausz-Hupé and Harry W. Hazard, New York:
Praeger, 1958, p. 7. This observation suggests an important historic contrast between the imperialism of the Eastern nations
and that practiced by the Western states in modern times. The
former, historically speaking, have extended their sway over
primitive peoples or senile cultures in the interior of the Eurasian
Continent (the Soviets in Outer Mongolia, for example; the
Chinese Communists in Tibet). The Western powers, on the
other hand, established hegemony over relatively civilized peoples along the borderlands of Asia and Africa, easily accessible
to ships. The primitives of Central Asia have neither the political
consciousness nor the communications resources to make an effective protest against Russian or Chinese Communist imperialism.
In contrast, even the primitives who have fallen under Western
colonialism have an opportunity, through trusteeship arrangements in the U.N., to air their grievances in the international
forum. But in the twentieth century, the enemies of the West
have turned the West's own revolutionary political concepts
against it. "The anti-Western movements, products of the deep
anti-Western resentment felt by the insufficiently Westernized
countries and classes, knew the argumentative vulnerability of
the West and exploited it. They took over concepts developed
in the free West since the seventeenth or eighteenth centuries
like 'democratic liberties,' 'right of self-determination,' or 'nationalism,' divested them of the moral and political context within
which alone they were meaningful, and used them in this subverted form against the West. . . . Thus in recent times the Russians 'liberated' Ukraines and Georgians, Lithuanians and Lat-

vians . . . in the name of nationalism and national self-determination." Hans Kohn, *Is the Liberal West in Decline?*, London: Pall Mall Press, 1957, pp. 45–46.

28. Throughout history, the garrison state has erected barriers against the contaminating effect of contacts with free societies, and modern Russia is no exception to this traditional behavior of totalitarian regimes. George F. Kennan has described this phenomenon as follows: "At the bottom of the Kremlin's neurotic view of world affairs is the traditional and instinctive sense of insecurity, stemming from the days when the Russians were a peaceful agricultural people, living on a vast, defenseless plain in the neighborhood of fierce nomadic tribes. To this, as Russia grew and came into contact with the West, was added a fear of the more competent, more powerful, highly organized societies which the Russian rulers there encountered. This latter sense of insecurity . . . afflicted the rulers rather than the Russian people, for Russian rulers have invariably sensed that their rule was relatively archaic in form, fragile and artificial in its psychological foundations, unable to stand comparison or contact with political systems of Western countries. For this reason, they have always feared foreign penetration, feared direct contact between the Western world and their own, feared what would happen if the Russians learned the truth about the world without or if foreigners learned the truth about the world within. And they have learned to seek security only in patient but deadly struggle for the total destruction of rival power, never in compacts and compromises with it." This is a paraphrase of the dispatch written by George F. Kennan while he was Chargé d'Affaires of the U.S. Embassy in Moscow, and which is recognized as the basis of his now famous article, "The Sources of Soviet Conduct." Walter Millis, ed. *The Forrestal Diaries*, New York: Viking Press, 1951, p. 136.

APPENDIX • COMMUNIST PSYCHOLOGICAL WARFARE *

During the Second World War, the term "psychological warfare" was brought into official use by Americans who wanted to employ propaganda against the Nazis, but desired to camouflage such ungentlemanly activities with a name sounding less offensive to American ears. Since the United States to this date has not waged psychological warfare, but restricted itself to propaganda undertakings, the term has given rise to unfortunate misunderstandings. It gave the exaggerated impression that something significant was being done, thereby hindering the investigation of what needed to be done. Desultory attempts at propaganda were mistaken for psychological warfare, a misconception which had disastrous results for the security of the United States.

AMERICAN LIMITATIONS

Most American propaganda is based on the assumption that people tend to act rationally and that "truth always prevails." [1] This conviction is an integral and inevitable part of the demo-

---

* This study by "Ferreus" (Stefan T. Possony) was previously published in *Orbis*, Vol. I, Spring, 1957, No. I. Grateful acknowledgment is made to the author and to the editors of *Orbis*.
[1] Nazi propaganda was nothing more than the obverse of these propositions: people tend to act irrationally, and truth—in addition to being indeterminate—prevails far less frequently than skillful lies. The discussion will show that the Communists are operating in far broader terms. At least in the sphere of psychological operations, the Communists are far more "totalitarian" than even the most radical Nazis.

cratic doctrine. This is not to say that American propaganda in each and every case is living up to its principles. Violations are unavoidable, but if they occur, they are resented and deplored. The principles as such are beyond challenge.

The American advertising and communications industries have worked out effective methods of appeal to audiences, and they have pioneered in the invention or development of "media." American propaganda is a continuation of publicity with the same means. Both political propaganda and publicity are most often predicated on the rationalistic postulate that the customer wants to be convinced about the excellence of the merchandise he is invited to buy. The customer expects and accepts proof, whether he is in the market for toothpaste or a political system. Conversely, American political propaganda assumes that, to the extent that a system, a creed, or a merchandise, cannot be proven to be satisfactory, it will be rejected.

Thus, the most usual American propaganda is an exercise in rhetorical persuasion, except that the strength of the logical argument is fortified by brevity, style, emphasis, omission, distortion and repetition, as well as "catching" devices to attract attention. Propaganda is applied to the mind as cosmetics are to the face.

Hence, propaganda affects only a small segment of the human psyche. If we were to take the term "psychological warfare" seriously, we would have to undertake many activities *in addition* to persuasion: we should aim at attaining a total psychological impact. Instead of limiting ourselves to "cosmetics," we would have to form or remold the entire face. Dr. Faustus, if he were to be a modern "target" of "psywar," would not just donate his soul to the devil but would have his soul remade by the "psy-warrior." In brief, psychological warfare aims at making *homunculum ex hominem*.

American literature does not indicate that anyone has as yet tackled psychological warfare as a problem of soul surgery. It is probably fair to say that there are no well-defined concepts of what psychological warfare is or could be. However, such a statement cannot be made confidently about the Communists. In fact, there are many disquieting indications that the Communists may have developed, or stumbled upon, an all-inclusive or a totalitarian doctrine of psychological warfare.

COMMUNIST PSYCHOLOGICAL ASSUMPTIONS

Perhaps the most striking characteristic of Communist propaganda is how dull and unconvincing it is. Its arguments are not logically persuasive and their presentation more often than not is repellent and not attractive. The fact that, nevertheless, Communism has been able to achieve considerable successes, even in the intellectual domain, has been puzzling to many analysts. One explanation of this apparent mystery may be found in the circumstance that the Communists do not at all aim to "persuade" the mind. Instead they seem to be orienting the *souls* of their audience. If we accept this as our first hypothesis, we should assume next that the techniques of soul surgery should become clearest in situations where they are easiest to apply. Hence, instead of looking for such techniques in the field of international diplomacy, we should expect that Communist psywar techniques are revealed most dramatically in the indoctrination of party members and in the activities commonly called "brainwashing" or "brain changing." The treatment of war and political prisoners, including party members, of young party recruits, and of captive populations may give more valuable hints about the Communists' secret doctrine of psychological warfare than their purely verbal efforts in so-called propaganda campaigns.

Perhaps the best method of coming to grips with this elusive problem is to review briefly the various schools of modern psychology and see whether or not their teachings have been applied, in one way or the other, by Communist operators.

The Communists have acknowledged that they owe considerable debt to Ivan P. Pavlov and to his discovery of the conditioned reflex. This theory, especially if reinterpreted, can be evolved as a supplement to the basic theorem of Marxism, that a change in social conditions will transform man. In addition to rejecting the "subjective" or "will" factor, the Pavlovian or post-Pavlovian theory asserts that man's reflexes and behavior are controlled by signals—social conditions, words and mass communications—which in turn are controllable by scientific procedures. Thus, man's behavior is decided by "objective" factors and, to the extent that those factors can be manipulated, is determinable. The person is "other-directed" by state or party or, in their absence, by economic "forces"; psychological processes can be managed, fixed, or altered; and man can be "transformed."

Fundamentally, the Communists hold that behavior, especially the behavior of groups, classes and nations, can be manipulated through the conditioning of reflexes, a circumstance which is particularly important for those situations where the human animal is denied food and treated to overdoses of ringing bells. To a large extent, this theory underlies Soviet propaganda, especially its insistence on monotonous repetition and its capture of all the symbolic words which, so to speak, "ring a bell." As usual in the case of "planners," it is not specified how the planners can be planned, or how the human "conditioners" can be conditioned. It can be deduced from this significant omission that the Communists assume their own elite's freedom from the conditioned reflex mechanism and construe Pavlov's theory not as an interpretation of behavior as such but as a tool of struggle and domination.

Undoubtedly, the Communists learned from Pavlov a great deal about the interrelationships between physiology and psychology. This knowledge allows them, in their domestic and intraparty operations, to influence behavior through proper regulation of work, food and leisure, that is, to get at the mind through the body. More important is the probability that the Communists are making conscious use of Pavlov's findings concerning methods whereby psychological disturbances can be induced in living organisms. Pavlov has shown that by the manipulation of stimuli, the desire for independent action, or what he called the "freedom urge," can be weakened or extinguished and neurotic behavior be induced.

The artificial creation of insanity—a device which the Communists have applied to their prisoners by subjecting them to various forms of "invisible torture" such as uncertainty, fear, sleeplessness, strong light effects, and kneeling or standing—may not lend itself to the treatment of large numbers of people. However, unpredictable behavior, the acceleration and calming of disturbances and crises, alternations between smiles and growls, i.e., variable creations and releases of fear, and the maintenance of tension in perpetuity may induce quasi-neurotic behavior, increase the values of the "signal" (as, for example, those of the bell as against the food), and facilitate the acceptance of new word-signals. Whatever one may think of the determinism inherent in Pavlovian thinking, a deliberate application of such techniques makes it possible to implant in human minds numerous notions such as "A follows B," which are not only false as to fact but also inhibit the learning of the proper sequences. The ensuing disorientation cannot fail but produce lasting mental crises or, at least, serious maladjustments.

Perhaps more surprising than the Communist loans from Pavlov are their unacknowledged adoptions of the findings of Sigmund Freud. By interfering with family life and placing major emphasis on public education of infants, the father image is vested in an external and nonhuman entity, the state or the party. This method of rearing children probably induces them to become more submissive to higher authority; it undoubtedly aims at restricting the sphere of private life and conceivably—if the theories of the cultural anthropologists of Freudian persuasion have any validity—alters the emotional structure. It has been observed that the role both of the father and the mother in the Russian family is somewhat different from that of the Western European family, the Russian family containing an agglomerate of aunts and nurses, and thus of many "mothers," while the father exercises more remote and, at the same time, more arbitrary authority.

The value systems which are being inculcated by the Soviets exploit pre-existing Russian patterns. The Soviets make sure that the human herd obeys the "signals" of authority, while individual consciousness, emotionality and initiative remain underdeveloped. The relegation of sex and other types of affection to minor and regressive roles—not only Hegel but also Freud has been stood upon his head—induces, or rather is expected to induce, "sublimation" through productive work and party chores. This particular technique is employed to transform human beings into mere cogs within a gigantic machine.

The Communists adopted, although not for curative purposes, the basic techniques of psychoanalysis, in particular the psychoanalytic interview. Normally, such an interview is designed to determine the causes of psychological disturbance. It aims at the removal of these causes through their identification and is predicated on the assumption that this identification is possible through analysis of dreams and verbal associations, and the discovery of semantic blockages and *Fehlleistungen*. The psychoanalytic interview between physician and patient obviously would be impractical if patients were to be treated in large numbers. Hence the Communists have developed more streamlined methods which allow the mass production, not of cures, but of "complexes" and "traumas." These techniques include the compulsory writing of diaries, autobiographies and histories of one's thought development; of oral interviews with party members; of hearings before organizational and ideological commissions and the political police; and of public "confessions."

The purpose of these interviews, which may be repeated many times, is to inculcate in the "patient" feelings of error, guilt, shame, and fear, as well as desires for repentance and revenge— and to make available to the party powerful levers of blackmail. The expectation is that, through this process, the patient's conscience will be weakened, his will to obey and believe increased, his survival instincts stimulated, and he be made pliable for party purposes.

Normally, these procedures will be successful: since practically everyone is actually or potentially "guilty" within the framework of the Communist code—because no one ever failed to doubt the dogma or to wish escape from party discipline, and because every sane person has family and property instincts—the average "patient" can be relied upon to produce the trauma by himself. Whenever a person in whom the party is interested shows himself capable of resisting, individual and active treatment is indicated. This treatment may vary between outright pressure and terrorization, and "persuasion" of the kind described in Arthur Koestler's *Darkness at Noon*.

Whether the treatment be self-inflicted or "other-directed," the very submission to this process is conducive to guilt and shame. Even if there is no specific treatment at all, the adoption of the artificial Communist creed must produce guilt complexes, as does, within a Communist-controlled nation or within the party, the negation of the "accepted" code. Many of these guilt complexes are essentially social and political in nature—"I have sinned against my class," "I am a saboteur and exploiter"—and they expose the person to the dangers of nonconformism. Whenever the Communists succeed in convincing people that they are a sort of incarnation of humanity's social conscience and that they are history's anointed arbiters of any action undertaken by non-Communists, a person will tend to be apologetic about any doubts he may be harboring concerning Communism. Opposition to or deviation from Communism is tantamount to a negation of mankind's loftiest ideals and of mankind's inevitable future.

The Communists try to exploit, negatively and positively, a person's relationship to communities such as his family. In this connection they have adopted or reinvented, in their own fashion, Alfred Adler's theory of the inferiority complex and the power urge; they evoke in the "patient" various feelings of insufficiency, thus hoping to stimulate him into compensatory action which would satisfy the power cravings of his own self and of the party.

These processes aim, as does psychoanalysis, at catharsis, or the cleansing of old thoughts and emotions. While the therapist wants to eliminate the sources of trouble, the Communist psychological manipulator works toward the destruction of the self-reliant personality. To employ modern terms, he tries his hand at "brainwashing." Once this operation has been completed, a supplementary activity, "brain changing," must be undertaken. In this effort the Communists, strange though it may sound, have either taken their cue from Saint Ignatius of Loyola, and perhaps from such mystics as Saint Teresa, or else they have rediscovered the mystical processes in their own way. The brain is being emptied of mundane thoughts, while simultaneously and wherever possible the body is being weakened and the sensuous drives are being subdued by fatigue, hunger, deprivation and anguish. The mind enters a state or receptivity and exaltation. At this point, thoughts, ideas, symbols and emotions—in short "visions"—are put into the cleansed mind. The "patient"—who may be a member of a Western Communist party or a student at a party "university"—is invited to learn by rote some of the basic texts of the Communist literature. He is asked to write down the various thoughts which he considers as the right ones, and to apply the doctrine to current and concrete issues. He may even be asked to participate in conspiratorial activities and to commit himself through acts of immorality, which may range all of the way from informing and spying to the betrayal of one's parents, from leading a lynching party to straight murder.[2] The propositions of the doctrine must be *attached to the person* by extreme emotions. Wherever possible, this process is eased by public discussions, such as "democratic criticism," confession, trials, etc., which may induce trance or, conversely, "hardening" the soul.

Hypnotic and suggestive techniques seem to be used extensively. The "patient" is invited to emulate Coué; he must indulge in autosuggestion and tell himself, often by mechanical repetition, that he is becoming a better Communist, that he is cutting

[2] This "tradition" goes back to Nechayev and was described by Dostoyevski in *The Possessed*.

himself loose from all the black shadows of the past, and that he desires to sacrifice himself to the cause. In addition, his manipulators follow the standard practices of hypnosis or, in any event, of suggestion, to make sure that the suitable thoughts really stick. An interesting aspect of this process is that the "patients" themselves, while learning and acquiring the proper reflexes, must emit the signals to which they themselves and the others must react. The insistence on parrotlike repetition is designed to harden the conditioned reflexes, to maintain a system of mutual suggestion or hypnosis, and to "fix" the desired complexes.

Two key terms of modern psychotherapy have special importance: frustration and guilt. By identifying existing frustrations and stimulating them, the Communists gain recruits and undermine foreign societies. Marx's early identification of the proletarian as the frustrated man *par excellence* has been abandoned, so has the notion that, psychologically, economic frustration is particularly potent. The Communists did not buy Freud's concept of the overriding significance of sex frustration. Instead they try to latch on to professional, social (and racial) status and intellectual-cultural frustrations, to the persons who place themselves outside the pale of their own society. The intent is not to allow these frustrations to incapacitate the man but, on the contrary, to transform them into aggressive impulses.

The international manipulation of guilt complexes comes out plastically in the Communist emphasis on the distinction between just and unjust wars. Command efficiency and troop morale are lowered through guilt feelings. A nation is more likely to win in conflict if it considers its cause to be just. Hence the Communists try to arrange matters in such a way that any war they are fighting will be a just war, while any war fought by a democratic nation will be unjust. The purpose is to inculcate into the Free World guilt feelings about resistance to Communism and at the same time immunize the "Soviet peoples" with a sort of ideological vaccination against any notion that Communist wars or even aggressions may be something less than emanations of an exalted sense of justice. The Free World has been infected to some degree by bad conscience and guilt feelings. Hence, partly at least, the often surprising paralysis of democratic will.

Apparently, the Communists have not much use for the teachings of C. G. Jung, except that they employ their own variations of the concept of the "archetypes" which says that the mind has a basic symbolic structure. One of the Communist concepts resembles the *"persona"* among Jung's archetypes:people are not what they seem to be or think they are; their true role is determined by objective factors. Ideology is of an apologetic and concealing nature; a person's thinking does not reflect truth. A capitalist, for example, plays a socially predetermined role. He may be subjectively honest—e.g., he may honestly wish for peace—but his true character is entirely different from such outward manifestations. He *must* be an aggressor and exploiter, and cannot help but act in accordance with this objective role rather than his ideological "mask."

The social universe is broken down into such archetypical relationships as classes and strata, exploiter and exploited, class-conscious Communists and backward elements, "comrade" and enemy, organizations and inert forces, etc. The craving for justice is monopolized in the sense that, according to the suggestion, only the Communists ever can really satisfy it. All basic human needs are to be satisfied by Communism; hence the *hic et nunc* Communist party member is the personification and the party the super-ego manifestation of ultimate human destiny. Communism, to put it differently, is both a myth which fulfills the eternal human requirement for myths, and a myth which satisfies the concrete needs of orientation—it gives direction and purpose to a man's daily chores.

This whole dimension of mythology does not replace the basic human relationships between parents and children, brothers and sisters, man and wife, friend and friend, but supplements them, thus modifying the personality structure in an important way. As a result of this change, expectation of punishment and reward, and emotional gratification are profoundly affected.

COMMUNIST SURROGATES FOR RELIGION

In this connection the Communists' drive against religion assumes particular importance. Modern psychology, partly in the wake of the findings of Jung and Karl Jaspers, has pointed to the interrelationship of religion and mental health: To the extent that a person like Prometheus overinflates his own ego, considers himself to be the ultimate judge of values, and preoccupies himself almost exclusively with his own desires, satisfactions, and frustrations—with the self rather than with his role in the universe—he loses balance and grows vulnerable to mental disease. If, however, he is able to evaluate his station in life properly and recognize objective "metaphysical" forces and obligations, his mental health is more or less secure.

In their attempts to undermine hostile societies, the Communists make every effort to destroy religious, ethical and other higher motivations, in the expectation that the preoccupation with immediate, mundane, material and private interests and the destruction of spiritual reserves will create frustrations and "atomize" society.[3] As religious beliefs wane, the number of possible recruits for Communism tends to increase. This is so not only because there is a mechanical relationship between Communism and atheism but, more significantly, because the human hunger for redemption and assurance must be stilled and because the archetypical desire for a God craves satisfaction. Communism redeems on earth and proclaims man to be "God." The revolution is seen as the crucial "religious" event which transforms man from the "object" into the "subject" of history, i.e., into the "creator" of the perfect society. Paradise is moved from the origin to the destination of man's wandering. Human limitations no longer are accepted as given but, in the Communist creed, the original sin is seen in the assumption of an anti- or nonrevolution-

[3] The term "atomize" was used extensively during the early thirties by romantic "national Bolshevik" writers in Germany: If a person ceases to be a member of a close community, he becomes a social "atom." Structural society transforms itself into an amorphous "sum" of atoms: persons become numbers.

ary attitude. Man is the maker of man, and the party re-creator of human relationships beyond the state of alienation.

The Communists' most powerful weapon in their onslaught on religion is "social criticism" addressed to situations of economic hardship, oppression, racial tension, delinquency, family trouble, and to shortcomings of religious organizations. The purpose of "social criticism" is to produce frustration-consciousness and persuade people that they cannot take such frustrations in their stride, let alone sublimate them by religious abnegation and hope for the hereafter. Instead they must overcome them by revolutionary and violent action, and by active sacrifice. Frustration, let us note, is a forerunner of aggressiveness, especially if aggressive impulses can be instigated or stimulated artificially.

Similarly, ethics are derived from religious precepts and divine commands. Although this should not be taken as an argument for or against a particular theory of ethical thinking, it tallies with a common habit of thinking, especially in less advanced societies. Yet again, to keep ethical motivation strong, the modern moralist must find better arguments than justifications from weakened religious beliefs. There is a vacuum in the "upper reaches" of modern man's mind. The Communists did not tarry to move into the void.

To the extent, therefore, that religion is eliminated as the Basic Premise, the individual is thrown back onto his own mental resources. He looks for another Basic Premise and abandons himself to hedonistic and other ego-centered drives. Most importantly, having been deprived of the basis of certainty, he loses judgment and, above all, the Job-like steadfastness in trouble. These changes in our thought patterns which were inevitable but which require hardy personalities, have opened up a major psychological vulnerability.

By contrast, the Communists must find for the societies under their rule a substitute for religion as a foundation of mental health. They cannot adopt religion, certainly not openly, because this would sensitize human conscience and thus undermine the foundations of their state and their world movement. Neither can they condone hedonistic tendencies or any objective, probabilistic, open-minded and multivalued thinking which would jeopardize their dogmatic ideology and, most significantly in our context, preclude the effective application of psywar, Communist style. Their obvious solution is, first, to peddle the pseudo-religion of materialistic Communism; second, to retain the archetypical aspects of religions: faith, brotherhood, initiation, salvation, redemption, grace, paradise, consecration, guilt, sin, sacrifice, atonement, ascetism—all of which have their counterparts in the Communist ideology; and third, to be excessively dogmatic about it all.

Communist dogmatism knows of saints and devils, incantations, indices of forbidden books, self-chastisement, anathemas upon heretics, ritualism, exegesis, apologetics, mysticism and talmudism (but not of a wailing wall for the leaders in power). This quasi-religiousness is at the bottom of the various psychoanalytic and hypnotic techniques which, without this "spiritual" foundation, probably would not "take."

There is still another way of looking at this problem. To the extent that Communism embraces a materialistic or atheistic cosmogony, it *is* religion. It answers one of the basic human questions by pointing to matter, the laws of nature, and accident as the causes and meaning of the universe and, by implication, to true death and extinction as the future. Communism admits the existence of a higher power, but it assumes that power—or force—to be "blind" and nonpersonal. Thus, it purges religion of the concept of a higher power which is purposive, and it rejects the notion of a higher power which has revealed its purposes in terms understandable by humans. Thus, it accepts the idea that higher forces are intervening in human lives, but it assumes this intervention to be entirely accidental and meaningless. Thus, it postulates that "science" may give man a capability to influence the higher forces, nay to dominate them, but it rejects any idea of a personal relationship of man with God. Thus, it accepts brotherliness and *Sobornost'*, so important in the history of the Russian Church, but it perverts both into party discipline. The ethical contents, and, in particular, the dimensions of love, are removed from religion. Politics are dehumanized by the denial of man's creation in the image of God (*ad similitudinem dei*).

There is, then, no choice but that the State incarnate the Supreme Being. The dictator becomes God, the only God for that matter; and the party becomes the church. As a variant, collective leadership becomes a sort of Trinity. The Central Committee and the local leaders take care of polytheistic needs. The parallels could be pressed further. The point is that all the essential mundane elements of religion except the Virgin Mother complexes are represented.

COMMUNIST SOCIOLOGICAL ASSUMPTIONS

Many schools of psychology are agreed on the importance of fear and anxiety. According to Pierre Janet, the higher functions of the human mind are dependent on an interplay of the various psychological forces operating at high tension but merging into a state of psychological equilibrium. If this equilibrium is disturbed or the tension (or energy) lowered, the higher functions, especially creative thinking and moral stamina, suffer regressions or become inoperative. Fear and anxiety are considered by Janet to be among the main factors which hinder the proper working of the mind. Karen Horney, though a follower of Freud in many respects, deviated from the master by assuming that fear and anxiety are responsible for many of the psychological difficulties which Freud ascribed to sex frustration. Whatever the specific theories, there is little doubt that fear is frequently a cause of human difficulty, that it diminishes survival capabilities of all kinds, and that it is the disintegrating factor *par excellence*. This, of course, is not a new discovery for the political practitioner. It is not surprising that the Communists always have laid great stress on terror, violence and purges, and nowadays have enlisted the specter of nuclear war in their strategy of terror. In the dimension of psychological warfare, they do not expect that much will come from further readings of the *Communist Magnifesto*, let alone of Lenin's *Empirio-Criticism*, but they usually obtain good results from military threats and movements, and from giving the impression that they are willing to go beyond the "brink of war." The "specter" of Communism now is in the nature of a ghost in the closet. The specter that really haunts the world is that of a technological *Golem* heavily armed with nuclei and bacilli and propelled forward by jets and rockets.

However, the Communists have added an "improvement" to the age-old art of inducing fright. Men no longer fear a phenomenon once its nature has been understood and once the phenomenon's behavior has become predictable. A danger that is perceived clearly may become a stimulant for action—a most unwelcome possibility. Consequently, the Communists have adopted the techniques of erecting impenetrable "curtains" and of acting unpredictably and capriciously, for example, by alternating smiles with growls, arresting the innocent and freeing the guilty, keeping prisoners in captivity beyond their terms but releasing them at any odd moment, and in general showing themselves impervious to reasonable argument and immovable by counsels of moderation. Deliberately, the impression is being created that one never can know what is going to happen next; even if everything is calm now, the "next" disturbance may be of unparalleled violence.

Let us look at one example of Soviet "irrational" behavior. The Soviet predilection of giving consistently an inflated impression of Communist strength is unsound, according to all rules of the military art. Schlieffen's motto, generally accepted by thinking soldiers, was, *"Mehr sein als scheinen."* Specifically, this method was considered as sound by a foremost Soviet expert, Marshal Boris Shaposhnikov. But the opposite axiom: "Appear stronger than you really are," is a most rewarding one for the purposes of psychological operations, especially if the victim's reactions to the Soviet strategy of terror can be inhibited by a show of phony friendliness. The technique of blowing hot and cold and of alternating confusing signals was used by Pavlov to instigate "neurotic" behavior in his dogs. It is entirely acceptable to international politics.

"Frequency modulation" in diplomacy is designed to dislocate a nation's fortitude. The technique is patterned after Hitler's pioneering attempts during 1936–1939. The ups and down from expectations of "peace in our generation" to fears of total war, and the frequent rearrangements between "business as usual" and war preparedness, led to a frame of mind best expressed by Neville Chamberlain's *"Il faut en finir."* Rational decision-making had become quite impossible. While in 1939 the decision at long last was for resistance, the Communists apparently expect that in future the democratic decision will be against nuclear war. The peace above all" theme, punctuated and made convincing by war scares, is designed to kill the *national conscience*.

Another important cause of mental disturbances has been identified by Emile Durkheim in his concept of *anomie*. Durkheim showed that anomic situations lead to acute frustrations which manifest themselves, for example, in rising suicide rates. Other sociologists, such as Ferdinand Toennies, have amplified this concept by pointing out that, to be psychologically healthy, the individual needs a close community life (*Gemeinschaft*). Precisely because society has changed into a functional and utilitarian association, the individual needs emotional security and close human relations. The structure of the over-all society must be intelligible so that the individual can orient himself within it. His dependence on the large group must offer gratifications sufficient to evoke in him feelings of loyalty, pride of membership, dedication, conviction, etc.

The Communists aim to produce *anomie* through propaganda, class warfare, infiltration, disintegration, policy sabotage and other revolutionary and subversive operations. The psychological effects are not long in coming. Given an anomic situation, it is relatively easy to obtain gratifying results with suggestive rather than persuasive propaganda and to induce in large numbers of people some kind of neurotic behavior characterized by hopelessness, obsessions, compulsions, and fears of failure. Protracted disturbances undermine motivation, dedication, loyalty, the community spirit, and all those attitudes which keep society going.

As this assault bears fruit and creates defeatism and listlessness, *anomie* grows with cumulative force.

The normal individual in a normal society experiences his society as a going concern and a working whole. His understanding of his own functions and positions is based on a—usually intuitive —apperception of social structure. In the absence of such an apperception—and the intuitive understanding can be weakened by verbal "cross-signals"—he will act atomistically, just as does the person who has lost religious or ethical motivations. In short, the Communists try to destroy what could be called the integrating elements of society.

COMMUNIST CROWD PSYCHOLOGY

It will come as no surprise that the Communists are close students of crowd psychology. They have learned Gustave Le Bon's fundamental postulate that crowd behavior is characterized by the temporary weakening or loss of restraint and reason. Crowds are suggestible, aggressive and destructive. "Crowd mentality," i.e., the loss of impulse and action controls, is contagious. Going beyond Le Bon, the Communists have discovered that "crowds" are not formed just by direct physical contacts among a mass of people, such as in meetings or demonstrations, but that, in modern times, crowd attitudes can be created among people who are physically isolated. It is merely necessary to arouse excessive fears, exploit a calamity, stimulate a panicky attitude, give signals for action against scapegoats or for actions with a symbolic character, and keep the majority of the population paralyzed. It is easy to see how the application of conditioned reflexes and fears to otherwise straightforward propaganda operations can contribute greatly to the *Vermassung* of modern man. One of the great objectives is to induce in all hostile groups the attitude of *nevolya*—"no will."

However, the Communists know that crowds do not originate or move by themselves but must be created and led. Activating concepts are as necessary as paralyzing ideas. Therefore, the principal aim of Communist activities is to render the revolutionary leadership group capable of performing the "rape of the masses." This leadership group must be endowed with one predominant characteristic: "iron will" impervious to the attrition of time. The Communists have borrowed Nietzsche's concept of the "length of will." Will is iron only if the commitment is total in all dimensions, time included. The Communist leader is a person who cannot turn his back on Communism, and the comrades see to it that defections of leaders do not really occur, even in the case of expulsions and purges.[4]

COMMUNIST SELECTION PROCESSES

In establishing their party cadres and developing proper leadership, the Communists make extensive use of elaborate methods of selection. There is no evidence that they have been employing so-called projective tests, for example of the Rorschach type, but they do not need those. Unlike the normal psychological investigator who is called upon to make *a priori* findings about people, the Communists are able to test their people *in action* and put them under strains of various types before selecting them for responsible positions.

There are essentially five aspects of the Communist selection process:

1. The candidate is requested to prepare extensive biographical accounts of himself and to repeat this literary effort several times for the purpose of revealing whatever personal weaknesses or strengths there might be in him.

2. The individual must show a capability of absorbing the Communist doctrine and at the same time eliminating non-Communist thoughts. This result is achieved by restricting his reading to approved Communist texts, by having him learn many

---

[4] It is noteworthy that the Russian language has quite a few terms for leader and leadership, some of which have the meaning not only of command but also of ordering in the sense of arranging. The term *upravlenie* refers to bureaucratic actions and denotes impersonal leadership. The term *rukovodstvo*, literally leading by the hand, is applied to leadership by the dictator and the presidium. The first is a society (*Gesellschaft*), the second a community (*Gemeinschaft*) term.

of these by rote, and by keeping track, through diaries, of the person's intellectual development. It is assumed, usually quite correctly, that the systematic recording of one's thoughts and feelings easily reveals doubts, uncertainties and dishonesties in thinking, although it may not always disclose a person's true intent.

Very frequently the method is amplified to embrace group tests. The individual is forced to participate actively in group discussions about current and theoretical problems to the point of being able to defend them convincingly, and thus show his proficiency in mastering the doctrine. Sometimes the Communists go one step further, especially in countries which they control, and stage "psychodramas," for example, in the form of party trials and public confessions. In many instances these psychodramas are employed to give satisfaction to sadomasochistic drives (punishments, lynchings, etc.). The public confessions in purge trials serve the double purpose of destroying undesirable comrades both physically *and* morally, while committing them to maintaining party discipline, even to the point of self-destruction, and of giving a dramatic signal for a general persecution of all persons who hold opinions similar to those of the accused and of setting the model for similar "confessions" in the lower echelons.

3. In accepting an individual into the party, and particularly into the apparatus, the Communists see to it that the party satisfies all his needs for community and personal life. The major needs are taken care of to such an extent that, even if the party member should lose faith, his personal attachments would keep him in the fold. He has no place to go and he fears separation from the party because it would deprive him of all his friends, perhaps of his family, and most frighteningly, of his thought patterns and his mission in life. (One of the central purposes of Communist selection methods is to find *extrovert* activists.)

4. Great emphasis is placed on evoking in the member an emotional attachment to his "iron will." He must develop an image of self characterized by such ceaselessly repeated words as merciless, implacable, irreconcilable, ruthless, relentless, fearless,

etc. He must work himself into a "burning hatred" and adopt the uncompromising thought pattern of *Kto Kovo*—who will destroy whom? Feelings of any subjective kind must be suppressed: there are only two types of people, the comrades and the "others," who are enemies. Fight is the sum and substance of a Communist's existence. If there is less than total commitment to permanent conflict, the candidate is not suitable.

5. The party employs the member for many chores and tasks, gladly pushing him into ever more responsible and perilous assignments. It is on the basis of his behavior in tight situations, his initiative and drive as an "organizer," and his ability to instill class hatred in others, that the final evaluation of his capacity and reliability is made. These methods are strengthened considerably by more brutal forms of pressure such as the splitting up of families, keeping of hostages, involvement in criminal acts, and in general the incorporation into the party of the member's entire family, including his children or, conversely, the encouragement of liaisons and marriages between party members.

Persons who submit to these various tests and pressures willingly, espouse the creed with unquestioning faith, show absolutely no propensity for critical and independent judgment, obey every type of order in strict discipline—but who also are capable of giving orders and running other party members firmly and ruthlessly—these persons are promoted to the highest ranks of the party. There they form a modern version of the old janissaries, the erstwhile protectors of the Turkish empire.

COMMUNIST COMMUNICATIONS THEORY

Within these various efforts, the modern tool of radio has played a great role, although older tools such as newspapers, posters and books have not been neglected. Inside the areas under Communist control, all audiences are "captive." The radios are ubiquitous and noisy, and cannot be turned off. The purpose is to prevent independent thinking, to make sure that whatever message goes into a person's mind is of an approved and planned type, and to drown out all messages which interfere with the process of conditioning. Through the propagation of noise, the nervous equilibrium is affected and people rendered more docile and easily manipulated.

Insofar as the countries outside of the Iron Curtain are concerned, radio also is used on a large scale. While the Communists find no "captive" audiences for their broadcasts, they have captured numerous listeners indirectly, by repeating a limited number of slogans or symbols, provoking anti-Communist speakers into replies and arguments, proposing and opposing solutions, and making "news." There is no doubt but that counterpropaganda, aimed at the Communists, if it is executed clumsily, may recruit followers into the Communist fold, simply because to refute, it must pick up Communist points. The danger the Communists must avoid is the "silent treatment."

In their radio and conventional mass communications the Communists simplify and sloganize their messages, employ exaggerations, distortions, sensationalism, human interest stories, and scapegoats, and slant the messages according to situation and target. They do not hesitate to use lies. They couch their message in an authoritative style, indicating that only they know the answers, while the non-Communists preach impractical solutions and, in addition, are inferior human beings. A seemingly positive message is presented in offensive terms: the opponent is put on the defensive and action alternatives are presented. Fundamentally, the message is simple: Communist victory is assured, anti-Communism is doomed; fight for Communism is just, fight against Communism is unjust; the Communists must be loved, the anti-Communists hated. Unlike Western propagandists, the Communists do not worry about tactical consistency, partly because their basic message remains more or less unchanged. And they do not worry overly about plausibility, since many of their most important messages are not addressed to people with common sense in the first place.

However, beyond this more or less conventional, though streamlined, propaganda technique, the Communists have developed three improvements:

1. They make a distinction between agitation and propaganda, that is, they address themselves to concrete issues and cleavages, as well as to the more fundamental and enduring problems. They try to create, especially among the more intelligent audiences, an understanding of the Communist doctrine as such. At the same time they try to capitalize on the grievances and desires of any group, especially of the "underprivileged" type, which by force of circumstances is contemplating, or engaged in, some kind of rebellious action. Propaganda addresses itself to broad and invisible audiences, essentially the reading public, while agitation is directed to small, more or less uniform, visible and active target groups. Propaganda uses books and magazines; agitation relies to a large extent on the spoken word. As action develops, agitation slogans tend to become directives for revolutionary undertakings. In other words, propaganda sets up the quandary, and agitation shows the Communist-desired *modus* of relief.

2. C. G. Jung once observed that modern society embraces people who are living, psychologically, in all phases of human development, from the most primitive types to "modern man" who has "estranged himself from the mass of men living entirely within the bounds of tradition," There are magical, metaphysical, Aristotelian, Cartesian, dialectic, and multivalued probabilistic thinkers, and to a certain extent, most of these modes of thinking occur in each individual brain. It also can be said that there are represented in each society all historical types of psychological and social frustration. The Communists make a serious attempt to reach most of these targets. Far from preaching one simple gospel, and addressing it to the mentally most advanced, they present many different teachings ranging all the way from pure Communism via crypto- and semi-Communism to "front doctrines" and even synthetic ideologies *ad usum delphini*, for such unlikely customers as nationalists, conservatives, liberals, and even anti-Communists. By and large, their best target among the educated and semieducated is the frustrated intellectual whose scientific thought habits are underdeveloped. The ideal devotee of the Communist gospel is one who seeks certainty, is emotion-

ally attached to a prejudice or a pre-established position, is unwilling to verify his preconceived notions, and has the wrong idea of "objectivity."

3. The Communists combine propaganda with organization. The propagation of their messages leads necessarily to the recruitment of additional members. The new members, in turn, must participate in the wider propagation of the faith.

Normally, a man just sins, and does not sin beyond redemption. Mephistopheles, however, sees to it that Faustus, besides sinning, sells him his soul, and does so in writing. Thus, true domination is established. The campaigns for collecting signatures in support of the alleged peace policy of the Soviet Union are not primarily designed to be convincing to anybody, but to get a man's handwriting on a piece of paper and thus initiate in his mind a commitment to the cause for which he signed. *Litera scripta valent.* The fact is that people do not like to go back on their signatures and continue, even when assailed by doubts, to feel that they were right to sign their names at the time they did.

Inside the Iron Curtain these propaganda techniques are combined with four additional devices. First, people are being worked to the extreme limit of their physical ability. Physical exhaustion increases people's susceptibility to all kinds of suggestions, while weakening their capacity of critical evaluation. Second, by maintaining standards of living and, in particular, diets at low levels, both suggestibility and difficulties of evaluation are increased. Third, the restriction of living space, the crowding of entire families into one room, the frequent calling of meetings, and the imposition of extracurricular chores also help in this process.

Lastly, there is the fact that in Soviet lands sex has been deprived of much of its glamour and importance. Restructuration of sex is the simple result of the normal physiological determinants under Communism, overwork, poor nourishment, overcrowding, lack of time, geographical immobility, slave labor, and other hindrances to the normal play of the sex urge. The development of untoward sex frustration, however, is prevented (a) by manipulating the sex drive as a purely physical craving and (b) by setting compensatory goals. Obviously, if the Communists were to change their policies in this field and allow personalized love, the Soviets would recognize in some fashion the importance of the individual and admit the validity of basic human rights, including the pursuit of personal happiness. To the mind of the totalitarian police, pairing and mating are the beginnings of conspiracy, and in a deep sense, this suspicion is perfectly justified. The Communists have learned that it is more efficacious to plant informers not under but in the bed, and thus to destroy all desire to confide and relax in confidence.

THE COMMUNIST ABUSE OF SEMANTICS

Perhaps the most basic Soviet technique in the area of brain orienting lies in the abuse of semantics. Alfred Korzybski's general semanticists, for example, have found that many mental disorders arise from the propensity of people to think in "two-valued," either-or systems. If, in addition, the two values apply to vague terms, it is very easy to produce frustrations.

Let us take the term "success." If this term is interpreted in a very strict sense and if expectations are put at a very high level, it can be proved that no one, particularly no one in a capitalist system and certainly no member of the poorer strata in a capitalist society, ever experienced anything like success or could be truly successful in the future. It is easy to show the failure of any form of idealism, thus setting in motion discouragement, hopelessness, and ultimately a commitment to radical solutions. The Communists employ this device in their "social criticism" of the imperfections of the free enterprise system. At the same time, the imperfections of the Soviet system can be glossed over by pointing out that the welfare of the masses is increased by slow process. Even the failures of Communist policies abroad can be negated by reinterpreting the term "failure," occasionally by having recourse to a multivalued apologia.

"Either-or" thinking, however, is less a device than an essential ingredient of Communist thought. The Communist thinks in simple alternatives, and only in them, such as friend-enemy, "who is not for me, is against me," "one or the other system will win." Thinking in all-or-nothing terms ("all capitalists are...") is a variant of this prescientific mode of cogitating. Sometimes this borders on the comical. For example, discussing a typhus epidemic Lenin said, "Either the lice triumph over socialism, or socialism will triumph over the lice." *Tertium non datur*. Conversely, the hold of Communist thinking usually is broken when the "either-or" habit is cast off.

Communist semantics aim at creating the impression that the free system is entirely static and has not changed in any substantial manner since the time of Marx while, on the other hand, the Soviet system not only expands but moves to a predestined goal where all frustrations will end. The Communists' notorious reluctance to "time-index" their statements allows them to invalidate all untoward experiences, to thwart the rules of evidence, and to assert brazenly that the truth of their assertions is "generally known" or beyond doubt.

The Communists are very adept at all kinds of semantic and sophistic chicanery. They indulge in *argumenta ad hominem*, for example, by pointing out that the originator of an unwelcome thought is a capitalist, a slave of capitalism or, in any event, not a proletarian and certainly not a class-conscious one. They artfully assign concrete reality to abstractions. Thus, a "class" is treated as though it were an individual. The individual's reality is "determined" by his belonging to one or the other "class." The term "capitalism" also is an abstraction; moreover, it is a generic term which covers many different economic systems. Yet the Communists assume that "capitalism" can be a *causa causans*, and they never fail to lump together non-Soviet economic systems under one and the same category. Moreover, the Communists have created terms which becloud the issues, distort the meanings, and allow them to choose the "semantic battlefield" which is most advantageous to the current argument.

The Communists also are defensively interested in general

semantics. Feeling that their doctrine is neither factually nor logically tenable, they have established a sort of "semantic interdict." The faithful are forbidden to analyze the Marxian terms and dogmas, and to take issue with the party's logic. The vocabulary has been stabilized, at least as it relates to the doctrine as such. The information which would invalidate the doctrine must be disregarded or falsified. While in the beginning Communism claimed to be scientific, rationality has been downgraded gradually and has been replaced by emotionalism behind a façade of pseudo-scientific nomenclature: hence the official rejection of modern schools of logic and the obsoleteness of Soviet economics. The "interdict" also applies to the history both of the party and of Russia: the myth is indispensable, but it could not be preserved if objective research were allowed outside the field of the natural sciences. This inhibition of knowledge and logic is hurting the Soviets to a degree, because it cannot fail but disorient them; yet as partial compensation, the disorientation spills over into the free world.

THE SPECIFIC GOALS OF THE COMMUNIST EFFORT

In summary it can be said that Communist psychological warfare aims at the following objectives:

1. The creation of a psychologically strong, obedient, disciplined, steadfast, and "iron-willed" leadership core which thinks and emotes in a certain way, in that way only, and in that way for a long time regardless of obstacles.

2. The creation of a larger group of "oriented" propagandists who spread Communist notions and are instrumental in creating and maintaining a suitable frame of reference which is imposed upon non-Communists.

3. The creation in both groups of a burning sense of hatred.

4. Docility, discipline, and controllability of subject populations which must be commanded by the unopposed will of the party leadership.

5. The creation, in the ruling, upper and intellectual classes of non-Communist societies, of frustration, confusion, pessimism,

guilt, fear, defeatism, hopelessness, and neurosis, of *oblomovism* or *nevolya*, in essence the psychological destruction of anti-Communist leadership.

6. The splitting of a society into many competing and mutually hostile groups and the sapping of the spirit of loyalty, community, mutual helpfulness, positive expectation, and willingness to take risks and to act.

7. The creation and stimulation of an all-pervading sense of fear and anxiety, whether it be fastened onto the dangers of nuclear war, or physical terror, or professional, social and human ruin.

8. The capture of the time dimension in the sense that an expectation of cataclysm and no-progress under "capitalism" is established and paired with the affirmed expectation that the future belongs to Communism.

9. The promise of relief from all troubles by means of an infallible as well as inevitable solution.

10. The semantic domination of intellectual, emotional and socio-political life as well as the semantic control of *all* political arguments.

11. The weakening and destruction of national consciences in the Free World and the inculcation of bad conscience about firm opposition to Communism and the ideals usurped and distorted by it.

In former times, the Communists perhaps had illusions about their ability to convince. They expected that the great majority of all peoples would become "proletarian" in status and conscience. With these early expectations gone, it seems that the Communists have adopted a more moderate but presumably more practical objective: *simply to frustrate the policies of the anti-Communists.*

The rationale of zigzag tactics is to cause the opponent to build up a defense against zig, and shortly before it becomes effective, to "annul" this defense (the term is Bulganin's) by performing a zag. Thus, the initiative is slated to remain in Communist hands. The West, it is hoped, never will reach its objective successfully—Sisyphus at labor. As a result of the Free World's near failures, the Communists achieve mental and psychological ascendency, in particular they *prove* that the stronger will is theirs. The recipe is simple: fears, guilt neuroses, lack of will power, and disoriented minds for the democracies, and fearlessness and resoluteness for a Communist elite acting with firm discipline and according to one doctrine. Psychological weakness must be produced in the Free World and be pitted against the psychological strength of the Communist janissaries.

Much of this may be wishful thinking on the part of the Communists, but to the degree that the most crucial decision of all, war or peace, has been allowed to slip into Communist hands, the Communists have achieved psychological dominance. The Kremlin almost has become the master of mankind's fate: harsh, jealous, revengeful, and unpredictable like Jehovah—a father image the like of which the world has never seen. John Foster Dulles described this unhealthy situation as early as 1946: "Few men in political life anywhere act without first thinking whether they will please or displease the leaders of the Soviet Union. Never in history have a few men in a single country achieved such world-wide influence." [5]

This world-wide influence is the true measure of Soviet success in psychological warfare.

The only redeeming feature is that the Kremlin Olympus is neither omnipotent nor omniscient. It is beset with its own fears and psychological difficulties which today are increasing at a staggering rate. Its methods work only for a time and to a degree. At the height of physical power the motivation and conviction of Communism have begun to wane. The *Männerbund* at the top of the Communist movement has been split up, because the image of the ferrously willed robot is an unreal one, because neither healthy psyches nor minds can be kept in a state of constant disorientation, and because the Communists bear a huge guilt for numerous crimes and gradually are beginning to feel the pangs of conscience.

[5] "Thoughts on Soviet Foreign Policy," *Life*, June 3, 1946, p. 124.

The psychological planning of man has remained impossible. Yet we would be foolish to ignore that the Communists have made great strides in the art of psychological manipulation. The West does not yet understand the nature of the psychological attack which has been launched. It does not comprehend the causes of its paralysis, and often does not even notice that its freedom to act has been impeded. Once the Free World will assess the conflict in its psychological dimension, the course of history will be reversed. Then there will shine, we trust, *ex occidente lux.* In the hopeful words of Friedrich Hoelderlin:

Wo Gefahr ist,
Wächst das Rettende auch.

HARPER COLOPHON BOOKS